T0260725

The Digital Party

Digital Barricades:
Interventions in Digital Culture and Politics

Series editors:
Professor Jodi Dean, Hobart and William Smith Colleges
Dr Joss Hands, Newcastle University
Professor Tim Jordan, University of Sussex

The Digital Party

Political Organisation and Online Democracy

Paolo Gerbaudo

PLUTO PRESS

First published 2019 by Pluto Press
345 Archway Road, London N6 5AA

www.plutobooks.com

British Library Cataloguing in Publication Data
A catalogue record for this book is available from the British Library.

ISBN   978 0 7453 3580 3   Hardback
ISBN   978 0 7453 3579 7   Paperback
ISBN   978 1 7868 0360 3   PDF eBook
ISBN   978 1 7868 0362 7   Kindle eBook
ISBN   978 1 7868 0361 0   EPUB eBook

This book is printed on paper suitable for recycling and made from fully
managed and sustained forest sources. Logging, pulping and manufacturing
processes are expected to conform to the environmental standards of the
country of origin.

Typeset by Westchester Publishing Services

Printed and bound by CPI Group (UK) Ltd, Croydon, CR0 4YY

Contents

Series Preface

Crisis and conflict open up opportunities for liberation. In the early twenty-first century, these moments are marked by struggles enacted over and across the boundaries of the virtual, the digital, the actual and the real. Digital cultures and politics connect people even as they simultaneously place them under surveillance and allow their lives to be mined for advertising. This series aims to intervene in such cultural and political conjunctures. It features critical explorations of the new terrains and practices of resistance, producing critical and informed explorations of the possibilities for revolt and liberation.

Emerging research on digital cultures and politics investigates the effects of the widespread digitisation of increasing numbers of cultural objects, the new channels of communication swirling around us and the changing means of producing, remixing and distributing digital objects. This research tends to oscillate between agendas of hope that make remarkable claims for increased participation, and agendas of fear that assume expanded repression and commodification. To avoid the opposites of hope and fear, the books in this series aggregate around the idea of the barricade. As sources of enclosure as well as defences for liberated space, barricades are erected where struggles are fierce and the stakes are high. They are necessarily partisan divides, different politicisations and deployments of a common surface. In this sense, new media objects, their networked circuits and settings, as well as their material, informational, and biological carriers all act as digital barricades.

Jodi Dean, Joss Hands and Tim Jordan

Acknowledgements

This book would not have been possible without the sympathetic support of many colleagues and friends who have contributed in different ways to its development. I would like to thank David Castle, my editor at Pluto, and the Digital Barricades series editors for their advice and support. Events and debates conducted through the Centre for Digital Culture at King's College London, and in particular the cyberparty conference in May 2015, were also useful in developing my thinking. I am grateful to the 30 interviewees who contributed their experience and ideas, and to all the people who volunteered to read an early draft of the book, providing useful comments: Maria Haberer, Graham Jones, Manfredi Mangano Francesco Screti, Lazaros Karavasilis, Antonio Calleja Lopez, Che Brandes-Tuka, Jasper Moriarty, Giorgios Venizelos, Felicia Panosoglu, Mawii Zothan, Asmita Jain, Patrick McCurdy, Vicente Rubio, Lorenzo Coretti, Julia Schönheit, Robin Piazzo, Francesco Screti, Enrico Padoan and Gavin Brown. My thanks also go to Alex Foti, who provided very insightful comments and advice on style for this book; to Javier Medina Lopez for discussions about the relationship between movement and parties in Spain; to Nick Srnicek and Mark Cotè for valuable discussion about digital capitalism and the logic of Big Data.

Introduction

On 18 May 2018, the registered members of the Movimento 5 Stelle (Five Star Movement) were convoked via email to participate in an important online consultation due to take place from 10 a.m. to 8 p.m. A window was created on the main dashboard of the Rousseau participatory portal to vote on the 'government contract', the agreement that had long been negotiated with Lega, the right-wing populist party of Matteo Salvini. There were 44,796 people who participated in the consultation, with 42,274 voting yes and 2,522 voting no: an overwhelming 94 per cent majority in favour of the agreement. Luigi Di Maio celebrated the vote on Il Blog delle Stelle, the official party house organ, as a democratic consecration of the Contract for the Government of Change and the pact with Salvini. A few weeks later, eventually the Five Star Movement and Lega formed a coalition government which was dubbed by the press 'yellow-green', or *carioca*, because of the colours of the two parties (yellow for Five Star and green for Lega).

How was it possible for an 'internet party' that had long been ridiculed by the mainstream media in Italy for its naïve techno-utopianism and dilettantism to enter government less than 10 years after its foundation? What led it to enjoy such a widespread popularity in the Italian electorate? What kind of political organisation and model of democracy does this formation put forward? And is the case of the Five Star Movement an Italian exception or also an indication of what is happening in other countries?

To broach these questions, it is useful to do a flashback to September 2017, eight months before these events, watching a YouTube video showing Luigi Di Maio, the Five Star Movement leader and current Vice Prime Minister, before the crowds of Italia a 5 Stelle (Five Star Italy), the annual national gathering of the Five Star Movement.[1] Just like prior editions, the event takes place in Rimini, a beach resort on the Northern Adriatic coast, which has a tradition of hosting political conventions at the summer's end, when hotels start emptying out as vacationers return to Bologna, Milano or Munich. Di Maio is chatting with his bodyguards as he approaches the entrance of the meeting area.

'Do not close the space at the front. I want to greet the people', he whispers. One of the so-called 'wonder boys'[2] of the Five Star Movement, Di Maio is a 31-year-old from Avellino, near Naples. His father was a local councillor of Movimento Sociale Italiano (MSI), the old party of hard right. His dark complexion, puppy eyes and perennial smile make him popular with female voters. He is widely considered by the press as not qualified for a leading political role as he did not complete his degree in law, and his CV, prior to becoming a politician, listed only some short stints as Web master and stadium steward for the Naples football team. However, he is hardly a political novice. Like many other leaders of the Five Star Movement, Di Maio has been active for many years in the political movement launched by comedian Beppe Grillo, what amounts to a great badge of honour amongst movement supporters and has had the important role of vice-president of the Chamber of Deputies.

As Di Maio crosses the main gate of Rimini's fair – topped by a cartoon portraying the party's founder and guarantor, Beppe Grillo, taking off on a spaceship – he is greeted by a friendly crowd. He generously shakes hands, gives hugs and kisses on cheeks and engages in small talk with supporters. People call him by his first name, Luigi, or by the endearing nickname Gigi, and treat him as if he was someone familiar to them. Some remind him of previous encounters they have had, much in the same way people often do on Facebook on the occasion of birthdays and such life events, to which Di Maio graciously assents. Others film him on their phones and ask him to take a selfie together, which he patiently agrees to with a smile that is reminiscent of Italian reality show celebrities. Proceeding towards the main stage, where he is due to deliver a speech, Di Maio passes by a big, inflatable, mouse-shaped stand called Villaggio Rousseau. This is where information and workshops about Rousseau, the movement's online decision-making platform, can be found.

Rousseau – an innovation Five Star activists are very proud of – constitutes the movement's 'digital heart', an online platform where registered members can discuss and vote about various political issues concerning the internal and external activities of the organisation. It is the system used to choose the movement's candidate for the general election, due to be announced this evening. Besides Di Maio, seven other people are running in the primaries, but they do not stand a chance of being elected. This is because they are nonentities – the movement's detractors have already dubbed them as 'Snow White's seven dwarfs' – while viable rivals, such as charismatic Alessandro Di Battista and Roberto Fico, have been persuaded not to stand.

Di Maio eventually reaches the main stage, and the proclamation of the winner, live-streamed on Facebook, begins. The master of ceremony is Beppe Grillo, the comedian party founder, who recently announced he would leave the stewardship of the movement to the chosen premier candidate due also to act as the future movement leader, while retaining the role of movement guarantor. Using his consummate theatrical flair and irony, Beppe Grillo tries to concoct some suspense, making the event resemble a scene from a talent show when the winners are announced. He starts from the bottom of the list, with Domenico Ispirato, age 53, 'a site manager with a passion for cooking',[3] who received just 102 votes, and moves up to the second-best, Elena Fattori, whose 3,596 votes are dwarfed by Di Maio's score of 30,936, 82 per cent of the total votes expressed electronically, though with a modest participation of only 27 per cent of the 140,000 registered party members. As soon as the winner is proclaimed, confetti in the three colours of the Italian flag is blown into the air. Grillo hugs Di Maio, and together they unfold the white party flag, which features a red circle containing the word *MoVimento* with a dripping-red capitalised 'V' borrowed from the cult movie *V for Vendetta*[4] and the signature five yellow stars. The party's internet address, www.movimento5stelle.it, is well visible below the logo.

Backed by the movement MPs flying the Italian tricolour, Di Maio goes on to deliver his victory speech. He argues that this is a moment when the Five Star Movement can finally rise to power and change Italy for the better. 'Participatory democracy is our DNA', he asserts, emphasising the party's well-known commitment to digital democracy. 'We enter the institutions not to seize them for ourselves, but to give the keys back to you', he continues, and then concludes the speech by saying, 'Long live Italy! Long live the Five Star Movement! Long live the free people!'

The rise of the digital party

This sketch of Five Star Movement's annual gathering, Italia a 5 Stelle (Five Star Italy) provides some insights about the emergence of a new party type, which I describe in this book by using the term *digital party*.

The digital party is the new organisational template seen across a number of new political formations that have been created in recent years, from the Pirate Parties that have emerged in many Northern European countries, to left-wing populist formations such as Podemos in Spain and France Insoumise in France, down to new campaign organisations such as Momentum, driving the surge in popularity of Corbyn's Labour Party in the United Kingdom. Despite their manifest differences, these various formations display evident commonalities in the way in which they promise to a deliver a new politics supported by digital technology; a kind of politics that – as featured by different elements of this opening scene – professes to be more democratic, more open to ordinary people, more immediate and direct, more authentic and transparent.

These parties present themselves as the solution to the democratic deficit that has turned political institutions into the preserve of technocrats and self-serving politicians. They respond to a generalised distrust towards traditional political parties caused by the effects of the Great Recession, by promising to deliver a democracy matching contemporary social and technological conditions. To this end, such organisations have heavily invested in the development of online decision-making tools meant to provide a more direct way for citizens to participate in political decisions, from the Five Star Movement's Rousseau platform that we have just introduced, to Podemos's Consul participation system and the Pirate Parties LiquidFeedback democracy app. Using these tools and adopting a number of rules promised to guarantee more transparency and to prevent political careerism and bureaucratism, this new wave of political parties promises to mend the crisis of democracy, starting from the organisation that has traditionally acted as the primary link between the citizenry and the state: the political party.

The digital party, or alternatively the 'platform party', to indicate its adoption of the platform logic of social media, is to the current informational era of ubiquitous networks, social media and smartphone apps – what the mass party was to the industrial era or the cynically professionalised 'television party' was during the post–Cold War era of high neoliberalism. This emerging party-type integrates within itself the new forms of communication and organisation introduced by Big Data oligopolies, by exploiting the devices, services, applications that have become the most recognisable mark of the present age, from social media like Facebook and Twitter, to messaging apps like WhatsApp and

Telegram, channels on which people can follow any sort of political event such as a Five Star Movement convention. The rise of the digital party thus reflects how technological innovation has also shaped the political party, a form of organisation that for a long time had seemed impervious to change amidst a frozen political system.

The enthusiastic adoption of new technologies aims at improving the efficiency of political organisations, tapping into the flexible organisational affordances and mass outreach potential of social media. But it also has a clear utopian element. It is presented as the means of making politics more democratic and direct by, on the one hand, doing away with a number of structures and processes of traditional parties that are accused of having contributed in making politics excessively bureaucratic, opaque and corrupt; and on the other hand, ushering in new processes that can make people more involved in the political process. To this end, digital parties have transposed to the political arena some of the typical features of the operational model of digital companies leading to impressive feats, but also displaying many flaws, as seen in a number of controversial online consultations as described in the opening sketch.

The digital party is a 'platform party' because it mimics the logic of companies such as Facebook and Amazon of integrating the data-driven logic of social networks in its very decision-making structure; an organisation that promises to use digital technology to deliver a new grassroots democracy, more open to civil society and the active intervention of ordinary citizens. It is 'data hungry' because, like internet corporations, it constantly seeks to expand its database, the list, or 'stack', of contacts that it controls. The digital party is also a start-up party, reminiscent of 'unicorn companies' such as Uber, Deliveroo and Airbnb, sharing their ability to grow very rapidly. The Five Star Movement, in less than a decade from its birth, has managed to become the largest party in Italy, and is currently heading the national government, while many other formations have had a similarly explosive growth trajectory. Like social networks, it is a party that feeds on the 'engagement' which its supporters and sympathisers provide. It is constantly busy eliciting feedback from its member/user base, crowdsourcing ideas from it, balloting on issues, measuring the response of the public, and modifying its strategy and messaging accordingly. It is a party that adopts the free sign-up process of social media and apps, to lower as much as possible the barrier to entry and its definition of membership, and exploit the close-to-zero marginal costs of communicating online with an ever-expanding base of members. In other words, the digital party is the translation of the business model and organisational innovation of digital corporations to the political arena and their application to the idealistic project of the construction of a new democracy in digital times.

The rise of the digital party constitutes a fascinating question for all those interested in the transformation of politics in a digital era, amidst a period of rapid political transformation, when normally stable systems, such as party systems, suddenly appear open to new interventions. Since the onset of the financial crisis of 2008, the political arena in Western countries has been invested by a veritable turmoil. This has been seen in a number of surprising developments that have defied the predictive ability of journalists, analysts and pollsters, from new protest movements like those of the 2011 movement of the squares that mobilised millions of people to the victories of dark horse candidates such as Donald Trump in the 2016 U.S. presidential elections. Many of these developments have been deeply intertwined with the use of digital technology and its capacity to disrupt deep-seated political equilibria. Yet the actual nature and implications of these transformations still escape our comprehension.

This book aims at developing a balanced account of this wave of organisational innovation, overcoming the twin evils of uncritical celebration and preconceived criticism that have so far dominated public commentary on the digital party. As with my previous work on social movements and social media, it stems from long-standing and in-depth empirical analysis, encompassing direct observations, 30 expert interviews with politicians, organisers and developers, as well as hands-on knowledge of the technologies utilised by these formations. Examining this material, I have focused on a number of key questions that should be of interest not only to scholars but also to political activists, and inquisitive citizens more widely. What is the nature and meaning of the digital party? How does it differ from previous party types, such as the mass party at the height of the industrial era, or the television party of the post-industrial era? How does it redefine processes of membership, leadership and participation? To what extent is this party type actually more democratic than previous party types? Is the digital party simply to be criticised or derided, as it has become customary for many activists on the left? Or should good democrats also take heed of its positive lessons?

In the course of the book, we approach these questions focusing on three formations that have epitomised the rise of the digital party – the Pirate Parties, the Five Star Movement and Podemos – while occasionally extending our investigation to other political phenomena that display similar organisational trends. For each of these formations, extensive empirical work has been completed, visiting party offices and campaign events, discussing with people involved in their organisational processes and in the development of participatory platforms and attending various campaign events. The discussion engages with the theoretical debates on political parties which have developed for over a century in political science, from evergreen classics as Gramsci, Weber and Michels to more recent scholarship of authors such as Otto Kirchheimer, Richard Katz, Peter Mair and Angelo Panebianco. A number of issues that are central to the understanding of the political party are explored: their root motivations and social composition; their ideology and values; their forms of organisation and participation; the nature of processes of decision-making; and the changing nature of leadership.

My wish is that this work will contribute in making some order in debates where analysis tends to be case-study specific and where there have been few attempts at systematisation, and that it will provide some insights not only to scholars but also to the organisers and developers who are directly faced with the organisational questions raised by the emergence of digital parties. Before, we venture on this journey, it is fit to begin with a brief history of these formations, to continue with some highlights of the main features of the digital party, which will then be developed over the course of the book.

From Pirates to Momentum

The term *digital party* attempts to capture the common essence seen across a number of quite diverse political formations that have risen in recent years, and which share the common attempt of using digital technology to devise new forms of political participation and democratic decision-making. The early embodiment of this ideal type is found in a series of self-declared 'internet parties' that have claimed the role of champions of the new digital society, vis-à-vis the rusty and collapsing structure of a crisis-stricken neoliberal society and its worn-out politics. The most famous early examples of this trend are undoubtedly the

Pirate Parties, a group of parties campaigning for digital rights, that have been particularly successful in Northern European countries.

The first Pirate Party was founded in Sweden in 2006 by entrepreneur and former liberal politician Rick Falkvinge. It was created in the wake of the uproar generated by the judicial shutting down of Pirate Bay, a popular file-sharing service which wore with pride the stigma of piracy levelled at anybody downloading movies, books and video games for free, and especially those facilitating the circumvention of copyright laws. The formation was officially launched by Falvinge on the Direct Connect file-sharing hub, with a petition to register a new political party focusing on issues of copyright, file-sharing and patents reform. The new formation adopted as its symbol a black pirate sail, so shaped to resemble the letter 'P', and rapidly gathered thousands of supporters. After polling a diminutive 0.63 per cent in the 2006 Swedish general elections, it managed to achieve an impressive result in the 2009 European elections, when it scored 7.13 per cent of the vote, thus electing two Members of the European Parliament (MEPs) for Sweden. In 2010 the Pirate Parties International was founded in Brussels, with local chapters making significant gains in a number of European countries. In the 2011 Berlin State election, the German Pirate Party obtained 8.9 per cent of the votes, winning 15 out of 141 seats in the local assembly. After a brief surge at the polls, the party was marred by scandals and internal disputes, from which it has yet to recover. Another Pirate Party success has been the case of the Píratar in Iceland, founded by a number of notable digital activists such as Birgitta Jónsdóttir and Smári McCarthy. The Píratar scored well at the 2016 and 2017 national elections, being involved at some point in talks to join a coalition government which eventually failed. The latest pirate feat recently occurred in the Czech Republic, where in the 2017 legislative election the Czech Pirate Party obtained over 10 per cent of the votes, making it the country's third largest. However, looked at from an international standpoint, Pirate Parties seem to have lost most of their initial momentum.

While not employing the Pirate Party moniker, and not adhering to the Pirate Party International (PPI) which coordinates most Pirate Parties worldwide, other formations have emerged in recent years that come close in ideology to the Pirate Party. These include the Partido de la Red (Party of the Net) in Argentina, the Wikipartido (Wikiparty) in Mexico, and Partido X (X Party, also known as the Party of the Future) in Spain, which, as their names attest, make overt claim to being parties of the internet. Like the Pirates, these formations propose a techno-utopian discourse which sees digital technology as leading us towards a better future. However, they have not been very successful in translating this vision into electoral results.

So far, the most impressive manifestations of the rise of the digital party have come from parties that, although drawing some inspiration from the Pirates and similar formations, and sometimes espousing a similar rhetoric of the 'digital revolution', are far more ambitious in scope and less single-issue oriented. Arguably, the most significant cases of recasting of the party form in the digital era are the Five Star Movement in Italy, in Italian MoVimento 5 Stelle (M5S) and Podemos in Spain, two populist formations that have heavily invested in the development of forms of digital organisation.

The Five Star Movement, which in the aftermath of the 2018 national elections ranks as the first party in Italy, was officially launched at an event on 4 October 2009 at Teatro Smeraldo in Milan. However, its origins go back to a series of mobilisations in the mid-noughties under the auspices of Beppe Grillo, the party's founder and long-time 'guarantor'. A charismatic comedian and satirist who had turned his theatre shows into raging attacks against the corrupt political class, Grillo promoted the development of activist groups that stood in local elections, in 'certified lists' called Friends of Beppe Grillo. A key step in this genesis was the anti-corruption Vaffanculo Day (literally 'Fuck Off Day') launched on 8 September 2007 in several squares around Italy. Fifty thousand people gathered in Bologna's Piazza Maggiore alone at the culmination of a campaign for 'clean parliament', highlighting the presence of dozens of politicians with criminal records. On this occasion the movement adopted the red 'V' symbol popularised by the cult movie *V for Vendetta*, which to this day appears in the Five Star Movement official name and logo.

The success of this mobilising effort was due to the way in which the street credentials and celebrity status of Beppe Grillo, presenting himself as a new Savonarola, chastiser of political malpractice and corruption, were combined with the media savviness of Casaleggio Associati, a digital consulting firm led by Gianroberto Casaleggio, co-founder of the movement. It was thanks to the support of Casaleggio that Grillo established his popular www.beppegrillo.it, which in 2008 featured among the world's most powerful blogs, according to the *Observer*,[5] and which, until recently, acted as the movement's official house organ, with its web address acting as a substitute for the party's official legal address. And it was following his advice that the movement structured itself around local groups, organised through Meetup, an online service that facilitates face-to-face meetings of people who share common interests. The party's policy platform initially resembled the one of a Green party, with the movement's five stars representing water (under public ownership), environment, free internet connectivity, sustainable development and low-carbon transportation (with electric cars, public transport a gradual build up in local elections between 2009 and 2012 and city bikes). However, it has progressively encompassed more populist issues, attacking political corruption and demanding law and order, and has not shied away from opportunistic attempts to win conservative voters over, especially on immigration issues.

Since entering the electoral fray, the party has experienced rapid success. After a gradual build up in local elections between 2009 and 2012, the party scored an impressive 25.5 per cent of the votes in the Chamber of Deputies in the 2013 national elections, to become the second largest party in Italy. It achieved further momentum in the June 2012 local elections, when the first successes in large cities arrived with the election of Virginia Raggi as the mayor of Rome and Chiara Appendino in Turin. This arc culminated with the Italian 2018 national elections, in which the Five Star Movement eventually became the first party in parliament with 32 per cent of votes in the Chamber of Deputies, well above the Democratic Party which had essentially ruled Italy since 2013, by humbling Matteo Renzi, who failed to have his party reach even 20 per cent of the votes cast. After protracted coalition negotiations, the Five Star Movement has gone on to form a government with right-wing populist party Lega, the other clear winner of this electoral round.

Fundamental to the party's identity, as a 'party of the Web', has been the question of digital and direct democracy, presented as a tool to skip party brokering and 'in-feuding'. Since its inception, the M5S has convened a series of online consultations with voters on local and national candidates (*comunarie* for local councils, *parlamentarie* for parliament, but also *quirinarie* to choose the candidate to support as the president of the republic, whose seat is on the Quirinal Hill in Rome), and online referendums on a number of issues, among others on the purging of representatives accused of having violated party rules. More recently, the M5S has created Rousseau, a discussion and voting system that was initially described as the 'Five Star operating system' and contains a set of further features, such as participatory legislation at regional, national and European levels.

Though quite different from the Five Star Movement, in terms of ideology and organisational structure, Podemos displays a similar enthusiasm for digital media which justify his description as a digital party. Podemos – a name that is an adaptation of unionist Cesar Chavez's 'Sí, se puede' and Barack Obama's 'Yes we can' – was launched on 17 January 2014[6] on the initiative of political science researcher Pablo Iglesias Turrión; he was supported by a group of colleagues and compatriots who orbited around the Complutense University of Madrid, including Juan Carlos Monedero, Iñigo Errejón, and various groups from the radical left and social movements, including the Izquierda Anti-capitalista (anti-capitalist left), a Trotskyist faction. The formation rode the wave of mobilisation initiated by the 2011 Indignados protest movement, also known as the 15-M for its starting date, on 15 May 2011, and capitalised on the celebrity status of Pablo Iglesias, a regular guest on political talk shows. Podemos's electoral force has proved itself since the European elections in 2014, when it received 8 per cent of the votes and five MEPs were elected just two months after its foundation. In the 2015 municipal elections in Barcelona and Madrid, two women, Ada Colau and Manuela Carmena, were elected as mayors, supported by civic lists assisted by Podemos. In the parliamentary elections of December 2015 and June 2016, Podemos came third behind the Socialist PSOE, and the centre-right Partido Popular. After opposing a coalition government of the PP and Ciudadanos, it is now externally backing a Socialist government led by PSOE leader Pedro Sanchez.

Compared to the Pirate Parties and the Five Star Movement, Podemos is more traditional in its leftist identity and its organisational structure, which incorporates various organs typically found in mass parties, such as the secretary and the party's central committee. However, it has been characteristic in its embracing of digital technology at all levels. For a start Podemos has used effectively social media as a mobilising tool and has quickly become the most popular Spanish party on Twitter and Facebook. Furthermore, it has pursued a digital democracy agenda similar to the one of the Five Star Movement, with the declared aim of bringing to the party the demand for 'real democracy' voiced by the 15-M movement. Soon after its foundation, it set up its own participatory portal, called Participa (Participate), through which members could get involved in proposals and discussions. All important decisions, such as party policies and elections to party office, are supposed to be taken on this platform rather than through an assembly of delegates, as happens in traditional socialist or communist parties. More generally, Podemos has tried to present itself as a force in tune with the spirit of digital culture, concerned with questions of transparency, and championing the rights of the new workers of the digital economy, including the self-employed often looked at with a bit of suspicion by the traditional left.

Pirate Parties, the Five Star Movement and Podemos can be seen as the most iconic manifestations of the digital party format, and this is why most of the analysis in this volume focuses on them. However, a number of further phenomena display similar organisational trends, such as France Insoumise and Momentum. France Insoumise is a left-wing populist party founded on 10 February 2016 by former Socialist politician Jean-Luc Mélenchon. Its name can be translated in English as 'Unbowed France' or 'Unsubmissive France', a stance also expressed in the party's *phi* symbol that looks like a person with a clenched fist. France Insoumise is even more remarkably 'left' than Podemos is, not only because of the long career of his main leader but also because it has been supported by the Parti de Gauche (Left Party). However, France Insoumise clearly differs from traditional left parties in its embracing of digital democracy and its doing away with traditional bureaucratic structures. The formation has used the political software NationBuilder to gather supporters and has developed its own dedicated platform to make decisions on policies and strategy and has resorted to social media, YouTube videos and even video games as propaganda tools.

A similar spirit of organisational innovation has been displayed by Momentum, a left-wing political organisation that was initially founded by Jon Lansman, Adam Klug, Emma Rees and James Schneider after Jeremy Corbyn's election as Labour leader in the autumn of 2015. It self-describes as an organisation that wants to 'build on the energy and enthusiasm from the Jeremy Corbyn for Labour Leader campaign, to increase participatory democracy, solidarity, and grassroots power and help Labour become the transformative governing party of the 21st century'.[7] Momentum has been widely applauded for its effective use of social media, and has recently established My Momentum, an online platform that allows members to participate in discussions and make decisions. Some trends of the digital party can also be seen in related phenomena, such as Bernie Sanders' presidential campaign in 2016, which, while not adopting digital democracy tools, has been innovative in its use of digital organising tactics, empowering the rank and file to organise the campaign locally.

It is fairly obvious that, at the stage at which the internet is on the point of becoming, if it has not already become, more influential than TV, all parties are compelled to 'go digital'. Political organisations of all stripes have by now adopted different digital technologies in their functioning, such as establishing party websites, and social media channels for the party as a whole and for specific candidates. In the United States, famous cases have been the internet savviness of Howard Dean and of Obama's first and second presidential campaigns and the tricks used by his social media team. Other mainstream candidates like current French president Emmanuel Macron have similarly leveraged digital platforms to achieve stunning success. And it is Donald Trump's cheap and dirty use of social media that contributed significantly to his conquest of the White House.

The reason for focusing on Pirate Parties, the Five Star Movement and Podemos – is that they are 'digital' in a more qualified sense. To this end, it is useful to distinguish between what David Karpf names 'legacy organisations', namely organisations that have been founded before the digital era and are now trying to adapt to it, and 'netroots organisations', formations that have emerged in recent years and have consequently been shaped from the very start by digital technology and connected organisational forms.[8] In older organisations, such as traditional political parties, the use of digital technology tends to concern intra-organisational processes and the external communication of parties to their targeted publics.[9] These organisations tend to be very prudent in absorbing digital technology in their operations, and continue to view television and the press as their main grounds of campaigning. In netroots organisations, instead, the use of digital technology directly concerns the ways in which parties are organised internally and the forms of 'intraparty democracy' through which decisions are made. In other words, in traditional parties the transformation ushered in by political technologies happens only in their relationship with the outside world; in the case of digital parties proper, the entire life of the party is cast open and rearranged around the idea of a more direct and participatory democracy.

Digital parties proper, as those discussed in this book, are the ones that bring digital transformation to their very core, to their internal structure of decision-making, rather than using digital communication simply as an outreach tool. But this transformation is not limited only to these formations. The hegemony of the digital party format can be seen in the fact that also some of the old mass parties of the left, including Labour in the United Kingdom, the SPD in Germany, and the PSOE in Spain, are progressively adopting online decision-making platforms and the discourse of digital democracy. The digital party thus designates both a specific party type that can be most clearly seen across a number of formations described as 'internet parties', and a trend of general transformation of the party system in the present era.

The promise of online democracy

What defines the digital party as a new party type is not simply the embracing of digital technology but the purpose of democratisation which digital technology is called to fulfil. Organisations such as Pirate Parties, the Five Star Movement and Podemos have presented their adoption of the logic of interactivity and participation, popularised by social media platforms, as a way to deliver a more direct democracy; a democracy which is sometimes imagined to be as smooth as the interactivity of social networking sites and as malleable as the data clouds these services rely upon. The 'platformisation' of the party is premised on evident strategic considerations: the platform logic is seen to be more effective and more fitting to present times than the old and bulky bureaucracy of traditional parties. Choosing this path, digital parties attempt to offset their weaknesses as outsider organisation, their lack of steady funding and of offices and similar infrastructures, and their competitive disadvantage vis-à-vis large and well-established organisations. They adopt a philosophy of 'distributed organising', to use the terms of Sanders' staffers Becky Bond and Zack Exley[10] to tap into the political labour of their diffuse support base, much in the same way in which social media companies extract value from the 'free labour' of their dispersed user base. However, this organisational revolution cannot be understood as stemming merely from strategic and economic considerations, as a translation of the 'lean management' and the 'disruptive innovation' philosophy adopted by several Silicon Valley firms to the political arena. Rather, it is also premised on, and justified by, the utopian vision of an online democracy using digital technology as a means to extend and deepen political participation, reintegrate in the polity many citizens who have for a long time been distant from the political arena and allow them to have a more direct and meaningful intervention in the political process.

This utopian vision is seen at different points in the opening scene of this book. It is displayed in the discussion of the Rousseau platform, from the very appeal to the philosophy of Jean-Jacques Rousseau, the theorist of direct popular democracy, famous because of his suspicion of any form of representation,[11] to the investment in the creation of a decision-making platforms trying to turn this idealistic democratic vision into an app, easily accessible to users. It is further seen in the Five Star campaign slogan that appeared everywhere in the Rimini party convention: *Partecipa, Scegli, Cambia* (Participate, Choose, Change), which expresses the idea of a post-representational democracy in which people do 'not settle for delegation but aspire for full participation',[12] as expressed by Davide Casaleggio the son of Gianroberto Casaleggio, whom he replaced after his death, as president of Casaleggio Associati in a Rousseau promotional video. The digital party presents itself as an organisation that is going to do away with the serious limits of representative democracy, and the distance it has created between citizens and their representatives. It bears the promise of *disintermediating* politics, making it more similar to immediacy, interactivity and instantaneity of social experience in the digital era, while doing away with a number of middlemen – bureaucrats, consultants, spin doctors – suspected of being responsible for many of the ills of contemporary politics and the way it distorts the authentic will of the people.

What we see in these and similar slogans is an ideology which I describe in the course of the book as 'participationism' given its almost obsessive emphasis on participation. Combining populist appeals to popular sovereignty with the libertarian promise of more individual autonomy, this narrative argues that many of the problems of contemporary politics stem from the way citizens have been excluded from decisions on the issues affecting them. To remedy this situation, it advocates the creation of 'open spaces', in which individuals, independently from their political values, beliefs and pre-existing partisan divides, may discuss and find a consensus on various issues of interest. Thus, digital technology is seen as ushering in a sort of digital version of Athenian democracy, an agora (a metaphor always heard in digital democracy debates), or a public square (Podemos's discussion space is called 'Plaza Podemos', a reference to the occupied squares of the Indignados movement), in which citizens may discuss without unnecessary mediations.

This emphasis on direct democracy is reminiscent of a long-standing strain of democratic idealism that typically resurfaces in moments of dissatisfaction with liberal democracy. Digital parties' utopian vision echoes the proposals of early democratic socialism, such as those of Moritz Rittinghausen and Victor Considerant, who proposed to use popular assemblies, referendums and popular initiatives. Furthermore, it incorporates a number of ideas coming from the project of a *Basisdemokratie* (grassroots democracy) proposed by 1970s new social movements and Green parties, including limits to consecutive mandates and the rotation principle among representatives, in order to avoid the formation of power cliques and political careerism. And finally it echoes demands for 'real democracy' issued by the popular assemblies of the 2011 Occupy movements. Thereby, digital technology is viewed as the means through which this vision, which has often butted its head against technical and political impossibility, may eventually come true. With its mass interaction capabilities, it is argued, digital technology offers an antidote against the oligarchic tendencies of organisation, famously denounced by Robert Michels, and, at least in the most radical version of this narrative, the means through which citizens can eventually revoke the mandate given to their representatives and participate directly in public life.

The embracing of the utopian project of online democracy is most evident in the deployment of online decision-making platforms, alternatively described as participation portals, which are discussed in two separate chapters in the course of the book. These 'participation tools' – Rousseau for the Five Star Movement, the Participa portal in the case of Podemos, and the early adoption of LiquidFeedback by the German Pirate Party – are mass online decision-making applications that facilitate the participation of members in various discussions, deliberations and e-ballots. But they are more than mere tools. Their introduction involves a radical revision of the party form which re-organises itself around the logic of the platform. Online decision-making is seen as substitute for the traditional system of party branches and delegates that still dominate the remnants of mass parties; it takes on the function of registering and steering the moods of the party base that was previously largely mediated by the party cadres.

The consequences of this organisational revolution are complex and controversial. The organisational template introduced by the digital party has the merit of updating the party form to the technological and social conditions of our era. The digital party has demonstrated the ability to operate efficiently despite extremely limited economic resources, and introduced new forms of membership involvement, as seen in processes of participatory legislation, where ideas for new parliamentary initiatives are crowdsourced from members. However, such organisational restructuring does not result, as some platform party advocates would like us to believe, in a radical diffusion of power in the organisation, nor does it lead to a situation in which 'everyone is of equal worth', as suggested by the Five Star Movement slogan (*ognuno vale uno*). Rather, we are faced with a more ambivalent trend, which may be described as 'distributed centralisation', to express the way which the opening at the party's bottom is accompanied by an increasing concentration of power in the hands of the charismatic party leader, whom I describe as the 'hyperleader', and his or her immediate *entourage*. Rather than the 'participatory democracy' promised on the tin, the reality of the online democracy seen in these formations and their 'participatory platforms' corresponds to what in the course of the book I describe as a 'reactive democracy' manifested in the dominance of forms of 'passive democratic engagement'[13] that are constantly retro-alimented by the leadership's top-down intervention.

The introduction of decision-making platforms is pivotal in the process of organisational restructuring affecting both the top and bottom of political organisations, that is, the party's central office and the party on the ground. Thereby, we see a highly reactive 'superbase' becoming allied with a charismatic hyperleader at the expenses of intermediate strata.

Characteristic of all these formations has been the adoption of a flexible definition of membership. Registering as a member is often as easy as signing up for social media such as Facebook, thus significantly lowering barriers to participation. Furthermore, new members do not need to pay to register: membership is delinked from financial contribution, with platform parties relying on donations rather than on membership fees, as is mostly the case with traditional parties. This choice is presented as a way of making the party more open to society and making political participation as immediate as participating in online discussion on social media. Following this open membership model has often allowed these formations to rapidly accrue a vast base of registered members, sometimes far surpassing more established political parties. Platform parties have heavily tapped into the free labour and the financial contribution of these supporters, resembling the way digital companies extract value from the data of their users.

Continuing to the party's top, it can be seen that these formations have a very light organisational structure, not only much smaller than the imposing bureaucracy of the mass party but also often tinier than the professionalised bureaucracy of consultants, spin doctors and policy advisors of more recent television parties. The political party comes to resemble the start-up companies of Silicon Valley, with their essential staffing, and the operations of digital advocacy groups such as MoveOn, which have very small central staff considering their scale of operation and large membership base. The process of disintermediation of the party decrees the death of the *cadre*, the old figure traditionally involved in the nitty-gritty work of organisation, propaganda and agitation on the party's behalf, that is disposed of much in the same way as bookshops were outcompeted by Amazon or cab companies 'disrupted' by the diffusion of Uber. However, this doing away with an intermediate representative does not simply eliminate power, as the narrative of participationism would want us to believe. Rather, it transfers it in the hands of the party leader and the party staff directly dependent on him.

Online platforms, besides being a space for discussions and deliberative processes, often become the space in which hyperleaders constantly verify the level of support they enjoy among the superbase. While encompassing deliberative elements, the democracy practised within digital parties is clearly skewed towards the 'quantitative' model of plebiscitarian democracy, centring on initiatives and referenda proposed by the top, rather than towards the 'qualitative' model of participatory democracy, with individual members intervening actively in strategy building and policy development. A clear demonstration of the implications of this tendency, and the power of initiative it assigns to the party leadership, is the fact that online consultations have almost invariably returned super-majority percentages ratifying the line proposed by the leadership, with very few cases of rank-and-file rebellion.

This problematic underside of the digital party was clearly on display in the events recounted in the opening sketch, and in the process of nomination of the Five Star Movement's candidate for prime minister. The fact that Di Maio won hands down with 82 per cent of the vote is a good illustration of the way the political selection process used by digital parties can fall short of basic democratic criteria. Similar trends can also be seen in formations such as Podemos, where internal referendums have almost invariably turned into seals of approval for the party leadership. Many online consultations of these parties have come to uncannily resemble the show elections of the Soviet bloc, which could not be further from the promise of a more participatory democracy.

Digital parties thus suffer from an evident mismatch between their idealistic discourse and their often deadpan practice, between the face-value promise of a participatory democracy in which members are given all the power and the leaders are mere figureheads, and a plebiscitarian reality where the opposite often seems to be the case. We move away from the decried party oligarchy only to find ourselves trapped into some sort of Caesarist rule, or a 'benevolent dictatorship' to borrow a term often used to describe digital guarantors of open-source projects as Wikipedia and Linux; one legitimised by popular consent, yet unmistakably autocratic and anti-pluralistic. Online democracy too often risks degenerating into sham democracy, and over the long term this is only bound to produce disillusion in party members and sympathisers. More generally, these parties belie the dangerous illusion that politics can be resolved simply through a change in process and restructuring of internal organisation rather than through a systemic overhaul of social structures and political institutions. It is therefore imperative that digital parties are approached with a combination of hope and caution, enthusiasm and reservation, attentive to their positive innovations but also wary of their practical failures.

In the course of the book, we explore the various issues that are relevant for understanding the digital party.

Chapter 1 outlines the theory of the political party and highlights how, far from having withered away, the party form is back with a vengeance in current times of economic and political turbulence. It goes on to discuss the existence of different party types that have emerged in different political eras, from the mass party of the industrial era to the television party of the neoliberal era, and ends with an examination of the relationship between party's structures and internal democracy.

Chapter 2 examines the root causes of the emergence of digital parties. It argues that the economic crisis of 2008 and the wave of digital transformation have created a new cleavage in society, centring on the 'connected outsiders', people who, despite their high level of connectivity, feel excluded economically and politically. The chapter continues by highlighting some of the key issues of interest to this constituency, which platform parties have championed, including digital rights, demands for new forms of democratic participation and for new welfare provisions.

Chapter 3 examines the platformisation of the political party. It argues that the platform logic of companies, such as Google and Facebook, has been mimicked by digital parties, leading to a new organisational template adopted by digital parties. This data-driven logic adopts the free membership model of social network sites, and their data analytics, to maintain a constant sense of the mood of public opinion. This leads to a party type that combines a renewed focus on mass participation with a very agile organisational structure, reminiscent of start-up companies.

Chapter 4 turns to the ideology of digital parties which I describe as participationism, given the central role assigned to participation over representation. I examine the utopian vision of constructing an open space of participation, as well as this party's rejection of the imaginary of traditional parties. Furthermore, I delve into the problems inherent in this cult of participation and the way it makes participation an end in its own right.

Chapter 5 explores the *pars destruens* of the digital party's organisational revolution. I highlight how the digital party does away with the skeleton of traditional parties, and in particular a structured central bureaucracy and a territorial structure of affiliation. This virtualisation of the party responds to the participationist desire of eliminating the intermediation of party bureaucrats, but this carries controversial consequences for the purpose of internal democracy.

Chapter 6 looks at the architecture of participatory platforms and the way in which they have come to constitute the organisational backbone of these formations. It examines how different decision-making software integrate different visions of democracy, with some leaning more on deliberative functions and others more on representative and plebiscitary balloting.

Chapter 7 discusses the process of online decision-making and how it is managed by the party staff. All digital parties involve some deliberative functions, crowdsourcing policy ideas from the party membership.

However, preponderance goes to more top-down functions, in particular to referenda through which the leadership seeks to constantly renew their mandate, with most ballots returning the expected results.

Chapter 8 explores the figure of the hyperleader. The hyperleader is a plebiscitary-charismatic figure tasked with representing the party in the media and internet spectacle, by attending TV talk shows and intervening obsessively on social media. Through his histrionic performances, the hyperleader makes up for the lack of a strong and dependable organisation. Nevertheless, the presence of the hyperleader is complemented by the continuing existence of a charismatic staff, a sort of micro-oligarchy that continues to exert much control on the party's direction.

Chapter 9 turns to the analysis of digital party membership. This takes the form of a highly active – or, better, reactive – 'superbase', which makes use of digital technology in order to participate in a number of online activities as well as to organise offline ones. The net result is an increase in the quantity of participation, sometimes at the expense of its quality. Furthermore, the opening up of participation creates new divides between 'super-volunteers' and 'lurking sympathisers', hyperactive and relatively passive participants.

The Conclusion summarises the findings of the present research and turns to an evaluation of the potentials and limits of the digital party and the need to revise both the conception and practice of digital democracy. At the end of the book, the reader will find an Appendix where all the interviewees this book is based on are listed. The research for this book involved 30 interviews with key informants, activists, organisers and consultants highly involved in the activities of these political parties. Unless otherwise cited, the quotes used in this book stem from those interviews.

1
The Party Strikes Back

Modern party organising starts with the French Revolution and the radical transformation in political culture and media that it triggered. The speeches of Brissot or Robespierre could resonate well beyond the crowd packed in the hall of the National Assembly, thanks to the mass circulation of revolutionary pamphlets and early newspapers. For two reasons, the Jacobins can be considered the founders of modern democratic politics. On the one hand, they were the first to implement the modern notion of popular sovereignty, which had recently been theorised by Jean-Jacques Rousseau. Although popular sovereignty was caricatured by the Whigs and Tories in Britain as a rule of the mob, it became the central logic of republican politics in modern nation-states, developing in electoral democracies based on mass suffrage. On the other hand, the Jacobins were the first to establish a centralised political organisation around a national party headquarters, the Jacobite convent that gave them their name.

Two hundred and thirty years later, we are witnessing a similar revolution in political media and party organisation, which is at the same time technological and political. Political media have evolved from café discussions and print media so that egalitarian aspirations are now conveyed on the screens of digital devices of all sorts, permanently connected to the Web. The 'new politics' of digital parties revolves around discussion on those social media platforms that have come to define political information and culture in the 2010s, as well as the development of new forms of online decision-making that promise to radically transform the internal democracy of political parties. To explore this novelty, it is necessary to lend one eye to the present, and its inventions, and another to the past and the long history of development of and reflections on political parties.

Taking this historical perspective, it is apparent that the birth of new political parties in the digital era is a remarkable turn that defies the expectations of most sociologists and political analysts. We come from decades in which it was widely assumed that political parties had weakened and would soon become irrelevant. In the year 2000, political scientists Russell Dalton and Martin Wattenberg argued that 'today mounting evidence points to a declining role for political parties in shaping the politics of advanced industrial democracies. Many established political parties have seen their membership rolls wane, and contemporary publics seem increasingly sceptical about partisan politics'.[14] Amidst growing apathy of the electorate and decline in membership, the political party seemed to many an outmoded type of organisation, a stubborn relic of a bygone past in the present 'post-political' society.[15] Political scientist Peter Mair famously asserted that we were at the passing of the 'age of party democracy'.[16] He argued that a number of phenomena, such as the volatility of voters and the rise of a widespread 'anti-political sentiment'. pointed to the decline of the political party.[17]

The diagnosis about the decline of the party was in line with post-modern theories on 'the end of history' that had become very fashionable around the turn of the millennium. Amidst the extreme differentiation and individualisation of the information society, the aggregation function of political parties appeared to be arduous if not impossible. As Manuel Castells wrote, we were entering the 'network society', in which all organisations would transform themselves according to the logic of the network, going beyond pyramid-like hierarchies.[18] This did not bode well for the future of the political party, possibly the most hierarchical kind of organisation after the army. Furthermore, the old identities mobilised by political parties, often based on social cleavages stemming from the industrial revolution and its class divide, appeared out of sync with the post-industrial transformation of society. According to Mair and his colleague Richard Katz, political parties were prey to a 'de-alignment', whereby 'long-term societal changes have at least partially undermined the political and cognitive basis of party identification in advanced industrial democracies'.[19]

To this sociology of extreme complexity, fragmentation and class dis-identification added the perception that in a globalised world the party would lose power for a rather obvious reason: because the nation-state, its traditional target of conquest and space of operation, was losing power in favour of global and unelected governance institutions. On the left, autonomist Marxist philosophers Antonio Negri and Michael Hardt described (and welcomed) the shift from nation-states to a global empire,[20] while on the neoliberal front *New York Times* columnist

Thomas L. Friedman waxed lyrical about the inevitable victory of globalisation over nations.[21] With the nation-state losing power, the political party seemed to be condemned to growing irrelevance.

This condition seemed to favour other types of collective organisations operating transnationally and focusing on single issues, such as social movements and non-governmental organisations (NGOs). As argued by Katz and Mair, 'the fragmentation of policy interests and interest articulation may make it more difficult for parties to represent a theoretical median voter', and 'the proliferation of citizen interest groups and other political intermediaries has provided alternatives to the traditional representational role of parties'.[22] In question was thus the very primacy of the party as the dominant type of political organisation, something that was explicitly proposed in the late 1990s by veteran political scientist Philippe C. Schmitter, arguing 'there is no longer any a priori reason to suppose that political parties should be privileged or predominant in this regard'.[23] So why is the political party making such a strong comeback?

Beyond anti-party suspicion

The assertion about the ultimate withering away of the party, accompanied by the cognate thesis of the withering away of the nation-state in times of globalisation, echoes a long history of anti-party suspicion – one informed by the rejection of party authoritarianism and totalitarianism – which has acquired new strength in neoliberal times. Personalities as different as George Washington, James Madison, Heinrich Von Treitsche, Moisei Ostrogorski, John Stuart Mill, Ralph Waldo Emerson and Simone Weil vocally criticised the political party.[24] They alerted to the fact that political parties militated against individuals' independent judgement, calling for obedience and uniformity, and highlighted that rather than pursuing the general interests of society, they mostly ended up defending the narrow interest of a faction. Emerson for example, famously argued that 'a sect or a party is an elegant incognito, devised to save a man from the vexation of thinking',[25] while Simone Weil noticed that political parties led to a situation in which 'instead of thinking, one merely takes sides: for or against. Such a choice replaces the activity of the mind'.[26]

The totalitarianism of the 20th century seemed to corroborate the strong suspicion towards political parties. Nazism and Stalinism demonstrated the extent to which the party could be turned into a cruel machine of obedience, pursuing ruthless repression. The image many people continue to associate with the political party is strongly tinged with such reminiscences of totalitarianism. The mind flies to the abomination of Hitler's Nationalsozialistische Deutsche Arbeiterpartei (NSDAP), described by Franz Neumann in *Behemoth*; or to the show trials and persecutions conducted by communist parties in the Soviet bloc, as dramatised in *Darkness at Noon* by Arthur Koestler; or as symbolised by the INGSOC party described by George Orwell in *1984*, an organisation constantly bent on manipulating its members and commanding unswerving obedience.[27] This is why the New Left looked with sympathy at Mao Tse-Tung's slogan 'Bombard the Headquarters' and Che Guevara's 'Focalism', despite the fact that these figures were also far from immune from totalitarian distortions. This tendency was reinforced by the anti-authoritarianism of environmental, feminist and urban movements in the 1970s and 1980s, which often styled themselves as purveyors of a different and more spontaneous kind of politics with respect to staid party politics. Starting in the 1980s, anti-party suspicion began to be also directed towards the neoliberal successors of socialist parties, and in particular the so-called 'astroturf parties', political machines lacking any real popular backing, led by careerists in the vein of Frank Underwood in the TV series *House of Cards*; party organisations mobilising voters thanks to clever media marketing paid for with the abundant proceedings accruing from lobbying and graft.

To this day, the very mentioning of the word 'party' evokes negative associations among leftist activists.[28] It is really telling that the World Social Forum, the main gathering of the anti-globalisation movement, excluded parties from its premises, as if they were morally reproachable. Interestingly such suspicion of political parties is also displayed by activists of digital parties, to the point that some overtly reject the definition of *party* altogether, preferring to be considered *movements*, and they are consequently described by sociologists as 'movement parties'.[29]

This anti-party suspicion is disturbingly in line with typical neoliberal distrust towards organised collectivities; with its disbelief in the artificial order (*taxis*) and trust in the spontaneous order (*kosmos*) of society originating from the free market, as proposed by Friedrich von Hayek in *The Constitution of Liberty*.[30] The party is thereby seen as a grey Leviathan, an authoritarian structure which imposes social conformism on individuals, undermining freedom, authentic expression, tolerance and dialogue. Such skepticism is well represented in internet studies where many people have come to deny the importance of organisations, claiming that we are now in an era where 'organising without organisations'[31] is possible and where collective action gives way to 'personalised action frames'.[32]

Given this widespread consensus in sociology and political science, the rise of new political parties poses interesting social and political questions. Phenomena such as Podemos, Pirate Parties, the Five Star Movement and Momentum, far from confirming the death of the party, point to a revitalisation of the party form, a trend that is finally being recognised, as shown, among others, by the work of Jodi Dean.[33] These formations have been impressive in the way in which in a short time span they have managed to win the support of major sections of the electorate, often getting 15–30 per cent of votes polled and establishing large membership rolls, sometimes totalling half a million people. Some of them, such as the Five Star Movement, are already in government, whereas others, such as the Pirate Party in Iceland and Podemos in Spain, have come close to power, having been in negotiations for the formation of coalition governments. They may well not call themselves parties, and have rebranded themselves as movements. But, as we shall see, parties they are, though of a very different kind than the ones we inherited from the 20th century. Like the Arab Phoenix, the party is rising from its ashes, but in the process it is also changing plumage.

The rise of a new wave of political parties is in and of itself a significant historical event. Party systems are notably durable structures that are resistant to change. Besides the comparative advantage of established parties over contenders, this inertia is due to the fact that political parties are anchored in deep-seated social cleavages that correspond to exceptional revolutionary turns of the modern era, such as the democratic revolutions of the 18th and 19th centuries that gave birth to liberal and conservative parties, and the Industrial Revolution that spawned socialist and communist ones.[34] One of the last notable cases of transformation of the party system has been the rise of new left parties in the 1970s and early 1980s.[35] These parties included the Green Party in a country like Germany or France, and the red Democrazia Proletaria (Proletarian Democracy) in Italy, all founded in the crucible of the radical movements of the seventies, and brought to the mainstream new demands about quality of life, gender and reproductive rights, and environmental issues.[36]

Similarly to what happened with the foundation of New Left and Green parties in the 1970s and 1980s, the impulse for the creation of platform parties comes precisely from activists who for a long time declared the futility of political parties while asserting the primacy of social movements and civil society. When economic crisis, social discontent and political repression strike, the need for structured political organisations fighting for state power tends to resurface, and many of the digital parties described in this book can be seen as the political projections of anti-austerity and pro-democracy movements of the early 2010s. Yet, the similarities between post-1970s parties and post-crash digital parties end there. As we shall see, although they absorb and develop a libertarian impulse which has typically been associated with 1968 movements and the cyber-anarchist left of the 1990s, they also introduce radically new ideological tendencies, sometimes described as 'populist' or 'communitarian', which reflect the social experience of the Great Recession and the consequent demands for social protection, collective solidarity and political community it has raised.

What is a political party?

Although constituting a central element of politics, the political party is surprisingly under-theorised, with a relatively small number of works pertaining to the canon of political science engaging directly with its nature. The mandatory starting points for any serious reading on this issue are such immortal classics as Alexis De Tocqueville's *Democracy in America*, Robert Michels' seminal work *Political Parties*, Max Weber's discussion of the party in *Economy and Society*, Moisei Ostrogorski's *Democracy and the Organization of Political Parties*, Antonio Gramsci's remarks on the 'modern prince' in the *Prison Notebooks,* and Lenin's *What Is to Be Done?*, written before the failed 1905 revolution.[37] In recent decades debate on this issue has been limited, with attention mostly focusing on the party system rather than on the party as an organisation.[38] The last major monograph on the organisational structure of political parties is *Political Parties: Organization and Power,* by Italian political scientist Angelo Panebianco, written in 1988.[39] Surprisingly limited attention has also been dedicated to the political party in Marxist theory, except for the classic work of Lenin and Gramsci, and the more recent but rather unsystematic observations made by Nicos Poulantzas and Galvano Della Volpe. One just need compare this with the over-flowing literature on social movements in recent years to get a sense of this anomaly.

Taken in its most basic sense, as a political 'part', or faction, it may be said that the political party is almost a universal and trans-historical entity that has already existed in some form in antiquity. In Ancient Rome for example, the conflicts that dominated the late Republican period from the Social War of the Gracchi up to the Civil War fought by Julius Caesar centred on the opposition between the *Populares* (the faction representing the interests of the plebs) and the *Optimates* (representing the interest of the patricians). Similar factions existed in the Middle Ages, as seen in the opposition between the Constantinople's Hippodrome factions of the Blues (*Venetoi*) and the Greens (*Prasinoi*), or the Guelphs and the Ghibellines, supporting the pope and the emperor respectively in the long-standing struggles that tore apart the territories under the jurisdiction of the Holy Roman Empire.[40] These ancient parties were mostly lowly organised alliances of power elites, 'patronage parties' having no resemblance to a mass organisation.

The party, as normally understood in common parlance, is however a modern phenomenon which originates from the social conditions created by the Industrial Revolution, the rise of capitalism, the forma-tion of national-popular states, the establishment of representative and parliamentary systems and universal suffrage. As Max Weber famously put it, political parties are 'the children of democracy, of mass fran-chise, of the necessity to woo and organize the masses'.[41] Parties have played a crucial role in liberal democracies, to the point that, as argued by Schnattschneider, 'political parties created democracy' and 'modern democracy is unthinkable save in terms of political parties'.[42] Simi-larly, American political scientist Susan Scarrow has described political parties as one of the transforming inventions of the 19th century.[43]

Although the public imagination continues to associate political parties in modernity with mass membership parties, and in particular with socialist and communist parties, these party forms were preceded by cadre and elite parties emerging between the 18th and the 19th centu-ries at the beginning of parliamentary systems. Early examples of parties in modernity are the aforementioned Jacobins, who were in power during the first part of the French Revolution; the British Whigs, synonymous with liberalism; and the federalists and the early Republican Party in the United States. These were parliamentary parties of notables, who made themselves manifest in the presence of separate parliamentary groups and had the backing of competing sectors of the bourgeoisie, who were among the few with the right to vote anyway because of limits placed on the political franchise.

It is at this time that the first explicit definitions of political parties, still widely cited by political scientists, start being issued. Edmund Burke, the Irish Whig politician and philosopher who lived at the time of the French Revolution, described the political party in a famous phrase as 'a body of men united for promoting by their joint endeavours the national interest upon some particular principle in which they are all agreed'.[44] A century later, Max Weber adopted a more stringent definition of parties as 'associations membership in which rests on formally free recruitment. The end to which its activity is devoted is to secure power within an organization for its leaders in order to attain ideal or material advantages for its active members [which may consist] in the realization of certain objective policies or the attainment of personal advantages or both'.[45]

Weber's definition of the political party highlights two fundamental characteristics of this organisational form, which continue to be relevant to understand new political formations emerging in the 21st century: the relationship of the party to the state and its voluntarist character. What is characteristic to the political party, vis-à-vis other forms of association, is the way in which it is devised as a means to assert power within a larger corporate body, namely a state, for whose control it competes. The zero degree of the party in the context of democratic countries is an organisation that competes for government power through elections. This is reflected in minimalist definitions of political parties, such as Joseph Schumpeter's 'a group whose members propose to act in concert in the competitive struggle for political power'[46] and Giovanni Sartori's 'any political group identified by an official label that presents at elections, and is capable of placing through (free and unfree) elections candidates for public office'.[47]

The second key element of political parties is the voluntary character of adherence: parties are 'membership organisations' which need not only to obtain votes but also to attract members. As we shall see in the course of the book, from the standpoint of the political party, members are crucial because they provide financial and labour resources without which it could not exist. From the standpoint of members instead, the party is seen as necessary in order to represent them collectively, thus allowing them to achieve aims that could not be attained individually. As German sociologist and syndicalist Robert Michels noticed, the political party is necessary, particularly to working people who would be unable on their own to have any influence on the state and no defence against powerful individuals. 'Organization, based as it is on the principle of least effort, that is to say upon the greatest possible economy of energy, is the weapon of the weak against the strong.'[48] The party thus acts as a 'structural aggregate', providing members with a way to unite their forces and oppose common enemies.

Janus-like entities looking towards society on the one hand and towards the state on the other, parties can be said to have three 'faces' that have been famously identified by Katz and Mair – the party on the ground, the party in the central office and the party in state government.[49] First, the party exists in its support base as a movement made of members and sympathisers; second, political parties rely on the presence of central organisational offices, headquarters that allow them to coordinate their operations; third, political parties compete for elections to win office and obtain representatives.

Each of these faces corresponds to a number of important social functions.[50] Parties are representative organisations that 'generate symbols of identification and loyalty' for their members.[51] They educate citizens, mobilise them and simplify choices for them. They aggregate and articulate political interests that are otherwise dispersed and inconsistent, as noticed by British Liberal politician and historian James Bryce when saying that parties 'bring order out of chaos to a multitude of voters'.[52] Parties recruit political leadership and train them. Finally, they organise government, control the state and implement policies, guaranteeing stability. These three faces of the party acquire varying degrees of importance and different articulations in different party types and can often find themselves at odds with one another, competing for power.

From the mass party to the television party

Different eras and social conditions have seen the dominance of rather different party types which reflect the technological and social tendencies prevalent at the time. To this day, historical comparisons aimed at identifying new party types tend to begin from the mass party, the form of political party that dominated the industrial era. The notion of mass party is mostly associated with the large parties of the left, social-democratic, socialist and communist. But it has also progressively become dominant on the centre-right (in Britain the Conservative Party and the Labour Party, in Italy DC and PCI, and in Germany the SPD and the CDU). The mass party came to constitute the foremost organisational structure of industrial modernity, one that still survives, though often in tatters, in some political parties as those of social-democracy. Classic theorists such as Ostrogorski, Michels, Duverger and Weber based their reflections on the political party on their direct experience and sometimes involvement in mass parties.

The mass party displays a number of distinctive features: a mass base which contributes to the functioning of the party both financially and with its political militancy; a large and permanent bureaucracy occupied by professionalised political personnel; a highly hierarchical and centralised organisational structure; a capillary territorial presence; the vertical integration of cultural and social annex organisations; a clear class base (the working class for the left and the bourgeoisie for conservative parties); an explicit and persistent ideological orientation of the party's strategy and policy platform.[53] Mass parties were the parties of a mass society and were instrumental to the functioning of these societies as the vehicle for the social integration of the masses in the political arena, in response to the atomisation created by industrialisation and secularisation, as proposed by Sigmund Neumann and Moisei Ostrogorski.[54]

Pointing to the analogy between the mode of production and the mode of organisation in different historical eras, Italian intellectual Marco Revelli proposes that the mass party was the political equivalent to what the Fordist factory was in the economic sphere. It resembled it in its 'gigantism' and its effort 'to incorporate large masses of men in a stable way, by arranging them in solid and permanent structures'.[55] The party was conceived as a factory where politics had to be produced through collective 'political work', inspired by Taylorist criteria of efficiency and rationalisation, as if politics were some sort of manufactured good. In this structure, the militants were, according to Revelli, the equivalent of workers in the assembly line, the local cadres being the production technicians and the central committee the corporate board of directors. Members were vertically integrated starting from their place of abode, through the presence of local sections and cells, in turn coordinated in regional or provincial councils, and from there in national assemblies responsible for electing the party leadership.

The analogy between the Fordist factory and the mass bureaucratic party goes a long way towards explaining why the crisis of the former has been accompanied by a decline of the latter. The crisis of accumulation of Fordist capitalism, signalled by the oil shocks and the stagflation crisis of the seventies, weakened both the organised working class and traditional sectors of the bourgeoisie, the mass parties' traditional bases of support. This in turn was compounded by the rise of new protest movements, like student rebellions environmental and feminist movements, and urban activists that signalled the emergence of new demands and sensibilities recalcitrant to the forms of representation offered by the political party, amidst a rising sentiment of anti-authoritarianism and resistance to *encadrement*.

As the mass party entered a slow but progressive decline, a new breed of political parties started to emerge, which presented themselves as 'light' and post-ideological alternatives to the modernist titan of the mass party while traditional mass parties also started to progressively acquire such post-modern characteristics. Already in the 1960s political scientists began debating the emergence of new party types, starting with Otto Kirchheimer's 'catch-all party',[56] then moving on to Angelo Panebianco's 'professional-electoral party'[57] to end with Peter Mair and Richard Katz's 'cartel party'.[58] Frankfurt School jurist and political scientist Kirchheimer used the term *catch-all party* to express the fact that political parties were increasingly flexible in their class base and ideological content, and attempted to adapt to the ever-changing mood of the electorate.[59] In the 1980s, Angelo Panebianco suggested the turn towards an electoral-professional party whose stress rested on the 'central role of the careerists and representatives of interest groups within the organization'.[60]

In the mid-1990s, Katz and Mair announced the rise of cartel parties, parties that were complicit with one another in their desire to control power and keep out possible contenders at the expense of an electorate deprived of meaningful choices.[61] They argued that parties were becoming stratarchical, namely that different 'faces' of the party – 'the party on the ground', 'the party in public office' and 'the party in central office' – 'were becoming independent from one another'. In this context, the party in public office was 'increasingly state-oriented, and corre- spondingly less firmly tied to civil society' as seen in its growing dependence on state funding. This evolution led to a 'sense of ... self- sufficiency', which often translated into a disregard for the sentiments of the base. In this context, 'the relevance of linkages which are based on trust, accountability, and above all, representation, tends to become eroded, both inside and outside the parties'.[62]

Catch-all party, electoral-professional party and cartel party are ad- mittedly quite different concepts which focus on different axes of transformation of political parties: their ideological and class nature, their organisational logic, and their relationship with the state and civil society.[63] Yet, these various notions may be taken as symptoms of the same trend: the crisis of the mass party and the connected rise of a post- industrial, post-ideological and post-class party that has come to dominate the neoliberal era and bears much of the responsibility for the growing disenchantment with politics. I shall refer to this party type as a 'television party' to highlight that the shift towards a new organisa- tional template, beyond the mass party was strongly influenced by the rise of TV as the dominant channel of political communication.

The neoliberal perversion of party democracy

The television party is that type of political party that has been depicted and satirised in TV series such as *The Thick of It*, *House of Cards* and *Baron Noir* – a party well known for the way in which it uses television as a key means of propaganda, often in highly cynical ways, while also relinquishing its bonds with the grassroots. Ever since the famous tele- vised debate between Richard Nixon and John Fitzgerald Kennedy in 1960, scholars have discussed how television has changed political com- munication, and these debates have continued to the present day to examine the political style of leaders such as Silvio Berlusconi and Donald Trump. Yet, often these discussions have overlooked how this transformation did not just concern political parties' external commu- nication but also their internal organisation.

The paradigmatic example of television party is provided by the po- litical venture of Silvio Berlusconi and his 'party-company', Forza Italia (Go Italy). Rather than a Fordist factory, the television party resembles a media or a marketing company, which has been considered as the vanguard of the post-industrial economy. It is significant that Silvio

Berlusconi founded Forza Italia on the media firepower of his television network and partly also on the territorial network of football fans' clubs of A.C. Milan, the club which he owned, providing a fitting substitute for the local militant support of traditional parties. The organisational change facilitated by the colonisation of the public sphere by TV can be appreciated at different levels.

First, the television party is a party that loses the support of an active base of militants. The prominence of television as a communication channel lessens the importance of a territorial support structure, and makes labour-intensive campaigning on the ground, such as through rallies, canvassing and the like, less important. According to Panebianco, 'Television and interest groups become far more important links (though precarious by definition) between parties and electorates than the traditional collateral organisations, the bureaucracy and party members.'[64] It is through its leaders' participation in TV shows that the television party mainly expresses itself and appeals directly to voters. This means that it can, by and large, do without a vast militancy rooted on the ground.

Second, it is a party that instead of the heavy and solid bureaucracy of the mass party adopts a light structure that looks more like an electoral committee, as it is suggested by the concept of 'professional-electoral' party. Echoing the tendency towards outsourcing of neoliberal capitalism, full-time salaried functionaries are substituted by professionals, such as consultants, pollsters and spin doctors often employed on a short-term basis as freelancers, in particular during election campaigns.[65] This goes hand in hand with the technocratic transformation of the 'party in public office', which enlists non-ideological policy wonks at his service.

Third, the TV party is a party that, unlike the mass party, no longer has a clearly defined class base and seeks opportunistically to draw its support from different socio-demographics according to circumstances. It is therefore a 'catch-all party' that attempts to intercept changing wishes and opinions, constantly polled by party experts, and then targeted through carefully vetted sound bites, such as those pronounced during TV interviews. The electorate comes to be approached as an 'electoral market', with marketing and advertising techniques used to understand and manipulate the people's desires as if they were little more than consumers, and the key market is usually identified in moderate voters, more likely to switch sides.

Fourth, the television party sees a strengthening of the party leader, with his persona becoming a recognisable image in the public eye and the leader's success being largely dependent on his telegenic appearance, often aided by heavy makeup, hair transplants and more than a few touches of cosmetic surgery, as seen in the case of Berlusconi and Trump. As noticed by Angelo Panebianco, 'mass media are driving parties towards personalized campaigns'[66] centred on candidates. Thereby the party leader is transformed into an actor that constitutes a key source of identification for party followers.

The dominance of the television party goes a long way to explain the detachment between citizenship and institutions, voters and elites, which we have experienced in recent years. With its mediatisation of politics, the television party type has eroded the role of the 'party on the ground' and strongly contributed to generating a passive attitude in the electorate, reminiscent of the 'couch potato' lifestyle attributed to TV viewers. In so doing, it has engendered political apathy, registered in nosediving citizens' trust in political parties and in the severe decline of membership in mainstream parties registered in recent decades.

In Italy, Christian Democracy and the Communist Party came to count more than 2 million members at their peak in the 1970s, while with the parties of the Second Republic, and in particular Forza Italia, the formerly communist Democrats of the Left and its successor organisation, the Catholic and Social Democratic Partito Democratico (Democratic Party), party membership never exceeded hundreds of thousands. In Britain, after having reached a peak of millions of members in the 1950s, the Labour Party collapsed to less than 200,000 members under Tony Blair's leadership. Turning towards television as the main channel to connect with the electorate, the television party ended up seeing its membership as a disposable asset, and in turn members came to see party participation as not being a very worthwhile pursuit. As a consequence, many mainstream formations have become 'parties without partisans' to use the expression of Richard Dalton, namely organisations that lack that vibrant internal life of the mass party at its apogee.[67]

The emergence of digital parties may be understood as a reaction against this trend of decline in political participation and party democracy. Informed by a widespread demand for the renewal of democracy, which in recent years has been expressed from many parts, including the protest movements of the Occupy wave in 2011, these formations promise to overcome the condition of apathy and passivity ushered in by the rise of the television party. They are presented by their leaders and advocates as forces that want to restore and reinvent party democracy, the set of mechanisms involved in deliberations and decision-making within political parties about strategy, leadership, candidateship and policy, in order to make the political party once again an authentic link between the citizenry and the state. By tapping into the participatory potential of digital media, it is claimed, these parties will lead people from the passivity of couch potatoes, to which they have been consigned by a televised politics, to a new era of mass participation led by 'netizens', who use digital media to participate directly in all the decisions affecting them.

Between democracy and oligarchy

The ambition of re-democratising the political party, which constitutes the prime mission of digital parties, needs to be understood in the context of long-standing debates about the relationship between political parties and democracy. For a long time, activists and scholars have debated the goods and ills of different democratic visions and connected organisational templates. A key influence on these debates has been played by German socialist activist and pioneering political sociologist Robert Michels and his 'iron law of oligarchy'.[68]

Writing at the beginning of the 20th century, Robert Michels developed a scathing analysis of political parties and their betrayal of democratic principles. In his book *Political Parties*, Michels argued that at the heart of modern democracies lies a paradox. Although democracy could only be fulfilled through the creation of collective organisations allowing otherwise powerless individuals to unite their forces, the creation of organisations ended up yielding oligarchies.[69] Power cliques emerging within political organisations would fight tooth and nail to preserve their power, making their own survival, rather than the official mission of the party, their actual end. For Michels, organisation is a conservative force that battles against democracy because it 'gives birth to the domination of the elected over the electors, of the mandataries over the mandators, of the delegates over the delegators'. As a consequence of the deep imbrication between organisational mediations and power dynamics 'who says organization says oligarchy'.[70]

This indictment of the political party stemmed from the bitter disappointment of Michels in seeing the German Social Democratic Party (SPD) turning increasingly bureaucratic at the same time as it was more moderate and cautious. The presence of a burgeoning bureaucracy and of an ever-growing army of cadres and functionaries ran against Michels' idealistic democratic ideals, informed by his reading of Jean-Jacques Rousseau and syndicalist leanings. He bitterly admitted that the 'gigantic number of persons belonging to a unitary organization cannot do any practical work upon a system of direct discussion'. Hence 'the need for delegation, for the system in which delegates represent the mass and carry out its will'. Having initially espoused a radically egalitarian view of democracy as direct government by the people, Michels was horrified to see how organisational necessities resulted in delegation substituting direct participation. This disappointment with socialist politics would later push Michels to become a sympathiser of Mussolini, in whom he saw a strongman capable of fighting against the oligarchy.

Such moral disappointment with party democracy is reminiscent of the objections raised to this day by anarchists, such as those involved in the Occupy Wall Street movement, who abhor the political party for being a hierarchical structure, what they equate to being necessarily anti-democratic. However, hierarchy is not necessarily the opposite of democracy. The dominant type of democracy in present societies, namely representative democracy, is actually highly hierarchical, centring on the elections of political representatives who go on to rule over the people. But this does not completely eliminate the possibility for bottom-up interventions from members, which can exercise influence in a number of ways, including the pressure they can exert on the leadership. Taking this relational approach, the degree of democracy depends on the balance of forces between the leadership and the membership and the degree of *responsiveness* of the former to the latter. Some parties, in this context, will appear as highly autocratic structures in which the leadership acts quite independently from the feelings of the base, sometimes even resorting to physical coercion to deal with recalcitrant members, as in the case of totalitarian parties. Other parties will instead appear more open to bottom-up stimuli coming from the base.

Early 20th-century political theorists such as Weber, Michels, Gramsci and elite theorists such as Pareto and Mosca[71] coincided in adopting a rather pessimistic view in which the leadership had a clear primacy. According to Weber, although the leadership is responsible for 'active direction of party affairs, including the formulation of programmes and the selection of candidates', the membership's role 'is notably more passive', but not as passive as the electorate's 'whose role is only that of objects of solicitation by the various parties'.[72] This view comes close to Michels' commentary about 'the general immobility and passivity of the masses' making the presence of leadership inevitable.[73]

Gramsci approached the question of party structure by identifying three elements: a 'mass element', namely the party's support base; a 'principal cohesive element', the leadership of the party and an 'intermediate element', articulating the two.[74] Without a mass element 'composed of ordinary, average men, whose participation takes the form of discipline and loyalty, rather than any creative spirit or organisational ability',[75] reasons Gramsci, a party could not exist. Yet, in and of itself the mass element, the support base of the party, is not capable of spontaneous self-organisation. It needs to be centralised, disciplined, organised. This task is assigned to the leadership, which is endowed with great 'cohesive, centralising and disciplinary powers'. The leadership has clear primacy over the membership, given that, as Gramsci proposes, though 'one speaks of generals without an army ... in reality, it is easier to form an army than to form generals'. This is in line with what Weber called the 'principle of small numbers' (*Prinzip der kleinen Zahl*) that is, 'the superior political manoeuvrability of small leading groups'.[76]

This view of the passivity of the mass, shared by Gramsci, Weber and Michels does not necessarily imply a wholesale indictment of democracy. Rather, what it entails is a model of 'competitive democracy' – in which, not too differently from Joseph Schumpeter's procedural theory of democracy,[77] the membership's power largely revolves around its ability to choose over competing leaders and the ongoing threat of revoking support. This may seem like a diminutive power, when compared with more idealistic theories of democracy as direct intervention of individuals in deliberative processes, which, as we shall see, strongly inform the vision of online democracy. However, it renders more realistically the nature of power struggles within political parties and the thorny relationship of conflict and negotiation that exists between the party's leadership and base.[78]

The working of this relationship depends by and large on an intermediary level, what Gramsci names the 'third element', or the articulating element. This is the entity which connects the first element (mass) with the second (leadership) and maintains contact between them, not only physically, but also morally and intellectually. This intermediate element comprises all the organisational, communicative structure and personnel that enable the leadership and the membership to communicate with one another. In the case of the mass party, the party type Gramsci has in mind, this can be seen as coinciding with the party's 'techno-structure', its apparatus of functionaries and representatives who act as the necessary point of connection between the summit and the base. In the case of the television party, this techno-structure is by and large substituted by the media system and specialised marketing personnel.

The key question is what happens to this third element in the context of digital parties, given their emphasis on disintermediation, which will be discussed in depth in the following chapters? Is this intermediary element eliminated in the name of directness and of that populist suspicion towards intermediary bodies that harks back to Rousseau? Or is it rather transformed and taken over by digital media and online participatory platforms?

The vexing relationship between power structure and intra-party democracy can be further developed by complexifying Gramsci's crystalline but perhaps all too schematic analysis and turning to more gradient representations of the political party's hierarchy. In a iconic passage of *Political Parties*, Robert Michels argued that participation in party life has an echeloned aspect. He represented the party as involving a number of levels and depicted it graphically, through narrower and larger lines, as the ever-decreasing runs of a stair which starts with voters (the largest group) and includes enrolled members, habitués of meetings (i.e. the militants), officials (those with office within or outside the party) and the central committee. As expressed by the metaphor of the stair, effective power is here in inverse ratio to the number of those who exercise it.[79]

Maurice Duverger utilised a different metaphor, the onion-like one of 'concentric circles'. According to this diagram, 'the largest [ring] includes all the electors who vote for candidates proposed by the party in local and national elections ....' The second corresponds to the sympathiser, 'a voter who recognises his inclination towards the party'. The third one, 'the inner circle, comprises the so-called militants, those people who consider themselves as members of the party, as elements of its community. They ensure its organisation and its functioning. They develop its propaganda and its general activity'. Finally, the fourth ring 'is the group of adherents, of members, which is inserted between militants and sympathisers. It is larger than the militants, but narrower than the sympathisers'.[80]

Establishing the degree of internal democracy entails exploring the relationship that occurs across these different elements of the party, the relative degree of porosity between different categories of participants and the overall balance of force between the membership and the leadership. The crux of the matter is to establish whether the more internal or upper levels are effectively controlled by the external or lower levels, and what kind of interaction between the two directions of influence is practically achieved. Indeed, as Duverger puts it, the 'central question is the relationship between these different circles'. In this context, 'the internal circles [are expected to] animate and conduct the exterior circles, but representing their orientation, and their general orientation coincide. In which case we speak of a democracy or, otherwise, of an oligarchy'.[81] The perennial risk is the insulation of the upper or internal layer of the party vis-à-vis the rest. Therefore a party will be considered democratic not when leadership is absent or weak, but rather when the leadership's legitimacy and strength depend on the validation and support of the membership.

The problem of bureaucracy

Key to ascertain the democratic quality of political parties and the relation between different elements within them is the question of bureaucracy, what perhaps constitutes the most classic and controversial issue in debates about organisation. Max Weber, the theorist of the 'iron cage of bureaucracy', cautioned against the possibility of the party central office becoming self-sufficient. If so, the party would appear in the guise of an 'inanimate machine ... busy fabricating the shell of bondage which men will perhaps be forced to inhabit someday, as powerless as the *fellahs* of ancient Egypt'.[82]

According to Weber 'wherever the modern specialized official comes to predominate, his power proves practically indestructible'. Therefore, politicians must resist this bureaucratisation acting as 'the countervailing force against bureaucratic domination'. This attempt however, Weber cautioned, will always be 'resisted by the power interests of the administrative policy-makers, who want to have maximum freedom from supervision and to establish a monopoly on cabinet posts'.[83] Michels had a similar perspective, in seeing the bureaucratic phenomenon as a fundamental cause of the anti-democratic distortions of the mass party: 'the oligarchical and bureaucratic tendency of party organization is a matter of technical and practical necessity. It is the inevitable product of the very principle of organization'.[84]

Gramsci shared similar fears about the risks of bureaucratisation. He asserted that 'the bureaucracy is the most dangerous hidebound and conservative force'. If this force 'ends up by constituting a compact body, which stands on its own and feels itself independent of the mass of members, the party ends up by becoming anachronistic and at moments of acute crisis it is voided of its social content and left as though suspended in mid-air'. In this context, 'when the party is progressive it functions "democratically" (democratic centralism); when the party is regressive it functions "bureaucratically" (bureaucratic centralism)'.[85] To summarise, it is not hierarchy and centralisation which in and of themselves constitute an enemy of democracy. Rather, the crux of the matter is whether the leadership and party staff are self-absorbed and self-reproducing or whether they serve members and deliver on their demands.

Bureaucracy can be seen as encompassing a variety of actors and functions. Most evidently it comprises the bureaucratic structure of the party in the central office, its functionaries and cadres, which constituted important figures in the mass party. It is worth noting that the television party was not entirely anti-bureaucratic either: while doing away with some of its salaried full-time staff, it hired a professional army of freelance consultants, pollsters and spin doctors. If anything, this 'externalised' bureaucracy is even more obnoxious, given that it lacks ideological loyalty and favours careerists over idealists.[86]

A further bureaucratic element is constituted by the party's organisational subunits and the forms of mediation involved in them.[87] As Duverger argues, two fundamental types of party exist: the direct party and the indirect party. Direct parties, by far the most common type, 'are composed of members that have signed a membership form, who pay their contribution every month and who participate more or less regularly to their local branch'. Indirect parties such as the UK Labour Party, to the contrary, are 'composed by trade unions, cooperatives, mutual societies, intellectual groups, who united to establish a common electoral organisation'.[88] Although the direct party is unitary, the indirect party is federal. However, in certain respects also the direct party is not really all that direct, built as it is on the back of territorial units, such as the 'section' of socialist parties, the 'cell' of communist parties and the 'militia' of fascist parties.[89]

All the basic elements of the party operate in accordance to the principle of delegation, the one which, as we shall see, is so decried by participationist ideology. Each of these basic units stands on its own as a sort of autonomous association, the site in which meetings are held and discussions are made which then feed into the broader party's decision-making process. It operates according to the principle of place, with one's locale of abode defining the necessary site of political participation. This system is represented in different guises in all the 'civic federated associations', which, as Theda Skocpol has proposed, constituted the dominant organisational template of the modern era, encompassing not only parties but also social, cultural and sports associations and even Masonic lodges.[90] It is at this level that the branch delegation system and bureaucracy are allied to one another. The management of the branch in fact requires the presence of cadres which act as local relays of the party's bureaucratic structure.

As we shall see, party bureaucracy, especially in its externalised and professionalised form as it has developed in the television party, constitutes one of the main targets of attack of the digital party. Emerging parties attempt to overcome the party's organisational apparatus to construct an extremely agile structure in which the most direct contact between membership and leadership may be achieved. In so doing, these organisations try to cater for an electorate grown wary of opaque state institutions and closed-off political organisations alike and wishing forms of participation that may approximate the directness and user-friendliness of apps and social media. But how do these parties actually go about this organisational restructuring? How do they integrate the logic of digital platforms in their operations? And most importantly, to what extent is this operation successful? Are these parties more democratic or more oligarchic than their predecessors? In other words, to what extent is the promise of online democracy realised in practice?

2
The People of the Web

As Gramsci proposed, 'The history of any given party can only emerge from the complex portrayal of the totality of society and state' and in line with this 'it may be said that to write the history of a party means nothing less than to write the general history of a country from a mono-graphic viewpoint, in order to highlight a particular aspect of it'.[91] What this means is that we cannot conceive of a political party in isola-tion from society, a mistake that too often is made by political science, when the party system is often studied from a formalistic perspective without taking into account its social determinants. Rather, at the outset of this project we need to be perceptive of the material and cultural con-ditions from which digital parties originate; to examine how these parties manifest a transformation of society in the present era of eco-nomic crisis and technological innovation; how they incorporate new attitudes, opinions and interests; how they express new social demands and connected policies, which mainstream parties appear unwilling or unable to capture. In other words, if we are to understand the architecture of the party, we first need to examine the ground it is erected on.

Capturing the social motivations behind the rise of digital parties entails exploring what we may call 'the People of the Web' to use an expression often utilised by Five Star Movement founder Beppe Grillo at his rallies, in his YouTube videos and in his Facebook posts. This notion can be seen as a symbolic rendering of the support base of digital parties, which in this chapter I identify from a socio-demographic perspective with the category of the 'connected outsiders', people who are caught in a condition of dissonance between their cultural and socio-economic conditions. These platform parties have in fact garnered massive sympathy from a constituency that, while often possessing a high level of internet access and education, as well as being younger than average, confronts economic insecurity and a perception of exclusion from the political process. The term 'people of the Web' stands to express a number of key features of this core electorate.

First, as the presence of the term *Web* stands to indicate, digital parties appeal to people who by and large identify themselves with the 'digital revolution', namely the rapid transformation of society produced by the penetration of digital technology into every aspect of our life and with its positive potential for social change. Digital parties rely upon people who are highly connected, and who by and large believe in the ability of digital technology to improve our lives and are informed by what scholar of digital activism Guobin Yang has described a 'cultural belief in the power of the Internet'.[92]

Second, as it is suggested by the use of the term *people*, this constituency is not mobilised by means of traditional class appeal, as it was prevalent at the height of the industrial era. Rather, it is invoked by resorting to populist subject interpellations, using notions such as the 'people' and the 'citizenry' which have by now become customary subjective referents for populist movements on both the left and the right. The use of this catch-all term belies the fact that the support base of these movements is highly varied and unstable, centring on a core constituency of digitally connected but often economically precarious millennials, but branching out into a host of other social constituencies, including the unemployed, older people and fractions of the working class and middle class.

Third – and this conjoins the first and the third element – digital parties appeal to people who live through a fundamental contradiction in which their extended scope of communication does not match up to their economic living standards and inclusion in the political process. These people may well be integrated in the communication system, as especially seen in the case of millennials who are famous for their media savviness. Yet, at the same time they are by and large socially and economically excluded, as they often fall prey to unemployment, precarity and stagnant wages. They are hyperconnected and hyperexploited; or, better, they are at the point of overlap between these two categories. Hence, the yearning for a new politics, one based on digital rights, social provisions and new democratic institutions, which may solve this condition of political marginalisation and economic insecurity.

In the course of the chapter, we explore the nature of this support base, paying attention to its socio-demographic dimensions and the new political demands that spring from it. We begin with a theoretical discussion of the idea of the social cleavage as a fundamental fracture that opposes different sections of society, proposing that the digital revolution is creating a dispute between connected outsiders and disconnected insiders that goes a long way to explain the rise of platform parties. We continue with a socio-demographic analysis of digital parties' supporters, which highlights the dominance of young and educated millennials with middling levels of income. Third, we expound the different wedge issues that have dominated these parties in their attempt to capture the support of connected outsiders: the demand for new digital rights; for privacy, freedom of expression and transparency online; the request for new forms of democratic participation adapted to present historical conditions and finally, the debate about new social provisions matching the transformation of the economy and work in a digital era.

The digital revolution and its connected discontents

The rise of digital parties has to be understood as stemming from a new fracture in society, a new division within the electorate which opposes social groups that are differentially positioned vis-à-vis a central social dilemma. A concept that comes handy when trying to capture the social determinants of political processes is the notion of *cleavage*, a term that has been popularised in political science by Norwegian political scientist Stein Rokkan and his colleagues in the 1960s and 1970s, to make sense of the ways in which, at key moments in the course of history, new conflicts and corresponding social fractures emerged, producing lasting transformations in the party system.[93] Rokkan, whose work was deeply influenced by the functionalism of Weberian American sociologist Talcott Parsons, described a number of key cleavages that have shaped politics in the West: the national/regional one, that was engendered by the birth of the modern nation-state; the church/government cleavage that was ushered in by processes of secularisation starting with the French Revolution and the Napoleonic era; the industrial/rural cleavage provoked by the rise of industrial capitalism and the strain it provoked vis-à-vis the rural economy and finally, the capitalists/workers cleavage pitting entrepreneurs against wage labourers.[94]

In this light, political parties may be viewed as the surface manifestation of deep rifts dividing society in conflicting camps. This analysis comes close to the way Marxist scholars discuss the existence of parties of the proletariat and of the bourgeoisie, but taking into account a greater number of social divides that do not necessarily have to do with economic conditions. For example, the government/church cleavage explains the existence of Christian parties defending religious morals against what they perceive as the dangers of liberal secularism. More recently some scholars have argued that the rise of libertarian New Left parties, and of right-wing populist parties that have emerged since the 1980s, points to a new cleavage having to do with differing cultural views, with New Left supporters being more secular and open to cultural diversity and non-conformist sexual and social behaviours, and right-wing populist supporters opting for cultural conservatism. Following this theory, we may interpret the emergence of digital parties as signalling a new cleavage which reflects the profound transformation that society has undergone in recent years as the result of two separate yet intertwined phenomena: the Great Recession beginning in 2008, and the 'digital revolution' produced by the diffusion of social media, apps, Big Data and personal devices.

When we speak of digital revolution, we refer to a wave of profound and highly disruptive social transformation, which is reminiscent of the effect produced by previous revolutions, and in particular the Industrial Revolution, or better the two industrial revolutions which took place between the late 18th and 19th centuries, and were instrumental to the development of modern society: the era of the factory, of oil and steel; of the modern corporation, and of the trade union. The digital revolution is a process beginning with the computing revolution in the post-war era and continuing with the developments in communication and networking that led to the creation of the internet. It is the era of optic cables, broadband internet and smartphones, in which society is regulated by complex processes of information and communication.

The manifold devices and services that epitomise such revolution are all *digital* in a very simple sense: because they operate on the basis of digital rather than analogue coding of information. Analogue technology, as for example predigital photography, cinema, painting the press, involves an 'analogy' with the object that is represented, for example the model in a life-drawing class, or the movement of a car in a Hollywood film. Information is stored on surfaces such as canvasses, magnetic tape, films or vinyl discs, already in the form of an analogue representation. Digital technology instead encodes all data, regardless of whether it is visual, audio or textual, in the same numerical form that has to do with discrete quantities (numbers) rather than the potentially infinite possibilities as they are available in analogue representations. This allows for the convenient storage of enormous amounts of information, and what is more important, it allows to 'program' such information through a series of instructions and algorithms, enabling the most complex applications. We see this incredible pliability of information processes in many wonders of the present era, from video games and virtual reality to social media sites hosting the interactions of millions of people, to video editing or text-to-speech software.

The consequences of this technological change are clearly visible in the economic field, both at the level of companies' management model and at the level of the changing nature of work. Until a few years ago, information and communication technology (ICT) was still considered to be an emerging area, with great potential, but subordinate to more established industries. These days, instead, the world's top companies by market valuation are almost entirely digital companies, with Apple worth over a trillion dollars and Amazon coming in the second place, before Google and Facebook. Thus, digital companies have displaced from the top corporate rankings, the oil and car companies – General Motors, Ford, Exxon, Shell and so on – that were the emblematic firms of the industrial era. This certainly does not mean that material production has disappeared. Cars continue to be produced, oil to be extracted, and the devices that make possible complex informational processes possible are hardwired in the mining of specific materials, such as silicon and rare earth minerals. Yet, these processes of production are pushed down the value chain, making the companies that produce them subordinated to the power of digital companies; that by now appear to have surpassed even banks in the echelons of global capitalism, and are in fact trying to become banks themselves, hoping to turn the millions of user accounts they have into credit accounts.[95]

The consequences of this technological transformation are out for everyone to see. From the way people produce, purchase and consume; to the way they get to know friends and sentimental and sexual partners; to the way they discuss films, art, current events or the latest musical hit – all aspects of our life, from the most public to the most intimate, seem to have been revolutionised by the ubiquity of laptops, smartphones and tablets in our homes, our offices, restaurants and parks.

This transformation has been widely celebrated by a number of intellectuals who see in technological development reasons for great optimism, and it has often been eulogised by digital parties' activists. Thus, in the declaration of principles of the Pirate Party the following is stated:

> We live in a time which is unique to human history. Never before have so many had the possibility to communicate so easily with each other. Never before have so many had access to so much knowledge. Never before has the spreading of information contributed to so many quick technical, cultural and economical advances, as well as having opened for new prerequisites and possibilities for participation and democracy.[96]

However, this transformation is far from being as overwhelmingly positive as Silicon Valley evangelists and followers of the New Age religion of 'digitalism' would want us to believe, in line with their 'solutionist'[97] narrative in which all problems, bar death, but perhaps eventually including it, may eventually be solved by wondrous digital tools.

The digital revolution carries a worrying underside of growing surveillance, shrinking privacy, ballooning concentration of ownership, increasing causalisation of labour and declining economic conditions for the majority of the population in Western societies. We live in times riven with a profound contradiction. On the one hand, this is, as the term *digital revolution* stands to suggest, a period of rapid technological innovation, severely transforming the way in which we live and leading many people to harbour great enthusiasms about the future. On the other hand, these are also days of great economic distress, resulting from the greatest crisis of capitalism in living memory.

It is ironic that the year 2007 – what most people consider as the beginning of the financial crash, though others postpone the beginning to 2008 – is also the year of release of the first iPhone, the product which popularised the smartphone, the killer device of the social media era. And indeed, exactly at the same time as our economic system was suffering such a profound economic shock, we have witnessed a wave of technological innovation, which seems to have few comparisons in its scope and rapidity. Although these trends may appear to be at each other loggerheads, they are not. In fact, economic crises have also often been moments of rapid technological innovation. Richard Florida, for example, highlights that during the Long Depression that started in 1873 there was a peak in patents, and the same may be said about the stagflation of the 1970s that led to the development of industrial robots.[98] Furthermore, we know from Joseph Schumpeter that capitalism is characterised by a tendency towards creative destruction,[99] in which incumbents in various industries are constantly threatened by the rise of new products and services, and we most clearly see this phenomenon in the so-called 'disruption'[100] posed by new companies, such as Airbnb, Amazon, Uber and Deliveroo, to existing companies.

The rise of digital behemoths such as the FAANGs – Facebook, Apple, Amazon, Netflix and Google – has created enormous economic unfairness. These companies have acquired monopoly status in the markets they have themselves largely created, with negative consequences for employment and consumers who need to eventually pay monopoly prices.[101] Furthermore, these companies have heavily engaged in tax avoidance tactics by moving their fiscal address to countries with low levels of taxation (e.g. Ireland and Luxembourg) and amassing huge cash reserves in fiscal havens. It has been reported that Apple alone has over $200 billion stashed away in tax havens.[102]

The digital revolution has also contributed to significantly worsening working conditions around the world as has been documented by Nick Dyer-Whiteford in *Cyber-proletariat*.[103] It is true that if one looks at the shining top of the digital economy, one will see the cropping up of highly qualified and highly paid jobs, from software development and engineering to marketing, community management and Web design, sometimes working in pretentious 'campuses' with lounges, sport facilities and the like. However, these attractive jobs continue to account for a very small share of the overall workforce. In fact, one of the most significant differences between the industrial and digital giants is that the latter have a far lower employees/turnover ratio compared with manufacturing companies that are notoriously more labour-intensive. For example, as of 2017, Google counted a total of 61,814 employees worldwide, far smaller than the number of General Motors employees, which stood at 180,000 as of December 2017, down from 600,000 in 1979, despite being a fraction of Google in terms of annual turnover. The bulk of new jobs that have been created by the digital revolution and its transformation of the world of work tend instead to be lowly qualified and lowly paid jobs.

This trend is epitomised by the rapid growth of causalised workers such as call centre workers, riders for delivery companies such as Deliveroo, Uber drivers or warehouse workers as those of Amazon[104] among many other typical profiles of the so-called 'gig economy'.[105] These figures can be considered as part of the 'precariat', an emerging class which, in his *General Theory of the Precariat*, Italian activist and theorist Alex Foti describes as 'the underpaid, underemployed, underprotected, overeducated, and overexploited'.[106] What is more, many fear the job-destroying avalanche of the incoming second automation revolution, with robots predicted to eliminate many manual jobs such as drivers substituted by self-driving cars, and artificial intelligence threatening to destroy clerical jobs, such as those in the legal and accounting sectors.

This ambiguous nature of the digital revolution provides useful insights to make sense of the support base of digital parties, which, as we shall see, centres on digitally savvy millennials living in urban areas. These people are 'connected outsiders' because they are all and at the same time the digital revolution's most enthusiastic advocates and its most vocal discontents. They are the people who prize the most the cultural and social innovations brought by digital technologies and services, which have seeped into the most remote corners of their lives. Yet, they also stand in the front line of the most obnoxious effects of this technological change. It is imperative to take into account this paradoxical state of affairs, if we are to understand the root motivations that have informed the establishment of digital parties, the mission these formations have set themselves and the way they are positioned vis-à-vis a variety of emerging conflicts that define our era. We shall concentrate on three key issues that have been raised by platform parties: digital freedoms, democracy and economic security.

The conflict around digital freedoms regards the condition of the individual vis-à-vis large-scale organisations such as corporations and the state and the emergence of new forms of online surveillance. The consequences of Big Data on civil liberties and individual privacy have become widely debated after a number of famous events, from the revelations made in 2013 by U.S. information analyst Edward Snowden about the way digital companies were collaborating with the National Security Agency to conduct mass surveillance on internet users, to the 2018 controversy surrounding Cambridge Analytica and its data misuse. A concern about privacy was also central to Pirate Parties' campaigning in defence of peer-to-peer file-sharing, as it was felt that preventing people from downloading copyrighted material would have involved large-scale surveillance. This conflict opposes the connected outsiders to all those authorities interested in maintaining forms of surveillance and control over individuals.

The second conflict regards democracy, and the mismatch between the institutional framework we have inherited from the industrial era and the conditions of life of a digital society. The profound transformation of our everyday experience has made many of the typical mechanisms of participation that were extant to the industrial society – from periodical ballots to Wednesday night meetings – unfit as a vehicle of organisation and mobilisation in the context of the digital society. Although some sections of the population, and in particular older and more economically secure 'disconnected insiders', still seem to feel represented by this system, this is not the case for connected outsiders, who demand new forms of participation, more in line with present technological and social conditions.

The third conflict regards the economy and involves the severe impoverishment and precarity suffered by many people, and especially young people, as a consequence of the combined effect of the economic crisis (which has disproportionately hit young generations) and of digital disruption produced by the diffusion of digital companies. In this context, the connected outsiders demand new forms of economic support, new social provisions and services that may guarantee them some security amidst economic uncertainty, vis-à-vis both corporations and the disconnected insiders who are resistant to pay the costs of this new social pact.

Young, connected, broke

Digital parties are parties of *outsiders*, of people who, because of their age, professional situation or economic security, feel excluded from society, and therefore harbour grievances against the existing system and establishment parties that are seen as keener on representing insiders. The *outsider* can be understood as a person who experiences an unstable social and economic condition, who is struggling to make ends meet and who often finds herself stretched because of the lack of welfare state provisions. This is a condition that has become widespread since the financial crisis of 2008, after which digital parties have emerged and grown, and which is particularly strong among millennials, the cohort providing the bulk of support for these movements, that face high levels of unemployment and job insecurity.

Pirate Parties have been well known to be 'younger and savvier about the Internet' as reported by the *New York Times*,[107] and particularly concerned about digital rights. This bias towards young people is also visible in the case of the Five Star Movement, for which age has long been the main predictor of support. A 2014 survey by pollster SWG[108] argued that the Five Star Movement was over-represented by those below 45 years old and under-represented among those over 55 years old, and was particularly strong among people between ages 35 and 44. More recent research after the 2018 elections corroborates this picture. While it has become more inter-generational than in previous years, the M5S continues to be over-represented among those aged 18–34 and under-represented among those over age 65, who overwhelmingly voted for establishment parties Partito Democratico and Forza Italia.[109] Podemos is even more skewed towards young voters. According to a survey by *El Pais*, the overwhelming majority of its voters in the 2014 European elections were below 35 year olds.[110] This trend continued despite the votes of the party more than doubling in the 2015 and 2016 national elections. According to research by the CIS institute in 2016, Podemos's voters were still in their majority below 35 years of age and in the elections that same year Iglesias' party won 44 per cent of the vote of young people.[111] The typical profile of Podemos electorate was said to be urban youth with higher education.[112]

This youth bias should be understood as part of a larger trend of political radicalisation of young voters as a consequence of the distress provoked by the 2008 financial crisis. This tendency is also seen beyond digital parties proper, and in particular in post-crash left formations and candidates that have in fact also experienced a spectacular growth in the young vote. In the 2017 French presidential elections, Jean Luc Mélenchon was by far the most popular candidate among young people, with 30 per cent of those between ages 18 and 24 turning to him. Jeremy Corbyn's impressive performance in the 2017 UK general elections was propelled by an avalanche of youth vote. In a post-election survey conducted by YouGov,[113] it was found that Labour share of votes was inversely proportional to voters' age. Labour scored 66 per cent among those ages 18–19; it only had 19 per cent of support among those aged over 70. Finally, the typical voter of Bernie Sanders was said to be below 45 years of age.

The sympathy of young people, especially those living in urban areas, towards digital parties is unsurprising for a number of reasons. First, young people enjoy higher than average levels of internet access, which means they are more likely to buy into the techno-utopian idea of the digital revolution as a positive change. Second, they have been disproportionately affected by the effects of the economic crisis, stagnating wages, unemployment and labour casualisation. Therefore, they tend to be more receptive to the message of social change offered by digital parties and their promise to redistribute wealth.

In terms of levels of income and occupation, it can be said that digital parties are neither working-class nor middle-class parties. Although more skewed towards middle and low incomes, these parties' support is quite inter-classist, something that is rather unsurprising in the era of 'catch-all politics'.[114] According to a research by CISE research centre conducted in 2014, the Five Star Movement was over-represented among manual workers and the unemployed, and under-represented among pensioners and the upper middle class.[115] Further research pointed to insecurity of employment as an important predictor of M5S vote, with more precarious voters, regardless of whether they were in manual or intellectual professions, more likely to vote for the Five Star Movement, and with more secure workers tending to vote more for Partito Democratico.

Podemos has been the first party among the unemployed, manual workers and the self-employed, but it has also drawn high level of representation among people with high income and high education in urban areas. A CIS research institute barometer in 2015[116] represented the vote of Podemos with a V curve, high among the unemployed and workers, low among people with average salary and highest among people with mid to high levels of income. Podemos thus encompasses a diverse coalition which includes many people who feel victimised by the crisis, regardless of whether they are part of the working class or the middle class.

Some post-crash left parties show a similar socio-demographic profile, which, though encompassing also people of the middle and upper middle classes, caters to the unemployed and sections of the working class. In the 2017 elections, Jean-Luc Mélenchon was the first candidate among the unemployed, where he won 31 per cent of the polls, but he was surprisingly low among industrial workers, scoring higher among employees and cadres.[117] Similarly, Bernie Sanders' voters in the presidential primaries in 2016 had an average income below $50,000 dollars. Labour under Corbyn was quite equally represented across all income brackets, though more pronounced among the DE classes of people on low income, where it had 44 per cent of the vote share. Finally, Labour was over-represented among those with a high level of education, scoring 49 per cent among those with a degree. Across all these cases we find a common inter-classist trend that reflects a 'catch-all' orientation, but with a significant representation of people experiencing difficult economic conditions and in particular insecurity of employment.

Further interesting is the level of education and internet connection of digital parties' voters. The Five Star Movement initially seemed to be on average regarding the level of education. However, in the 2018 elections it outperformed all parties concerning voters with a university degree.[118] This took commentators by surprise as it did not seem to conform to the view of the Five Star Movement as the party of the excluded.[119] Its electoral heartland was in small cities between 50,000 and 100,000 inhabitants and among people with higher levels of internet access.[120] Podemos voters are known to be above average in terms of education, with many of them holding a degree. They are over-represented among people living in cities above 100,000 inhabitants and with higher levels of education. Podemos enjoys 30 per cent support among people with a university degree and among students.[121] Young and educated people living mostly in urban areas are also the categories that enjoy higher than average levels of internet connection, a variable which has been demonstrated to be a predictor of vote for Pirate Parties, the Five Star Movement and Podemos.[122]

It is significant that some of the aforementioned biases are also visible in the composition of the 'party in public office'. The Five Star Movement's MPs after the 2013 parliamentary elections were impressively young on average, with the average age in the Chamber of Deputies at 33 years old. Of the 109 MPs in the lower chamber, 13 were students (an impressive number), 30 employees, 19 self-employed, 14 teachers, 10 unemployed (also a remarkable figure) and 1 researcher; there were also 3 doctors and 9 lawyers, both groups active and practising, and 4 manual workers, including a plumber. In terms of educational background, science and technology degrees came first, with 17 engineers and a conspicuous number of geologists and biologists.[123] Regarding Podemos, the elected Congress representatives in the aftermath of December 2016 elections[124] were found to be quite young, with 40 years as the average age, compared to an overall average age of 47. Out of 65 members of Podemos and allied 'confluences' 26 per cent were professors, while 7 per cent were technicians and 5 per cent social workers, and there was a conspicuous number of students.[125] Furthermore, Podemos MPs had a higher than average level of education as seen in the number of foreign languages they could speak.

Overwhelmingly young and highly educated, yet often also 'broke' and economically insecure, the *connected outsiders* are an emerging constituency that, dissatisfied by establishment parties existing parties, has found in digital parties a channel to voice a new series of demands on privacy, transparency, democracy and economic justice; demands which establishment parties have been incapable or unwilling to capture and on whose support digital parties have established their impressive electoral success.

Claiming digital freedoms

No hook, no eyepatch, no parrot on the shoulder. Christian Engström disappoints those who expect to meet someone looking like Johnny Depp's Jack Sparrow in *Pirates of the Caribbean* – one of the films that have the most illegal downloads – or a dishevelled young hacker spending all-nighters in front of a computer screen. When I met him in spring 2009, shortly before the European elections that would make him one of the first two Pirate Party MEPs, this activist, with a long history of involvement in copyright reform and internet privacy campaigns at national and European level, came across as a typical computer scientist, serious and methodical, but with a good sense of humour. The only detail that betrayed his radical political leanings was the pin fixed on his lapel, the symbol of the Pirate Party, with the threatening black sail shaped into a 'P' for Pirates.

The Pirate Parties owe their existence to the emergence of new demands: for 'digital freedoms' or 'digital rights'.[126] Digital rights have to do with the way information and communication technologies have transformed the relationship of individuals with large-scale organisations, and in particular corporations and the state. They include the following: the right to privacy; the right to freedom of expression online; the right to freely exchange material with other internet users; the right to maintain control over one's own data; the demand for free access to government information and transparency in public records; the right to a free or inexpensive internet connection and a reform of copyright laws to adapt them to present social conditions.

This demand for digital rights was central to Pirate Parties. These were born as single-issue parties concentrating on the defence of peer-to-peer file exchange, what the political mainstream and film and record companies would simply consider as 'piracy', hence the ironic choice to call themselves Pirates. The Pirate Party founded in 2006 by Rick Falkvinge, really grew in popularity in the aftermath of a decision by Swedish judges on 17 April 2006 to condemn the manager of Pirate Bay, a site that indexes the torrent files used by millions of users around the world to download movies, music and software – to one year in jail and 3 million euros in damages for breach of copyright law. After the ruling, the party members went in a few days from 10,000 to over 40,000, setting the basis for the spectacular growth in support experienced by the party in the following years.

Starting from this narrow demand for a reform of the copyright law, which Engström alongside other activists had advocated for many years, the Pirate Parties have progressively come to encompass a number of other issues that concern our digital life. This evolution can be seen by looking at the more recent versions of the Party Declaration of Principles. The first and perhaps most important is privacy, against the perception that citizens are left with no defence in a world of constant surveillance for commercial or security purposes, waged by digital corporations and governments. In fact, since Pirate Parties' early days, one of the arguments in defence of peer-to-peer file exchange was precisely that in order to block it, governments would have had to conduct very intrusive controls on people's online activities. The urgency of this issue has become all the more apparent in the aftermath of the 2013 Edward Snowden revelations about the doings of the National Security Agency mass surveillance operations, and after the Cambridge Analytica scandal which highlighted the scale of Facebook's mishandling of user data. Activists have proposed various solutions, including the use of encrypted communication and the development of the Tor (the onion router) tunnelling service, which shields internet users from control over their internet activity. In the Pirate Party's Declaration of Principles 3.1, it thus is stated, 'The postal secrets act shall be elevated to a general communications secrets act. Just as it is prohibited to read someone else's mail today, it shall be forbidden to read or access e-mail, SMS or other forms of messages, regardless of the underlying technology or who the operator may be.'[127]

A further question involves freedom of expression online, and the fight against censorship, in the face of various attempts to encroach on this freedom, not only in the context of autocratic governments often mentioned as part of a digital axis of evil – Iran, Russia and China – but also in Western democracies, in which bloggers are often subject to harassment and legal repression. This is an issue that the Five Star Movement has tried to appropriate, creating what it calls *Scudo della Rete* (Shield of the Net), a service that provides legal advice to movement activists and bloggers who have been targeted by legal suits.

Connected with this claim for freedom of expression is the demand for transparency in government acts. Although in the case of privacy the demand is made that the information of the individual is not made accessible to the state or companies without explicit consent, here the converse is the case. According to this vision, government information should be freely accessible to the public, allowing individuals to closely monitor the action of officials. The demand for transparency is one that is extant in digital culture, as seen most spectacularly by leaking websites releasing confidential information of public interest such as Wikileaks. In its declaration of principles, the Pirate Party has strongly sided with the demand for 'transparency from those in power'.[128] Similarly, the Five Star Movement has often advocated that the state needs to open all its proceedings to the scrutiny of citizens and in this spirit it has often live-streamed political meetings, countering its openness to public oversight with the secrecy of more traditional parties. Furthermore, it has organised the restitution of part of M5S MPs' monthly salary with a dedicated website, tirendiconto.it (alluding in Italian to the process of accounting), in which all the sums given by M5S reps are listed. Similar measures have been adopted by Podemos, which has a salary restitution programme called Impulsa financing social and community projects, and which publishes all its budgetary information on the party's website.

Many of these demands and policies that are part of the 'digital freedoms' platform have by now transcended the confines of digital parties. This is seen in governmental initiatives such as the Digital Bill of Rights proposed in the United Kingdom by Jeremy Corbyn or Brazil's Internet Bill of Rights (*Marco Civil da Internet*) which propose to update rights and freedoms to the digital condition. It may thus be said that whereas the early defining issue of digital parties – digital rights – has been progressively absorbed by mainstream politics, digital parties, including the Pirate Parties that were most strongly single-issue in their original design, have progressively come to encompass a greater variety of issues, starting from the question of updating democracy to the digital condition.

Hacking democracy

Although the demand for digital rights is the one that first signalled the rise of digital parties, the demand for a digital democracy updating the spirit of the democratic project to present technological and social conditions should be considered the real 'wedge issue' of this new wave of political parties. Digital parties originate from a widespread feeling of dissatisfaction with present democracy, at a time when many citizens feel that they have little say on important questions affecting their lives, and that the institutions that are supposed to represent them are out of tune with contemporary life.

This 'out-of-sync' condition of political institutions was represented by protestors in Sweden when, three days after the Pirate Bay raid on 31 May 2006, they shouted out of a government building, 'give us back our servers, or we'll take your fax machine.' Thereby, political institutions are viewed as dinosaurs that use outdated technology and are out of place in the modern era. To remedy this situation, platform parties have experimented with a variety of tools geared at constructing an online democracy that may set democratic processes in line with present technological and social conditions. We discuss these new tools, their affordances and political implications in the course of the book. But at this stage, some observations about the motivations that drive this process are necessary.

The dissatisfaction with democracy that explains the appearance of digital parties is a phenomenon that has quite a long history and can be traced back at least to the 1970s.[129] It is signalled by a range of converging signs of crisis of liberal democracy, including the decline of mass membership organisation, increasing individualisation and atomisation of the citizenry, as well as the role played by TV and mass media.[130] This dissatisfaction affects both the relationship between citizens and institutions and between citizens and political parties.

Confidence in political institutions has been dropping significantly in recent decades, manifesting a growing distance between the citizenry and the state, which increasingly seems to operate just as a service provider funded by taxes. Trust in political parties has also undergone a severe decline, as party members and citizens feel increasingly disillusioned about the unaccountability of a political leadership, that has often appeared as more concerned with winning elections and maintaining power at all costs than addressing substantial policy issues. Part of this distortion has to do with the changing relationship between parties and voters, as seen 'in the growing reliance [of parties] on the state apparatus for support instead of their own voters/members' amidst 'a growing public detachment with political parties', as described by Katz and Mair.[131] Namely, it is as if parties have by now stopped representing citizens within the state, turning instead to representing the state among citizens.

The sense of a democratic crisis has distant roots and has been discussed for decades now. But it has been significantly exacerbated with the financial crisis of 2008. Faced with the reality of a political system in which politicians seemed to be worried only about large banks and corporations needing public bailout money, while being unconcerned with the hardship of large sections of the electorate, many citizens have become amenable to the promise of new forms of democracy doing away with the privileges of the political class. Existing democracy is often painted as corrupt and distorted, bearing little resemblance to the lofty ideals associated across history with this idea. Hence the frequent description of politicians as part of an elite, an establishment or a caste, namely a class unanchored from society and the electorate, and uniquely bent on self-preservation. This distrust towards representative democracy echoes the criticisms voiced by the movements of the squares of 2011 – Occupy Wall Street, the Indignados and many other anti-austerity movements, whose flagship phrase was, famously, 'They don't represent us' and which have been an important inspiration for digital parties.[132]

Counter to this, platform parties often project the picture of a better democracy or a 'real democracy', to use a famous slogan of the Spanish Indignados during the 2011 protest movements. In the essay *Il Grillo canta sempre al tramonto* (The grasshopper [*grillo* in Italian] always sings at sunset), Dario Fo, winner of the 1997 Nobel Prize in Literature, along with Beppe Grillo and Casaleggio senior celebrated the power of direct democracy as a means of overcoming the present corrupt political system. They referred to Thucydides' rendering of Pericles' funeral oration, where the Athenian leader asserted, 'Our form of government is called a democracy because its administration is in the hands, not of a few, but of the whole people. In the settling of private disputes, everyone is equal before the law.'[133]

Authors such as Simon Tormey[134] have referred to the idea of a post-representational democracy to explain the common spirit behind a number of initiatives that have emerged in recent years, from participatory budgeting in Puerto Alegre to online deliberative consultations like those held in the city of Barcelona, all taken as examples of a new model of democracy that may point towards an overcoming of representative democracy as such. This suspicion towards representation is made visible in the popularity acquired among party activists by Jean-Jacques Rousseau, the theorist of direct popular democracy, after whom the Five Star Movement participatory platform is named. The basic idea is that digital technology enables overcoming, partly or wholly, the forms of representation and delegation that have so far dominated our democracy in mass societies, ushering in a digital democracy in which citizens participate directly in all important decisions.

Digital democracy has been defined as 'a collection of attempts to practise democracy without the limits of time, space and other physical conditions'.[135] Alongside similar terms – *online democracy, e-democracy, cyber-democracy, e-government, e-voting* or *open government* and *teledemocracy* – it has been used to capture the way digital technology can enhance political participation by: lowering barriers to information and discussion; extending the ways citizens can intervene on policy-making and allowing citizens to follow policymaking more closely.[136] This notion operates with a rather concise and intuitive techno-deterministic narrative: digital technology offers the opportunity to go beyond the process of representation to develop a more participatory politics, tapping into the participatory architecture and culture of the social web. Although for many years this idea appeared as a vapourware, with little impact on politics and society, digital parties have turned it into a key plank of their new politics and enacted it in the creation of decision-making platforms often involving hundreds of thousands of people.

The ambition behind the idea of online democracy is making citizens' involvement in the political process more direct and authentic. As argued by Davide Casaleggio, son of Five Star Movement guru Gianroberto Casaleggio, in an article published on *The Washington Post*, 'The Internet has made the established parties, and the previous organizational model of democratic politics more generally, obsolete and uneconomic.' He proposes that the effort of the Five Star Movement was to offer citizens direct democracy and that 'representative democracy – politics by proxy – is gradually losing meaning'.[137]

This yearning for a more direct democracy is an aspect that the Five Star Movement largely drew from the Pirate Parties and their experimentations with alternative forms of democracy and their use of the LiquidFeedback decision-making platform. In the declaration of Principles of the Pirate Party, it is proposed that the 'fantastic tools' of digital technology can produce an advancement in democratic mechanisms and that we need to go towards a form of democracy that 'assumes free, unsupervised communication'. This approach is echoed in Podemos's intention of 'hacking democracy', a phrase that was often used to describe the party's development of a participatory decision-making system with the aid of coders hailing from the 15-M protest movement.

This vision of democracy applies both to the transformation of political parties and more generally to political institutions, which digital parties want to reform after their own image once they take power. And in fact, many of these parties have proposed the creation of new institutions of direct democracy. The Five Star Movement has advocated the introduction of national referendums without quorum, and since entering government it has established a ministry for direct democracy. Davide Casaleggio went as far as suggesting that parliaments at some point may become superfluous, igniting a wave of indignation and accusations of authoritarianism from political commentators. In its electoral programme, Podemos has proposed that once in government 'the implementation of digital democracy tools will have special relevance'[138] as a means to achieve a more direct participation of the citizenry in decisions. As we shall see, this yearning for a new democracy supported by digital platforms has been central to the organisational restructuring introduced by these parties. But this is also an area of great controversy because of the mismatch between the idealistic discourse of these movements and an often hypocritical implementations.

Re-booting the economy

The claim for new personal freedoms and for new democratic processes does not exhaust the array of policies pursued by digital parties, which are also concerned with more material and economic questions. Common to these parties is the diagnosis that the old forms of economic organisation and regulation are failing and that therefore it is urgent to change the way we address economic problems. On the one hand, this diagnosis involves the demand for an hastening of the innovation drive in the economy, facilitating the diffusion of digital technologies and accelerating the turn towards renewable energy sources. On the other hand, it comprises the demand for new forms of social protection and new public services that may address the widespread experience of insecurity in the digital society.

In their techno-optimistic vision, Pirate Parties have often argued for a rapid diffusion of technological innovations, reforming antiquated laws on copyright and patents, providing people with free internet connection and facilitating a transformation of society with the support of digital tools. This techno-optimism is also visible in the Five Star Movement. One of the highlights of the M5S 2018 election campaign was the promise of making Italy a 'Smart Nation', an adaptation of the famous notion of smart cities. In this vision, Italy, one of the most technologically underdeveloped countries in the Organisation for Economic Co-operation and Development (OECD) group, will eventually shake years of inaction and sclerotisation and become attractive to digital companies of all sorts.

Although not as techno-optimistic as the Pirates and the Five Star Movement, Podemos has also taken a quite positive stance on the promise of technology especially in regards to renewable energy. Thus, for example, Podemos in the 2015 and 2016 elections has proposed the need for a new model of production that involves the 'promotion of self-consumption facilities, giving small direct aids to the purchase of solar panels or mini-generators for self-consumption without spilling into the network' and the 'the establishment of fiscal measures that tax the consumption of non-renewable and polluting energies, as well as the provision of tax incentives for the use of renewable and non-polluting energies'.[139] Solar energy is seen not only as a source of cheap and sustainable energy but also as a means to break the monopoly held by oil-producing countries on the global energy supply, and as a way of empowering ordinary people to produce electricity at home. Furthermore, Podemos has promised to fight against the digital divide, improving accessibility to telephony and the internet, especially for people in peripheral areas.

All in all, these proposals paint an image of digital parties as progressive modernising forces that want to usher in new technologies, allowing for a more efficient, environmentally sustainable and inclusive society. Nevertheless, many of these parties are also cognisant of the new social problems that characterise the digital condition, and the need to establish new forms of social protection, in a society in which job structures, forms of employment appear to be increasingly unstable.

One of the key measures advocated by many digital parties is Universal Basic Income (UBI). This policy, which aims at providing all citizens, irrespective of their employment situation or wealth, with a state-provided subsidy, has been widely debated in recent years and experimented in a number of countries including Switzerland, Finland and the Netherlands. Basic income in its various denominations is often framed as a response to the imbalances created by technological evolution. In Autonomist Marxist debates, starting from the times of Potere Operaio in the 1970s, it was viewed as a means to remunerate that productive activity which happens outside the workplace, at a time at which value production is dependent on social, cultural and linguistic processes. More recently, UBI has been proposed as a solution to the automation revolution and its negative effects on employment. Personalities from the Silicon Valley, including Mark Zuckerberg, have thrown their hats in favour of basic income, signalling a growing interest also from some capitalist sectors towards this measure.

Podemos has proposed the introduction of this measure on a universal basis. The Five Star Movement has instead adopted it as a synonym for a jobseekers' allowance, along the lines of the one available in the United Kingdom, or the Hartz IV welfare reform in Germany, with the transfer being conditional on the acceptance of employment opportunities.

For its advocates, basic income will free people from the blackmail of wage labour and provide them with a buffer to engage in volunteer activities, contribute to their community, educate themselves and attend to the needs of their family and community. For critics, basic income is, in fact, little more than a charity provision, which ultimately entails an assault to the post-war social compact or what remains of it. They point to the fact that this measure comes very close to the negative income tax proposed by arch-neoliberal Milton Friedman and argue that basic income will contribute to the further impoverishment of the proletariat because employers will feel confident that their workers were already provided with the bare minimum for survival, and will consequently pay their employees lower wages. Furthermore, it is feared that this measure will be then used as a justification to do away with pre-existing institutions of the welfare state, such as unemployment benefits.

Some scholars and activists have proposed universal basic services (UBS) as an alternative to basic income. They propose that the state model of universal healthcare should expand to other domains of life such as transport or communication services. This measure is aimed at protecting citizens, especially those at the lower end of society, and shielding them from the effects of automation and their impact on employment and stagnating wages, as well as providing all citizens with a job guarantee through extended state employment. What is interesting across these policies, regardless of their specific orientation, is the way they illustrate digital parties' efforts to devise a new model of social insurance in a society marked by extreme diversification and occupational instability.

All digital parties express a suspicion towards Big Capitalism, banks, large multinational corporations and the like, which they perceive as being bent on profiting from their dominant position. However, they are not necessarily anti-capitalist. Digital parties often value small and medium business and have proposed measures to support entrepreneurs and the self-employed whom they see as creators of wealth and who have been facing major difficulties to survive since the beginning of the economic crisis. It is significant that the founder of the Swedish Pirate Party, Rick Falkvinge, was previously an entrepreneur and an activist of the Liberal Party. The reform of copyright law that has become the flagship policy of Pirate Parties is understood as being, among other things, also a way to give more power to small business, to the amateur and the creative entrepreneur, by doing away with outdated regulations. By lifting the grip of large corporations over the market, it is hoped that distortions will be eliminated, and a healthy market economy reinstated. Despite advocating forms of state intervention in the economy, including the nationalisation of transport services, the Five Star Movement may be described as having a soft liberal element. At one point, in the European Parliament, it tried to move from the right-wing populist group Europe of Freedom and Direct Democracy (EFDD), where it stood with Nigel Farage's UKIP, to the Alliance of Liberals and Democrats for Europe (ALDE) i.e. the liberal-democratic group. Left-oriented digital parties such as Podemos, while being more oriented towards redistributive policies, have equally encompassed proposals to support small business.

In conclusion, despite the diversity in digital parties' economic views, which is testament to the ideological diversity that characterises them, ranging from liberal to socialist proposals, all these formations are concerned with transforming the economy, adapting it to the changing conditions of a digital society and redressing some of its most glaring imbalances. Digital parties thus present themselves as actors that are not simply riding the wave of the digital revolution, but also trying to direct it towards more democratic and social ends and usher in a more just and inclusive society.

3
When the Party Mimics Facebook

Despite its association with immobility and conservatism, the political party is a rather pliable organisational template that integrates the forms of organisation and communication that are prevalent at the time. Whereas in the industrial era, the party styled itself after the Fordist factory, in these times of social media and apps it has come to adopt the quality of Facebook and other digital companies known under the collective acronym of FAANGs. Looking at the doings of formations such as the Pirate Parties, the Five Star Movement and Podemos, it soon becomes apparent that what these organisations propose is a political translation of the operational model that brought to success figures such as Facebook's Mark Zuckerberg and Amazon's Jeff Bezos, applying the logic of the digital company to the political arena to reap economies of scale in the way they reach out to their supporters and involve them in online discussions and decisions. This tendency has been seen in their enthusiastic adoption of social media of all sorts, with many of these formations rapidly gathering a large following on Facebook, Twitter and Instagram. However, the adoption of the logic of platforms runs much deeper than a change in the party's political communications since it crucially affects the level of internal party organisation. Besides using available commercial platforms, these parties have also developed their own dedicated online participation platforms, which provide a space for members/users to be involved in deliberations and ratifications.

This transformation revolves around the attempt of updating the political party to leverage the power of digital technologies. The disintermediation achieved by FAANGs in several areas of information, culture, knowledge, commerce, entertainment, is being translated by digital parties in the promise of a more direct democracy that would disintermediate between voters and representatives. By tapping into the affordances of digital platforms, these parties aim at doing away with the bureaucratic 'third element', which – as we discussed at the end of chapter 1 – was considered central to the operation of the mass party and which is now considered not only an unnecessary intermediary but also as a bias factor in projecting the will of the people. In the same way in which social media bear the promise of eliminating bottle-necks in the system of communication and information, and other intermediaries such as the mainstream media, retail malls, restaurants and the like, so the digital party promises to use digital media to facilitate the direct participation of the citizenry in all the important decisions that concern the public interest. As we shall see in the course of the chapter, this project affects different facets of the party, such as its definition of membership, organisational structure, and the design of policy and political content. As a consequence of this shift, the digital party acquires the virtualised quality of the cloud, which is present anywhere and nowhere in particular, centralising all information in one virtual place while distributing interactions. And, like successful start-ups, platform parties become unsaddled by heavy organisation and material infrastructure, allowing them to grow at a spectacular rate. In this 'platformisation' trend lies the identity of the digital party and both the element of superiority and the vulnerability of this party form.

Organisation in a digital society

As with all forms of organisations, parties are closely tied with technology, with the way different technological conditions and connected modes of production end up facilitating different party forms, as discussed in the previous chapter. As argued by British/Canadian management theory author Gareth Morgan, organisations have always been technological, and more so since the Industrial Revolution, when 'concepts of organization became mechanized' and 'the use of machines, especially in industry, required that organisations be adapted to the needs of machines'.[140] Organisations are often themselves understood as instruments to achieve certain ends, with the word *organisation* deriving from the Greek *organon*, meaning 'tool' or 'instrument'. Hence the way in which, during the industrial era, parties have often been conceived of as *machines*, a term used pejoratively, to express the way many political apparatuses act cynically as conveyor belts of votes.

Technological effects proceed from the material properties of media apparatuses, or, to use a term that has become trendy in media studies, from their 'affordances'.[141] Different technologies 'afford' different actions. Banally, one cannot make a telephone call using a TV set, nor watch a viral video using a fax machine. Each technology elicits certain kinds of behaviour and carries significant organisational implications. Think, for example, of how it was different to convoke people to a meeting in 18th-century Britain vis-à-vis contemporary society, or the trouble an organisation had to go through – and still goes through, as is the case with many trade unions – to ballot members on given decisions when deprived of the possibility to resort to an e-ballot.

However, technology's importance for organisation goes well beyond its mere material affordances and its consequences for individual behaviour. As Karl Marx argued in *A Contribution to the Critique of Political Economy*, technology is a 'world-fact', a condition that defines the very plane on which society and the economy operates.[142] It not only determines the *mode of production*, but within the mode of production it *mediates* social relationships among different actors, whether they be relations of domination, as the one of the feudal lord over the serf or of the capitalist over the proletarian worker, or relationships of cooperation, as those among the members of a guild or a trade union. This technological mediation can take radically different forms. Think, for example of how entrepreneurs have started using wearable devices to track the behaviour and performance of their workforce, thus ensuring new forms of control and domination, or conversely, of the way digital activists the world over use social media and instant messaging apps as a means of co-operative organising.

From an organisation theory standpoint, communication technologies are important to fulfil two different tasks. On the one hand, and perhaps most obviously, they serve to communicate *externally* to reach out to people who are not in the organisation, to mobilise them as sympathisers, voters, supporters and so on; or to attack them as competitors, adversaries or deadly enemies. All parties are constantly seeking to attract public attention through press conferences, press releases, photo opportunities, media stunts and other 'pseudo-events',[143] and in the present era also through YouTube videos, Facebook likes and social media posts of all kinds. On the other hand, communication technology has a strong bearing on the *internal* organisation of the party and the way in which the party leadership interacts with members, and members interact with one another. This second aspect is the most relevant for the understanding of digital parties, given the way in which this organisational template centres on the revision of forms of intra-party democracy through the introduction of online decision-making platforms.

Platform politics

The digital party bears the alternate name 'platform party' because it translates the logic of digital companies, to the political field, as seen in its adoption of 'participatory platforms' – styled after the social media platforms – that have become the signature feature of companies such as Facebook, Google and Netflix. The party recasts its operations after the image of the 'platform', to the point that its platform becomes the party's 'digital heart' to use the expression adopted by the activists responsible for developing Podemos's participatory platform.

The platformisation of the party reflects the analogy between the mode of production and the mode of organisation in every historical era, which we have previously discussed. Just as the mass party reflected the nature and tendencies of industrial society, the digital party internalises the platform model of management and collective coordination that has been popularised by companies such as Google, Facebook and Amazon. It reshapes itself in light of the new affordances of digital media and its interactivity, which is seen by party leaders and ideologues as the carrier of new democratic possibilities that are going to solve political apathy and remedy the deeply entrenched oligarchic tendencies of the political party. The old and clunky armour of the political party is re-arranged in a more open and light organisational structure. In the same way in which social life has been reshaped at the 'point of a click', so digital parties propose to do with politics, to allow for a more direct participation of citizens in the political process. Coming to grips with the functioning of this party requires, therefore, firstly grappling with the logic of *digital platforms*, a term that has become central in both IT and popular discourse to describe these services.

Platforms are digital systems that act as execution environments of various programs and applications. Media theorist Joss Hands has defined platforms as 'software modules available online and cloud-based [clouds] that act as a portal to different types of information, with applications that aggregate content often generated by the users themselves'.[144] Communication researcher Tarleton Gillespie has focused on the computational metaphor of the platform as both an infrastructure on which to build applications, 'something to build upon and innovate from', and as a site for freedom of expression, 'a place from which to speak and be heard',[145] as the speaker's platform that was a signature feature of politics in the 19th and 20th centuries. Platforms lie at the core of various social media and apps, enabling users to accomplish a diverse set of goals: socialising with friends and acquaintances (Facebook); publishing one's thoughts or news (Twitter); finding sentimental and sexual partners (Match.com, Tinder); ordering a ride (Uber) or a meal (Deliveroo) and booking accommodations (Airbnb). What we see in these companies is a new business model that differs from Fordist and post-Fordist models in a number of ways.

First and most glaringly, platform companies are data businesses that collect massive amounts of personal data produced through our everyday interactions, by writing a post, uploading a picture or in the form of meta-data (e.g. our location data), traces that we leave without even realising it. These companies analyse user data to develop complex forms of profiling and market intelligence on the behaviour and consumption choices of their users. Thereby data become the main source of value extraction, hence the talking of data as 'the new oil'.

Second, these companies are based on a free membership model in which users do not need to pay for access, sometimes having to pay only for additional services (the 'freemium' model). Funding comes mostly from advertisement and from sale of user data and connected services to third parties. Such openness goes hand in hand, paradoxically, with the closed or 'enclosed' character of such systems, fencing in users and their data as a means of leveraging 'network effects'.[146] Hence the talking about these platforms as 'digital enclosures' which, while open to users, end up progressively trapping them.

Third, in order to gather data, digital companies vastly rely on the free labour of their members and 'user-generated content', namely information that is produced not by paid staff, but by ordinary people as they interact on the platform. Theorists such as Italian cultural studies scholar Tiziana Terranova has thus spoken of internet users as 'net slaves'[147] whose free labour is exploited, while digital gurus such as Jaron Lanier have campaigned for digital companies to pay users in exchange for their data.[148] Reliance on free labour goes a long way to explain how these companies, though titanic in market size, have very limited salaried staff.

These structural features can be better understood when approaching the functional logic of digital companies and the disintermediation process which lies at their core. Indeed, these companies' justification narrative revolves around the promise to allow users to do directly things that before had to be mediated by a number of middlemen; for example publishing their thoughts directly on their Facebook wall instead of sending a letter to the local newspaper, or calling a taxi on the Uber app instead of using a mini-cab company. Disintermediation is thereby associated with customisation, convenience and ultimately personal freedom, with the promise of making everyday life easier and more creative. However, what this narrative conceals is the fact that, though indeed these companies eliminate pre-existing mediators, they do so by establishing new forms of mediation at a higher functional level. De-centralisation of access goes hand in hand with greater functional integration resulting in a gigantic centralisation of control.

In his book *Platform Capitalism*, Canadian writer and academic Nick Srnicek describes platforms as 'digital infrastructures that allow two or more groups to interact. They are therefore positioned as *intermediaries* that connect multiple users: customers, advertisers, service providers, manufacturers ... and even physical objects'.[149] Namely, although these companies promise to do away with middlemen, bottlenecks, impediments and barriers to participation, they are in and of themselves intermediaries of sorts. Counter to what libertarian techno-evangelists would want us to believe, disintermediation does not stop at the level of erasing existing structures and hierarchies. Disintermediation always implies an act of *re-intermediation*: while eliminating old brokers, digital companies are themselves brokers introducing new higher-level intermediations.[150] The ideological function of the discourse of disintermediation is obfuscating this reality of re-intermediation and the power relations that are involved in it.

The higher-level intermediation offered by platforms revolves around *standardisation*: the definition of a number of protocols and rules regulating interactions. As argued by U.S. sociologist and architectural and design theorist Benjamin Bratton, platforms operate by means of a 'standardization of functional components that allows for the most diverse and unpredictable combinations within a given domain'.[151] They thus appear as 'generative mechanisms – engines that set the terms of participation according to fixed protocols (e.g. technical, discursive, formal protocols)'.[152]

Think, for example, about Facebook and its information architecture. In and of itself, Facebook is an empty shell, a *container* that acquires meaning only by means of the user-generated *content* that is produced by individuals interacting on it. The platform provides a format, with a set of basic rules which define the *process* which takes place, and according to which an infinite number of possible interactions can be performed. Thereby we are confronted with 'the apparent paradox between a strict and invariable mechanism (autocracy of means) providing for an emergent heterogeneity of self-directed uses (liberty of ends)', as proposed by Bratton.[153] The process of standardisation has important power implications in terms of the centralisation it facilitates and the biases that are inherent in the rules and protocols of the platform.

First, digital platforms are the enforcers of a spectacular process of centralisation, which is seen most glaringly in the titanic dimension that has been reached by companies such as Facebook and Google. As argued by Bratton, the platform 'simultaneously *distributes* interfaces through their remote coordination and *centralizes* their integrated control through that same coordination'.[154] The setting of common standards, defined by algorithms such as Google PageRank or the Facebook newsfeed algorithm, constitutes a central knot which centralises all the interactions. Contemporaneously distributed and centralised: this is the paradoxical logic of digital platforms. Hence, my use of the term *distributed centralisation* to speak about the platformisation of the political party.

Second, while presenting themselves as neutral and unsupervised, platforms display evident *biases*. They favour certain types of interaction over others and implicitly prescribe desirable and undesirable behaviour. The claim to neutrality is something we ourselves find frequently in the declarations of Facebook and other firms that emphasise their indifference to content, with no influence on the interactions that are played out within them, except in the case of major infringements such as hate speech or slander. This attitude reflects digital companies' intention to shield themselves from legal suits on the content they convey and on copyright infringement, and also the attempt to present themselves as radically open to any kind of desire and interaction, that is, ultimately, as radically democratic. However, this posturing could not be farther from the truth. *The platform is never neutral.*

As Bratton elucidates, the paradox is that 'platforms are formally neutral but remain, each and every one, uniquely 'ideological' in how they realise particular strategies for organizing their publics'.[155] The apparent impartiality and disinterestedness of the platform obfuscates the existence of a 'design', an architecture of interaction that is by its nature political. Its protocols and algorithms allow for certain actions and not for others, and accommodate certain types of engagement while disapproving of others. Furthermore, they often imply a hierarchy of roles, with certain categories of users – admins, moderators, contributors – able to do things normal users cannot do. Finally, the apparent complete automation of the platform conceals the process of management that is conducted in the back end of the system, with flesh-and-bones 'human operators' still responsible for different acts of control, gatekeeping supervision and moderation of user-generated content. These largely invisible biases and hierarchies embedded in platforms have evident political implications that are the more apparent in the context of digital parties.

The platformisation of the party

Digital parties display evident analogies to the platform logic of digital companies. This is visible at the most superficial level in the way these formations have integrated in their operation a series of digital services, from social media, such as Facebook and Twitter, for purposes of external communication; to various instant messaging apps, such as WhatsApp and Telegram, for internal communication. Social media have been instrumental for the success of movements like Podemos, the Five Star Movement and Momentum. These organisations have managed to skilfully utilise these channels, often becoming the most popular political organisations on social media in their countries.

But the turning towards a platform logic goes further and deeper than the adoption of corporate platforms at their service. Digital parties have also established their own platforms, 'participation portals' that act as the gathering point for a digital assembly of registered members, where to conduct internal discussions and deliberations. The most famous cases, which will be described in this book, are LiquidFeedback widely used by Pirate Parties, the Five Star Movement's Rousseau system and Podemos's Participa portal.

As summed up by Table 3.1, several are the structural similarities that exist between digital platforms and platform parties.

First, like digital companies, these political formations are data driven. Not only are they organised around social media, given the importance these play for their propaganda and internal discussion, but they also adopt the logic of collecting and aggregating user data in the course of their decision-making processes. By establishing their own

Table 3.1 Similarities between platform companies and platform parties

	Platform Companies	Platform Parties
Operational logic	Data gathering	Political data gathering
Membership	Free sign-up	Free membership
Value extraction	Free labour	Free political labour

participatory platforms, platform parties leverage user data aggregation, not too dissimilarly from what happens with companies such as Facebook or Amazon. They unite in the same 'database' hundreds of thousands of citizens, organising them around common interests, demands and wishes. Using the polling and rating mechanisms built into the architecture of social media and online platforms more generally, they engage their members/users in all forms of consultations, constantly charting their shifting opinions and with the ultimate aim of adapting to their evolving tendencies, in ways not too dissimilar from those practiced by digital companies and their data science teams.

Second, platform parties operate with a free registration model in which membership is disconnected from financial contribution. For example, in the case of France Insoumise, it is sufficient to write one's name and email address, and hit the button '*je soutien*' (I support) to become a member. Beppe Grillo has repeatedly celebrated the fact that becoming a member of the Five Star Movement is completely free as a move that opens up the formation to anybody, irrespective of their income and condition. However, the purpose of this move also belies the less idealistic end of momentous growth. Adopting this free membership model, digital parties are following on the track that has been paved since the late 1990s by digital advocacies such as MoveOn, Change.org or Avaaz, whose nominal members are simply users who agreed to be on their mailing list, or participated in online activity such as signing a petition.

The redefinition of membership has been key to allow these formations to grow at unprecedented rates and thus harness monstrous economies of scale. Like commercial platformism, political platformism is chiefly concerned with quantity and scale. It is geared towards gathering ever-increasing numbers of members in its 'stack'. As argued by Falkvinge in *Swarmwise*, 'All swarms are a matter of quantity. Quantity of people. Like army ants in the Amazon rainforest, it is a matter of overpowering your opponents with sheer biomass through superior ability of organization and ability to channel volunteer energy.'[156] Turning to the free registration model allows these parties to lift traditional barriers between members and sympathisers, such as those described by Maurice Duverger. However, this can also mean that membership becomes devalued, with the risk of enlisting a vast but largely de-responsibilised, and therefore de-mobilised, base, with little more commitment than the occasional petition signers of websites such as MoveOn.

Third, digital parties rely on the free political labour of their members, made available through their involvement in digital campaigning. In *Swarmwise* Falkvinge explains that 'a key aspect of the swarm is that it is open to all people who want to share in the workload'.[157] He suggests that supporters should be 'encouraged to pick work items off a public list, without asking anybody's permission, and just start doing them'. A similar philosophy has been proposed by Bernie Sanders' staffers Bond and Exley in their 'distributed organising' blueprint. As expressed by their flagship motto, 'The revolution will not be staffed', instead of relying on salaried organisers, progressive campaigns need to tap into the volunteer political labour available by their most ardent supporters, what they describe as 'super-volunteers'.[158] Besides, the contribution of these highly active volunteers, the smaller and extemporaneous interactions of sympathisers also play a significant role for the success of digital parties' campaigning. This is due to the architecture of social media, and the importance played by social media 'fans', as 'likers' and 'sharers', extending outreach by making political content visible to their own personal network of contacts.

In their complex, these developments feed into a model of organisational disintermediation, which promises to do away with all sorts of middlemen and parasitical organisations and institutions. 'Disintermediation' has indeed become an oft-repeated keyword in the discourse of Beppe Grillo and other digital leaders. What is promised here is a direct participation of citizens in political decisions overcoming the distance between citizens and politics. Ushering in a more direct participation is seen as premised on the elimination of the party apparatus, the 'third element' represented by the party's bureaucracy and its local cadres which Gramsci considered as a necessary articulating texture between the leadership and the membership. In its stead, digital parties install participatory platforms, which in their apparent 'horizontality' and 'openness' are considered as providing a more direct and unmediated link between the base and the summit of the party.[159] However, also in this case, the discourse of disintermediation belies a reality of re-intermediation in which doing away with previous forms of mediation is accompanied by the construction of higher-level mediations. Thus, rather than leading to an elimination of the 'third element', the platform can be seen as a rearrangement of this intermediary structure.

First, as happens with FAANGs companies, the role of intermediation performed by digital parties consists in the centralisation of organisational functions, which is the necessary counterpart of more distributed and open access. This may be described as a 'distributed centralisation' as a process of organisational polarisation that empowers both the leadership and ordinary members at the expense of the cadres and the bureaucracy. This trend is echoed in Becky Bond and Zack Exley's discussion of big organising, where 'the plan is centralised and the work is distributed'.[160] Namely, in the digital party there is a greater openness and flexibility in the way in which people can participate, but this goes hand in hand with a strong central control about strategy. The key way in which this centralisation is attained is through the construction of a centralised database of members which is constantly 'queried' by the various scripts used in participatory platforms. This situation contrasts sharply with the custom of traditional branch-based parties in which lists of members were often maintained locally and local cadres had much influence over the decision-making process. On this front, platform parties seem to continue on a track of development that was already visible embryonically in the plebiscitary transformation of 'cartel parties', which introduced primaries and direct leadership elections.[161] Although justified on the basis of greater organisational efficiency and a more direct membership democracy, this centralisation of the members' list and of the decision-making process obviously raises questions about its consequences for internal power dynamics, particularly in view of the significant advantage it accords the existing leadership vis-à-vis possible contenders.

Second, even though the platformisation of parties is often presented as a means to allow the membership to be listened to in an unsupervised manner without any top-down control or bias, this is in practice hardly the case. Advocates claim that digital platforms will champion spontaneous and authentic engagement, allowing 'the people to decide' on whatever issue, without any pre-defined decision or indication coming from the leadership. Hereby, emphasis is laid on the process, where 'the workflow becomes an iterative, evolutionary process of trial and error, of constantly adapting and improving, without anybody's supervision to make it happen', as proposed by Falkvinge.[162] This narrative casts an image of the platform as a transparent and purely technical apparatus, a digital version of the square of any physical gathering space that serves merely to bring people together. This metaphor of the agora often goes with proclaims of leaderlessness, voiced by politicians in the Pirate Party and the Five Star Movement, or more moderate attempts to say that leadership is simply a 'spokespersonship' or a 'facilitation' of what people have decided collectively. Yet this narrative serves precisely to conceal the persistence of power structures within the party, and of forms of management and influence over the decision-making process. Gramsci's third element thus is not eliminated. Simply, it is the platform with its biases and hidden forms of control that becomes the intermediary.

This hidden bias, as we see in chapters 6 and 7, is apparent at different levels: in the leanings inherent in decision-making software and the way they allows for certain behaviours while prohibiting others; in the process of management of decision-making and the way in which the party staff can influence the results of digital ballots through their control over the timing and the formulation of questions submitted to the base. Examining these processes it will be seen how, far from the edifying picture of a digital 'basis democracy', digital parties often correspond more to a model of plebiscitarian democracy, strongly top-down in its orientation.

But there is a third important implication of platformisation that should not be overlooked. Platformisation results in a subordination of content to process, sometimes at the cost of the loss of a coherent party line. To understand this point it is worth musing upon the changing meaning of the term *platform* in party discourse. Traditionally, in political contexts, the term *platform* was used to indicate the set of policies pursued by a political party, typically presented before elections in a party programme. By inverting the order of the terms *platform* and *party*, the digital party also inverts the meaning of the notion of party platform. Emphasis moves away from content and towards process. What keeps the party together is not anymore the adherence to and pursuit of a given set of policies that are seen to embody the party's objectives in accordance with its ideology, but rather the ethos of open participation and the members' experience of common involvement in decision-making and campaigning efforts. The party becomes process-oriented, the temporary and never finished product of an ever-changing dynamic, constantly responding and adapting to the transformation of the environment; a trend which carries evident risks for the party's identity and strategic coherence.

A hybrid party type

The digital party's 'specs' can be best summarised by contrasting it with previous party types, and in particular with respect to the mass party and the television party. This digital party type combines two elements that seemed irreconcilable in past parties: an agile directive structure and an active militant basis. With the mass party, the digital party shares the former's yearning for mass participation. Breaking with the long-standing tendency towards a fall in party membership and the disempowerment of members, platform parties have been characteristic in their ability to recruit and mobilise thousands of people, many of whom were previously marginalised from politics. Using digital technologies and the new interactive features they afford, these members are provided a larger room for participation than traditional political parties, as seen in the possibility for individual members to intervene directly on important political decisions. Differently from the mass party, however, the platform party does not have the former's imposing bureaucratic apparatus, a large salaried staff and capillary presence in every town and borough, something that allowed the political party to be a powerful machinery of social integration. It is party that gets rid of the cadres, those actors that constituted a fundamental articulating link between the leadership and the rank and file, who now stand accused of being parasitical middlemen; this while party branches and annex organisations are also sacrificed in the same way that bookshops and cab companies have been forced to shutdown by companies such as Amazon and Uber.

With the television party, the platform party shares agility, malleability, ability to respond in real time to the feelings of public opinion and sometimes even opportunism. Further, like the television party, the platform party has a strong mediatised and personalised character. It navigates a 'hybrid media system',[163] in which the internet complements but does not completely eliminate television and newspapers as channels to build direct contact between voters and representatives. It is also a party that resembles the television party as it constantly seeks to analyse, measure and predict the changing opinions and moods of society, only that in this case it also measures the reactions of users to social messages in which metrics on 'likes' and retweets become instantaneous indicators of public opinion moods. The most obvious difference between the TV party and the platform party lies in their media of reference: television for the first, and internet for the second. In front of the perception that TV's dominance has led to political apathy, turning citizens into couch potatoes, the digital party operates with the utopian assumption that the internet and digital technologies can serve as means of reintroducing a mass-participation element; a promise that while debateable has in fact been matched by some substantial results, as seen by the ballooning membership of these formations. Where the television party ended up concocting the triteness of a political talk show which made the supporter a pure spectator, it may be said that the digital party turns participation into something aking to a video game, accompanied, at least at face value, by an ethos of active participation, as the one that corresponds to the communicative experience of the social media era.

Such a hybrid nature of the digital party can be condensed through a series of images often associated with digital communication in the era of Web 2.0: cloud, start-up and forum.

The digital party is first and foremost a *cloud party*, whose digital assets, virtually accessible by any device, become a substitute for physical infrastructure as offices, circles and sections that characterise the traditional parties. Hereby, political participation is invested by a tendency towards virtualisation, where it loses its physical presence and gets rid of that heavy infrastructure that previously sustained its local articulation, as we see in chapters 5, 6 and 7. This placelessness of the party is the reflection of a digital placeless society in which the complexity and fragmentation of everyday life experience seem to impact pre-established spatial and temporal routines because of the presence of contrasting everyday life patterns and timetables. This tendency can, on the one hand, open up the party to various people who were previously barred from participating because of geographic remoteness, disabilities, family commitments or limited time. However, the participation offered by the cloud party can be much like real clouds, quite ethereal, and exclusionary towards those 'disconnected' citizens who find themselves on the other side of the digital divide.

Second, the digital party is a *forum party*, a party that, like social media platforms, which constitute the evolution of early internet forums, is a space of discussions, involving members, sympathisers and organisers. Although in previous parties these discussions mostly happened more discreetly within the party, and its manifold committees, debates are now supposed to be conducted openly, to abide by the principle of transparency derived from hacker culture, this is seen, for example, in political meetings being live-streamed, as is often done by the Five Star Movement in Italy. The emphasis here is laid on the *process* rather than the structure, on the attempt to constantly adapt its strategy and policy platform to a changing environment and changing mood that are constantly polled through consultations and interaction metrics. This goes with the assumption that, through its horizontality, the platform will allow the authentic voice of the people to emerge spontaneously. However, as we see in chapters 7 and 8, this is in reality hardly the case, as participatory platforms carry deep biases and are tightly managed by staff under the control of the leadership.

Third, the digital party is a *start-up party*, a form of organisation characterised by rapid growth and high scalability, but also high mortality. As happens with Silicon Valley companies, digital parties adopt an extremely light organisational structure that allows them to cope with an unstable and uncertain environment. In fact, some of them refer to juridically commercial enterprises, as is the case with Grillo registering the Five Star Movement logo as a trademark, or Momentum relying on a limited company to manage the data collected through its campaigns. Following the model introduced in the political domain by advocacy organisations such as MoveOn, digital parties have a very small central office, employ a phantom staff on specific projects, and most importantly they rely on the volunteer labour offered by supporters. Due to this 'lean management' structure the platform party is an osmotic and adaptive system, with porous borders and organic rather than mechanic tendencies, which enables it to rapidly respond to stimuli coming from the surrounding environment. This adaptability is the key reason for the spectacular success they have achieved in a very short time. However, as we shall see, this is also the Achilles heel of the digital party, whose agility risks too often turning into fragility, with the risk of exacerbating political disillusionment.

4
Participationism

The rise of the digital party does not just concern a technical and organisational change, facilitated by the diffusion of digital technologies and responding to considerations of organisational efficiency. It also involves a political and cultural transformation manifested in the emergence of a new set of values and beliefs deeply informed by digital culture and organised in a common ideology that we may describe as 'participationism'.

Participationism is a radical democratic creed which considers participation rather than representation of the ultimate source of political legitimacy. Participation is thereby framed as the normative criteria of a good politics, making legitimate only those processes that actively engage ordinary citizens while being suspicious of top-down interventions. Participationism is clearly seen when looking at digital parties' discourse and practice. The Five Star Movement has argued since the beginning that to overcome political corruption it is necessary to involve citizens, and that, as proposed by Davide Casaleggio, 'one should not settle for representation when one can achieve *participation*'.[164] This orientation is seen in the emphasis on the fact that all decisions should be open to public scrutiny, with meetings being live-streamed and the party's financial information being publicly available. The developers of the Podemos platform claimed that their goal was to 'develop free technologies that would allow massive online *participation*' and introduce 'methodologies of work that tend to improve internal democracy and make decision-making more horizontal'.[165] Similarly, France Insoumise thus describes the process that has led to the party's electoral manifesto: 'The method used is the image of the France Insoumise movement: rich, collective, *inclusive* and unprecedented.'[166] All in all, the idea is cracking open the old husk of the political party, making it responsive to the public, and allowing for a more direct involvement of citizens in the political process.

This valuing of participation is predicated on notions of openness, spontaneity, transparency, authenticity and immediacy, values that are deeply influenced by digital technology and by a number of subcultures that have developed alongside, such as hacker culture, remix culture and participatory culture. It expresses the desire for a more authentic and un-distorted intervention of the citizenry in the political process, beyond the disappointments of the neoliberal era and of the television party. But what is actually meant by participation here? Why is this concept normally utilised to designate a component of the political process in all institutions and organisations, elevated into a sort of guiding aim for political parties? What are the sources of inspiration for this emerging ideological narrative? And to what extent are we to lend any creed to this notion given the failure of previous attempts to democratise polit-ical parties and state institutions?

Participation: from means to end?

The normative valuing of participation that informs digital parties is clearly seen in the statutes and declarations in which they present themselves as open and participatory spaces that are very different from traditional parties. Across the formations, such valuing of partici-pation combines populist ideas such as popular sovereignty, the people's will and the fight against the elite with a strong cyber-libertarian feel, expressed in notions of openness, self-expression, freedom and au-tonomy, leading to a synthesis which is at the same time individualistic and communitarian.

Take, for example, the Pirate Party's declaration of principles, version 4.0, released in May 2012, in which it discusses what it calls the 'partici-pating society':

> The Pirate Party believes in a society characterized by *participation and participation* [sic]. We believe in people's ability to form volun-teer groups to do different forms of projects and efforts. Thanks to the Internet, these can be global and decentralized. We see Wiki-pedia and Linux as signs in time and believe in a future where people swarm around tasks to solve them in common. We believe in a cultural sphere where people jointly create, distribute, interpret and transform various cultural expressions. We believe in a political conversation where people participate and discuss with each other. We believe in an economic sphere where people get together in a fairly large network to realize their ideas.[167]

Hereby, participation is presented as a process liberating people's imagination and giving free rein to their creativity, thus radically transforming the way politics is conducted.

The Five Star Movement has adopted Italian singer Giorgio Gabber's quote 'freedom is *participation*' (*libertà è partecipazione*)[168] and its paraphrasis, 'democracy is participation', as one of its main mottos. Grillo has proposed in his speeches overcoming representative democracy with a 'hyper-democracy without parties but with citizens at the centre'.[169] Thereby, it is argued, the collective intelligence of internet users shall replace an aging representative democracy, with citizens assembling digitally any time they need to make important decisions. Charismatic and left-leaning Five Star leader Di Battista has argued that 'the absence of participation has bred monsters' and that 'the Italian people should uphold their responsibility' of being active participants in politics.[170] Thus, participation is not seen as just a right but also as a civic duty, in ways that are reminiscent of the civic-republican view of citizens as engaged participants in the polity.

A similar emphasis on the importance of participation is seen in Podemos, beginning from its statute where it is stated that 'citizen participation' is the hallmark of Podemos and that it is necessary 'to add a greater number of citizens to the analysis, decision and management of public issues'.[171] France Insoumise follows a similar line in its statute, where it says, 'We can promote the *direct participation* of all its members in the decision-making processes that significantly affect the organization, using all the face-to-face and telematic tools that can expand and guarantee democratic political *participation*' [italics mine].[172] And we find the same theme echoed in the statute of Momentum, where it is said that 'Momentum seeks to reach out across the community and encourages the *participation* of people who may not have been involved in political activities before' [italics mine].[173] As displayed by these examples, participation is thus turned from a means into an end in itself: participation for participation's sake, one may well say.

The prominence of the idea of participation in these movements reflects the importance this notion has acquired more broadly in contemporary society. We live in a society where we are told in a way that seems to echo the words of the inventor of the modern Olympic Games, De Coubertin, that the important thing is to participate. Participation is key in the internet and in the logic of data-driven business and of social media conversations with their centering on acts of sharing, commenting and 'liking'. Famously, Tim O'Reilly, the coiner of the *Web 2.0* term, argued that the difference between Web 1.0 and Web 2.0 would be that whereas the first followed the logic of publishing, the latter would follow the logic of participation,[174] as seen in the importance of user-generated content, crowdsourcing, and the recommendation culture of evaluations and reviews posted by users on different websites. There is no way for companies such as Facebook, Twitter or YouTube to operate unless users actively participate, and a more flexible and convenient 'participation' is precisely what we are sold by such consumer apps as Airbnb and Uber.

Digital media are widely viewed as tools that have brought back voice to the masses and are going to deliver us from the central control of mass media and mass society. Forums, social media, internet memes, and practices of remediation and bricolage described by Henry Jenkins are all examples of a 'participatory culture', enacted by internet users 'who engage in recreating and remixing content at their pleasure'.[175] According to Mark Deuze, the emphasis on participation reflects a changing notion of the citizen towards a 'rights-based, monitorial and voluntarist citizenry' and the rootedness of digital culture in a DIY (do-it-yourself) culture, particularly flourishing during the 1990s, with 'people claiming the right to be heard rather than be spoken to – such as is the case of the traditional mass media broadcasting mode'.[176]

An emphasis on participation has also become prominent in the political arena, with local government, the state, NGOs and sometimes even dubious development projects presenting themselves as participatory.[177] Curiously, similar trends are visible also in the art world, where *participation* has become a trendy term. This is seen in the relational aesthetics promoted by French art critic Nicholas Bourriaud,[178] and exemplified by the work of artists such as Claire Bishop, and various 'participatory practices'. Participation has also been a prominent theme in recent protest movements, with their criticism of representative democracy and their holding on popular assemblies in public squares, as a means to facilitate a more authentic participation.

When it comes to platform parties, this valuing of participation can be seen as stemming from the perception that representation in all its forms is not working anymore and that it is therefore necessary to start 'from the ground up', from the individual level, from concrete individuals with their problems and desires, rather than from collective categories – workers, women, unemployed and so on, who are the usual objects of representation. This logic reflects the fact that in present times individuals are reluctant to being absorbed entirely by the party, or any other organisation, for fear that their unique individuality may be overshadowed – an attitude which is clearly informed by neoliberal hyperindividualism. Individuals, we are told, want to have control over every step of the process, over the way in which they contribute to the movement, over the trust they place on the organisation and its leaders, over the 'mandate' that is given to them, if a mandate has to be given at all.

Approached from this viewpoint, where we take participation as a correlate of the distrust of participation and collectivity, we may see that participation is in fact not totally distinct from representation. Participation actually does, in certain circumstances, appear as an act of representation, though of a very specific kind, a 'self-representation' in which individuals take care of representing themselves directly, without having to give up their right of political expression, and delegate their power and voice to the leader and the party. It is as if the 'unrepresented', the aggrieved citizen of our era, now moved onto the stage and said, 'You do not represent me', then continued, 'In fact, now I represent myself directly and without mediations.' Participation, in others words, may be viewed not so much the substitute for representation as perhaps more of a zero-degree modality of representation, which befits times of extreme individualism and distrust in collective organisations.

Ceci n'est pas un parti

The framing of participation as an end onto itself is combined with a shift away from the traditional imaginary of the party as a bureaucratic organisation, towards the imaginary of the party as a spontaneous movement. With its suspicion towards representative structures and bureaucracies of all sorts, participationism implies a distancing from the discourse and practice of mass parties. In fact, rather than as *political parties*, a term which in common parlance in the present era carries highly negative connotations, digital parties want to be seen as *movements*, fluid aggregations of individuals, participatory spaces, which do not have all that solid and bulky structure which we normally associate with political parties. They present themselves as 'open spaces' where the citizens can gather in order to cooperate, without the implications of conformity traditionally associated with the political party.

The Five Star Movement has adopted a 'non-statute' (to distinguish it from a normal party statute) as well as similar non-prefixed terms (non-leader, non-office) so as to emphasise its departure from political officialdom. In this document it is proclaimed that 'the 5-Star MoVement is not a political party nor is it intended to become it in the future'.[179] The party claims to facilitate 'effective exchange of views and demo-cratic confrontation outside of associative and party ties, and without the mediation of leading or representative organizations, recognizing to the totality of the users of the Network the role of government and address normally attributed to a few'.[180] This denial of being a party is stated in its anthem, where it is said: 'we are not a party, we are not a caste, we are simply citizens, that's all. Everyone is of equal worth. Everyone is of equal worth.' Similarly, Podemos has consistently described itself as a movement, also in the attempt to present itself as the electoral projec-tion of the 15-M movement of 2011. This is seen, among other things, in the naming of its online discussion space as Plaza Podemos, alluding to the occupied plazas of the Indignados movement. At the launch of the formation on 17 January 2014, Pablo Iglesias promised that Podemos was 'not a party, nor one more product in the political supermarket' but 'a method to facilitate the protagonism of the citizenry'.[181] In a similar vein, on the website of France Insoumise it is clearly stated that FI 'is not a political party. It is a movement of individual citizens who recog-nise themselves in the approach of Jean-Luc Mélenchon without joining a political party or association'.[182]

This imaginary of the party as a movement is predicated on a notion of openness which digital parties derive from the world of hacking. Pirate Parties present themselves as the political equivalent of open-source projects as Wikipedia and Linux, 'wiki-parties' whose construction is open to the intervention of the citizenry. In the Podemos statute it is claimed that 'it is not possible to think of a distinction between activists and citizens, between an inside and an outside of politics'. The founding idea of Podemos, as expressed by Miguel Ardanuy, the former director of participation of the party, was 'to construct a different model of party than the one of the 20th century, a party *open* to society, where you did not need a membership card in order to participate [italics mine]'. He argues that what defines Podemos vis-à-vis older parties is that 'you do not need to pay' in order to participate. This approach, ac-cording to Ardanuy, would ensure that 'your militants look more like the country'.[183] This idea of openness is often mobilised by activists across the different formations that have been hereby described. Jorge Lago, a member of the citizen council of Podemos, thus presents the party as an 'open system', an organisation marked by an 'indistinction between who is a militant and a cadre and who is civil society'. It is a formation that prizes its 'porosity', allowing citizens to easily enter the party, also as a measure 'to break with the internal bureaucratization of traditional parties'.[184]

For Falkvinge a key feature of the swarm, which he conceptualises as the organisational logic of the digital party, is 'being open and inviting'.[185] Activists need to avoid the tendency of traditional parties to spend more energy on keeping people out of the party rather than allowing them in. Similarly, in the statute of France Insoumise it is stated that 'each *insoumis* can create or join one or more groups of action as long as he respects the framework and the approach of France Insoumise in a spirit of openness, benevolence and willingness to project itself into action'.[186] As explained by Guillaume Royer, who coordinates the participatory platform of France Insoumise, the idea was to create 'a structure, that was flexible, open and without clear frontiers between the member and the sympathiser'.[187] This stress of openness is based on the idea that, as argued by Emma Rees of Momentum, 'digital technology has been key to making political activity more accessible'.[188] According to these statements, digital technology enables an openness that would have otherwise been impossible and it is imperative for truly popular movements to tap into this possibility.

This emphasis on openness sometimes goes hand in hand with a celebration of the ephemerality of the party, of its being there only for limited period of time. Senator Vito Crimi of the Five Star Movement asserted in a debate I organised that the Five Star Movement was a 'biodegradable party',[189] one that, once it had fulfilled its goal of cleaning up Italian politics, would self-destruct – a radically different imaginary of the party from the one of the mass party, wanting to establish itself for eternity. Similarly, Jean-Luc Mélenchon spoke of France Insoumise as a 'gaseous' formation,[190] which was very different from the hardwired structure of traditional left parties and was 'neither horizontal nor vertical'. These formations typically like to present as open 'spaces of debate and consultation' structures that, like social movements, are not aiming to maintain themselves in the long run, even though in practice many of these formations have demonstrated quite the opposite urge. This shift also involves a rethinking of the role of politicians, who are not seen as having to act as professionals of politics, but are rather conceived of as 'poeticians',[191] to use the expression of Icelandic Pirate Party leader Birgitta Jonsdottir – that is politicians who practice politics as an art and a temporary endeavour rather than as a career, or as, 'citizens spokespersons', people who are just giving voice to the will of the people. Significantly, both the Five Star Movement and Podemos have adopted rules on limits to mandates, and Mélenchon has proposed the institution of recall referendums to ensure representatives are kept under check by the electorate.

The reason for this rejection of the imaginary of the traditional party should be quite easy to understand at this point. It is rooted in the widespread cynicism about institutional politics and the suspicion of political parties, and in particular of 'cartel parties', and their 'partitocrazia' (party-cracy) – to use an expression current in Italian political discussions – namely the tendency of political parties to monopolise political decisions and engage in practices of horse-trading while at the same time disempowering citizens. This suspicion appears to be directed both at the neoliberal TV party and its quintessential cynicism and opportunism, and at the mass party and its perceived tendency towards excessive discipline, collective action and isolation from the rest of society.

The Five Star Movement has been the most adamant in pursuing this argument. Its politicians have often quoted anti-party thinkers such as Simone Weil, who, in her famous pamphlet *On the Abolition of All Political Parties*, accused political parties of poisoning public life by exciting their militants in collective passions that led to conflict and violence.[192] Weil famously took aim at political parties because of the way in which they betrayed the Rousseauian ideal of popular democracy. She argued that although 'we pretend that our present system is democratic ... the people never have the chance nor the means to express their views on any problem of public life'.[193] Another important reference for the Five Star Movement has been Adriano Olivetti, the owner of the eponymous typewriter and IT firm during the post-war boom, and the founder of Movimento Comunità (community movement), which combined centrist communitarian ideas and a strong emphasis on the values of Christianity, with radical democratic views about the need to transfer power from the central state to local communities.

In his programmatic essay *Democrazia senza partiti* (Democracy without parties), Olivetti attacked the distortion of representative

democracy, and the way in which parties were becoming institution-
alised and concerned only with their own survival.[194] He proposed
that 'the task of political parties will be exhausted and ... the distance
between the means and the ends will be eliminated; ... the structure of
the state and society will come to an integration, a balance in which
society and not the parties will create the state'.[195] In the place of party
democracy, Olivetti hoped to create political orders, styled after religious orders, that would provide the structures of a Christian *civitas*,
with all the power assigned to local communities, conceived of as 'a
small homeland ... the living space where our social life is expressed'.[196]
Following these inspirations, and adopting a typical populist rhetoric,
the Five Star Movement has sometimes argued that its ambition was
representing not a part of society, but all citizens; hence, the declarations of people such as Davide Casaleggio about the coming superfluity
of parliaments as the space where different partisan views confront one
another.

This anti-party attitude is strongly tied to digital parties' advocacy of
direct democracy. In the previously cited book *Il grillo canta sempre al
tramonto*, Grillo, Casaleggio senior and Fo claim that it is necessary to do
away with parties and to create direct democracy institutions through
which citizens can decide, without mediation, on important political
matters. They propose to move from a party democracy to a direct democracy where there will be no need for a party:

> Our goal ... is to introduce direct democracy tools within the institu-
> tion, which means ... referendums without quorum, the obligation to
> debate the popular initiative laws deposited in parliament [...] and an
> interaction between electors and elected [operating] in an absolutely
> transparent and continuous manner, through the network.[197]

By shedding itself of the old imaginary of the party, of the straitjacket
of its bureaucracy, the digital party wants to become something else,
more of an instrument for the citizenry than a group representing a
part of society: an inclusive service platform whose content depends on
the results of an open process, registering in real time the fluctuating
mood of the citizenry.

This suspicion towards the traditional party form and this almost
obsessive emphasis on openness has important consequences for organisational forms. As we shall particularly see in the next chapter,

platform parties try to resemble social movements in their informal organisational structures and their facilitation of bottom-up participation. This allows them to achieve impressive feats at times of enthusiasm and mobilisation. Yet, it also raises serious problems of sustainability at times of demobilisation, when euphoria risks turning into dysphoria, and the hope of change all too frequently gives way to disappointment.

The pitfalls of participation

If we approach participationist discourse with a bit of critical perspective, it soon becomes apparent that the celebration of participation, or the 'cult of participation', to use the expression of Christopher Lasch,[198] that lies at the heart of the ideology of digital parties has significant ethical and political problems, and that reflects typical psychopathologies of the neoliberal era.

First, the turning of participation into an objective in its own right carries significant risks. Traditionally, participation was considered as a means to an end; as a necessary effort, or even the necessary *sacrifice*, in terms of expenditure of individual labour, money, time and energy, to be performed in order to attain the final end, namely socialism, or the good society. Now participation has somehow become an end in and of itself, in a utopia of participation, in which ends and means coincide. What matters here, one may say, is not what politics can achieve, but how it can achieve it; not the ultimate result, but the procedure adopted to obtain goals, the feeling of recognition and the transformative experience earned by those involved in the process. The focus on participation thus seems to be bent on a certain narcissism that Christopher Lasch already retrieved in the consumerism and countercultures of the 1970s, and that has become by now a common feature of digital culture and protest movements, with the danger of diverting attention from more substantial objectives.[199]

Second, participationism also raises serious problems for the legitimacy of intra-party democracy. Far from leading to a situation of equality among participants, where one person is worth one vote, to use an oft-repeated theme of the Five Star Movement, a strong emphasis on participation can lead to new forms of inequality, with high differentials in the intensity of participation, and the emergence of an 'aristocracy of participation' that ends up having a disproportionate say on decisions. Participatory processes – as suggested by Guillaume Royer, platform coordinator of France Insoumise – can usher in a 'tyranny of people with time',[200] those who have the possibility and dedication to engage in complex qualitative discussions. This problem reflects that aristocratic tendency expressed by Jakob Nielsen's famous 1-9-90 law of participation, which indicates the split of active and passive users. In any community, the great majority – 90 per cent or more – is made of passive users who are, for the most part, simply the recipients, or consumers, of information produced by others. Then, there is a 10 per cent of active participants, but inside which, once again, we find significant polarisation, and where only 1 per cent is really active and dedicated. This phenomenon has been found in a number of online communities, starting from Wikipedia, where 0.003 per cent of users create two thirds of the website content, and it is common to many online communities.[201] Thus, paradoxically the openness of participation creates a new digital divide, a 'participation divide' that separates those who are able and willing to participate from those who are not.[202] This conundrum raises the question of whether, rather than opposing participation to representation, what should be pursued instead is some form of accommodation between participation and representation. And indeed, as we shall see in the continuation of the book, some activists are starting to discuss the need for a synergy between participatory and representative practices, what may be described as a 'participatory representation', working towards a balance between deliberative bottom-up intervention and top-down preference aggregation.

Third, what participationism tends to obscure is the continuing presence of power structures. Participation, in fact, is not a process that happens in a void. It rather always unfolds in an organisational framework that by definition needs to pre-exist the act of participation. As discussed in chapter 2, the discourse on platforms tends to obfuscate the continuing presence of biases and power dynamics. This can lead to an illusion about the complete spontaneity of online democracy, overlooking the fact that decision-making is constrained by a number of rules embedded in software design and processes of management and moderation of collective discussions. To counter this risk, it is necessary to unveil the power relations that are mediated by platforms and examine the way they substitute, rather than merely eliminate, pre-existing power structures.

5
Death of the Party Cadre

In the political thriller *Murder in the Central Committee*, the late crime novelist Manuel Vázquez Montalbán opens with the assassination of the leader of the Spanish Communist Party. After a sudden blackout during a party meeting, committee members find their secretary stabbed on the floor in a pool of blood.[203] With the digital party, it is as if the rest of the central committee were assassinated during the blackout. As the lights, and the Wi-Fi connection come back on in the room, only the leader and a handful of his loyal supporters are alive. But it is not just the central committee, the foremost symbol of the party's central office, that falls under the axe of the technological and organisational disruption introduced by the digital revolution. It is the entire bureaucratic and organisational structure of traditional political parties that is unceremoniously consigned to the dustbin of history as space is made for a new structure – or better, for a new 'process' – to take its place.

The question of organisational structure is central to understand political parties and their internal democracy. In the mass party this organisational system was not just metaphorically a 'structure'. It comprised a physical apparatus hardwired into a brick-and-mortar infrastructure made of offices, branches, clubs, workingmen's schools, libraries and entertainment associations. It was a Leviathan staffed by a large number of full-time, salaried employees who often spent all of their lives at the party's service. As previously discussed, the mass party was analogous in the political field of the factory in the economic field. To follow the famous metaphor of Zygmunt Bauman about the opposition between the contemporary liquid society and the 'solid' industrial society, the party was an eminently solid structure based on mechanic top-down processes of information transmission and collective coordination.

As we see in this chapter. which deals with the *pars destruens* of the present organisational turn, the digital party points to a very different picture of party organisation: a flexible and cybernetic system, to the point where using the very word *structure* becomes questionable; hence people resorting to less encumbering metaphors of 'scaffolding', as proposed by Falkvinge, to express the party's organisation.[204] The digital party is not just a *liquid party*, a term used in debates in Italy to describe the postmodern party that politician Walter Veltroni wanted to turn the Italian Democratic Party into, shedding the last vestiges of the wondrous 'war machine' inherited from the Italian Communist Party after the fall of the Soviet bloc. Rather, it is an aeriform organisation, a 'gaseous' structure, to follow the metaphor adopted by Jean-Luc Mélenchon to describe France Insoumise: a 'cloud party' as it resembles the online clouds in which data and services are stored, to be accessed from virtually everywhere, while not being – or pretending not to be – anywhere in particular. The party turns into 'thin air', to use a famous Marxian quip on the process of capitalist modernisation. It becomes abstracted from geographic space to the point where it seems ineffable, impossible to pinpoint to any place.

This virtualisation of the party is seen at different levels. Digital parties shed typical signature features of traditional parties such as the presence of official headquarters in a recognisable location, whose addresses often became their alternate names, and of a capillary network of branches at the local level. The digital party seems to be pervaded by something akin to a *terror loci*, the fear of place or, better, the fear of being identified with a specific place. Offices, branches, clubs – all those places which gave parties a concrete presence in geographic space – are mostly absent in movements such as Podemos, the Five Star Movement or Pirate Parties; and whenever they are present, they are hidden away, lest they disturb the impression of a clear break with the antiquated rituals of traditional parties. Betokening the liquid quality of a digital society in which social experience is ever more fickle and dispersed, the digital party trades its erstwhile physical infrastructure for the virtual infrastructure of the platform.

This virtualisation of the party, where online media of different sorts come to act as the structure or, better, as the 'platform' or 'process' which ensures internal organisational coordination, is a trend that responds to efficiency considerations, given the high costs involved in maintaining buildings, annex organisations, and hiring a large permanent staff. At this level the digital party seems to follow the pattern of downsizing, outsourcing and reducing overhead costs of the new capitalism, taking it to more radical consequences than was the case with the television party. The digital party is the translation of the philosophy of lean management utilised by many Silicon Valley firms into the political field. It operates very much like start-ups, with small initial capital investment and a very small central staff, using its small size and high manoeuvrability to disrupt the market and attract 'customers' who are not satisfied with the products currently on offer in the political market.

Yet, combined with these economic considerations, one also finds ideological ones that stem from participationist ideology. The transformation of the party after the image of the cloud is premised on its promise to being a participatory space, a space in which, like the utopian yet all too dystopian world described in David Eggers' *The Circle*, one of Gianroberto Casaleggio's favourite books, in the digital party everything is supposed to be transparent and open for everyone to see. The party carefully avoids any connection with place, with official buildings and offices, because of their associations with secrecy and opaqueness, with water-cooler talk and close meetings. It wants to be seen as an organisation that is not controlled by anybody, where everybody knows who is in charge, and that it is so open to society that it almost becomes indistinguishable from it.

Party HQ not found

During my research visits to Madrid between 2014 and 2017, I was often baffled by the evanescent character of Podemos, by its apparent lack of location: a place that people – be they supporters, journalists or opponents – could locate, direct their admiration or hate towards and rally in on the occasion of electoral victories. This is traditionally done by the supporters of the Popular Party who, after each election, gather in Calle Bolonia in central Madrid, where the PP headquarters are located. The formal headquarters of Podemos were at 21 Calle Zurita, a narrow street in the popular and bohemian neighbourhood of Lavapies in central Madrid. It is in this neighbourhood that many early supporters of Podemos lived, and it is in its cafes, bars and nightclubs that the discussions that eventually led to the party formation took place. Here, Podemos was officially launched, with a highly staged presentation at the Teatro del Barrio, where Pablo Iglesias, displaying his compelling theatrical skills, made a powerful call to arms.

The party's office in Lavapies comprised just a pair of rooms on the ground floor of a very modest building, and it was closed on the two occasions when I went there. What a difference from the party head-quarters I had been accustomed to in my childhood in Italy! For me, the headquarters of the party were large buildings such as the Botteghe Oscure, in which the Italian Communist Party and its successive meta-morphoses had their centre of operations, or the nearby Piazza del Gesù building, in which the Democrazia Cristiana, the long-standing rivals of the PCI, had theirs. Indeed, symbolic places have always played an important role in party identities. Think about the Jacobins, who earned their name from having made their headquarters in the convent of the Jacobins, the nickname that was given to the Dominican order in the Middle Ages. This relation between the party and the place does not seem to apply to parties such as Podemos that have a ghostly pres-ence: their visibility on news media and social media alike is as great as their physical impregnability.

Podemos is far from being an outlier among digital parties in this *terror loci*. All of these formations display to different extents a ten-dency to avoid a physical structure. The lack of office space was one of the signature features of the Five Star Movement vis-à-vis the old parties in Italy. Thus, in the non-statute it is proclaimed that the legal address of the party is Beppe Grillo's blog, a circumstance often cele-brated in the movement's propaganda. As proposed by Roberta Lombardi, a top politician of the Five Star Movement, the party has 'a very fluid structure – there are no locations. These in the Chamber [of deputies] and in the Senate are the only physical places, alongside the spaces used by regional and municipal councillors. Our places are the institutions'. Roberto Fico, the current president of the Italian Chamber of Deputies and one of the leaders of the party's left, argues that 'it was a great innovative factor not to have an office. It was a great innovative factor to say we meet in a non-venue, or have a non-statute, and be a non-group, and have a non-leader'.[205]

The shedding of a vast and recognisable HQ, what under the Italian Communist Party went under the name of '*la centrale*' (the central), evi-dently responds to economic considerations. Maintaining office space comes with a high price tag, one that is, beyond the reach of parties that have been newly formed and whose funds are severely limited. Yet, one may say that platform parties make a virtue out of necessity, adding ideological considerations to economic ones. The reason for the *terror loci*, the fear of places, that seems to infuse many of these forma-tions stems from the fear of being identified with traditional bureaucratic organisations barricaded in their HQs, cut off from the streets and the citizenry, and conducting their business in the secret of closed rooms and *in camera* meetings.

In the eyes of digital parties, headquarters symbolise opacity and secrecy. They are perceived as the emblems of a professionalised politics which activists are fighting to overcome. They contrast with the emphasis on transparency these parties derive from digital culture and hacker culture. Rick Falkvinge recommends radical transparency at every stage of the process in order to avoid distrust, what he considers as the most dangerous enemy of successful mobilisations.[206] This makes a strong departure from traditional organisational structure in which it was accepted that some information had to remain secret, as indicated by the fact that at the top of all parties sat a 'secretary'. The rejection of headquarters thus belies a rejection of bureaucracy, and of its most visible features, the 'bureaus'. Party bureaucracy, which once counted thousands of salaried employees, stands accused of being a force that has placed a wedge between ordinary citizens and institutions, corrupting the legitimacy of democratic decision-making and accountability, through the byzantinism of committees and the pedantry, uselessness, and corruption of functionaries. Hence the party's central office becomes a symbol seen as clashing with the 'participationist' narrative of disintermediation and of a seamless and unmediated intervention of the citizenry in the political process. Instead of the physical site, the party identifies with a website. This trend is similar to the one seen in digital advocacy organisations, such as MoveOn, which studiously avoided having a central office, convinced that it would have created 'water-cooler talk' and distorted its aims and objectives.[207]

Obviously, we should take this rejection of bureaucracy with a pinch of salt. In certain circumstances, as is the case of Podemos and France Insoumise, they maintain some of the typical structures of traditional parties, such as the central committee. They mostly do have a central staff, though often numbering only a few dozen salaried employees. Furthermore, they do have offices, though very inconspicuous ones, which are made as invisible as possible to avoid associations with bureaucracy. In the course of my fieldwork, I had the opportunity to visit those of various organisations described in this book, the ones of Podemos, the Five Star Movement and Momentum. In the case of Podemos, the real centre of operation was not at the legal address, but at a back office space in Calle Princesa, near Plaza de

España. The party occupied the sixth floor of a commercial building, but there was no indication in the entrance, nor at the office door. Other digital parties have similar meagre premises to host central party staff, like the office of the Casaleggio Associati firm in the case of the Five Star Movement, which has long acted as the Five Star Movement's unofficial and shadowy 'war room'.

Despite the presence of some barebone central office space, this should be seen as only the hub of an expansive and distributed network of operations, of a vast 'phantom office' in which the party's work is conducted. Beyond the party's modest headquarters, one can imagine the simmering of work that is conducted at a distance, from home, from the workplace, from coffee houses and on the move by hundreds of activists, not too dissimilarly from what happens in the digital economy, from the Silicon Valley and San Francisco to Bangalore and Hong Kong, where much of the work is outsourced to other locations. The party bureaucracy is substituted by a dispersed micro-bureaucracy – a 'coffeshop-cracy' one may quip – that is everywhere, and nowhere in particular.

Farewell party cell

Contributing to the process of organisational virtualisation of the digital party is also the radical reshaping of the party territorial structure, that accounts for a large portion of that 'third element' which, as we saw, constituted the political party's backbone, allowing for its 'branching out' into society. Hereby, the party's branch that once occupied space in every city, town and borough, and was the most outward redoubt of the 'party on ground', is also abandoned. It is displaced by a more fluid or evanescent structure, based on informal groupings, deprived of that degree of integration in and control over the central party that was proper to traditional political organisations. This tendency may appear to be rather paradoxical, given these parties' ambition to recreate an experience of mass participation. But, as it should be clear by now, the mass participation that is on offer here is radically different from the one offered by the mass party during the industrial era. The party on the ground becomes by and large the party on the Web.

Official party branches are altogether absent in all the parties discussed in this book. Rather, what we find are more loose, informal and networked local structures, such as the M5S Meetup groups, Podemos's circles or France Insoumise *groupes d'appui*. These groups resemble movement assemblies or activist groups, often lacking a dedicated meeting space, with a small degree of formalisation and high fluctuation in participation. Falkvinge advises to create a flexible 'scaffolding' with local groups organised geographically in city groups and district groups. It cautions against having any group be larger than the Dunbar number, 150 people, in order to prevent that it becomes too large to cohere. Each local group will have two spokespersons who are then integrated at a higher level in the organisational 'scaffolding' with other 'go-to people' in the same geography, to allow for coordination.[208]

Differently from the 'sections' of socialist parties, these groups are not conceived as sovereign decision-making centres whose deliberations are then funnelled up to the higher rungs of the party. Rather, they are conceived as 'spaces of action', where people can debate, develop activities, plan local campaigns, in the spirit of the general strategy of the organisation decided by the leader or via online consultations. Jorge Lago, a key strategist of Podemos, for example argues that Podemos circles 'are not a space for decision but a space for action'. This organisational rearrangement involves separating decision and action. As proposed by Jorge Lago, 'the decision is taken by the party as a whole, not by its parts. Local circles follow these decisions and can choose which lines they want to concentrate on'. What is important about that is that 'militant work becomes outward-, rather than inward-, oriented'.[209] Thus, meetings of local groups, instead of being concerned with deliberation on various issues of national relevance, are more concerned with how to act locally on decisions already taken collectively, while retaining almost exclusive control over local political matters. This is compounded by the fact that membership in the movement is mostly not premised on membership in one of its local groups, as was the case in traditional parties, thus depriving local groups of the role as organisational access points.

Even more radical in its doing away with the local branch logic is the organisational philosophy of France Insoumise. In its official website, the party is described as 'a network movement. It federates action groups that are formed by the will of supporters and have an autonomy of action in the respect of the programme "The future in common"'.[210] Yet, this 'autonomy' of local groups, this anarchy at the base, is not in terms of their decisions, but in terms of the way in which they want to act on them. Local groups are significantly called 'groupes d'appui', namely support groups. As the text regulating the functioning of local groups goes on to state, 'Each insoumi [rebel – the name given to party members] can create or join one or more groups of action as long as he respects the framework and the approach of France Insoumise in a spirit of openness, benevolence and willingness to project itself into the action.'[211] Support groups, recently rebranded as 'action groups', are thereby designed as small informal cells or as 'affinity groups', such as those used in various direct-action movements, for example, against nuclear power or on other ecological issues. They should consist of a minimum of 2 and a maximum of 15 people, and they should split in two once they overcome this size. This arrangement is justified by the fact that 'small groups allow the real involvement of each member, avoid obstacles to setting in motion and promote a finely meshed territory'.[212] Further significant is the recommendation about the internal decision-making process of these groups, which avoids voting and favours consensus decision-making in order to 'reject majority/minority divisions' and 'encourage individual initiatives'.

What is at stake here is, to some extent, the very 'principle of place', according to which place of residence is what determines and legitimises one's own political participation; a principle that lays at the core of the representational democracy of civic-federated associations. Interesting in this context is the experience of Julia Reda, MEP of the German Pirate Party, who in her youth was active in the German Social Democratic Party (SPD – Sozialdemokratische Partei Deutschlands), the prototypical mass party at its height, and who highlights the great difference in the two parties' organisational systems. For Reda, 'the Pirate Party is less geographically structured'[213] and not based on local branches, as is the case of the SPD. This lesser local structuring has to do with the perception that forms of participation supported by internet use are not as localised as they were in the past, and people do not need a local delegate to represent them. Interestingly, this also has consequences for political careers. In the SPD, people would typically follow a traditional *cursus honorum*, starting with offices at the local level, for example as city councillor, to then progressively rise in the scope of their activity at regional and national level; now 'it is easier to run for a higher office without having done a previous career at the local level'. This marks a key difference between the digital party and the cartel party, where, as argued by Katz and Mair, only professional politicians could run for office.[214]

Perhaps the most interesting case study to understand the functioning of local groups in this new party form is provided by the Five Star

Movement and its Meetup groups. These activist groups were created in 2005, just 6 months after Beppe Grillo opened his blog, through the social network Meetup,[215] which allows users sharing a certain interest or cause and living in the same area, to discuss online and meet offline. Meetup groups were fundamental in the early formation of the movement and came to involve several thousands people. They were organised as open assemblies working on different issues, including environmental ones, and on questions of corruption and inequality, and they would hold monthly general meetings, often focusing on specific topics. As described by Roberto Fico, people would meet

> to talk about various things and how to organise things locally, always in public spaces, depending on availability at the time. Indoors during winter, and sometimes outdoors in spring and summer. We saw each other in all places, in pubs, with beer and sandwiches, or sometimes in theatres of a local church. The important thing was to never meet in the same place in general, in order to move around as much as possible.[216]

As Fico goes on to explain, this structure was in tune with the ethos of the movement in its early stage, before it became an electoral organisation with the ambition of contending for public office.

> The idea was to create new forms of participation, which were also aimed at new ideas of life in common. So, for example, we wanted to change the way things are purchased, and started using the GAS system (Gruppi di Acquisto Solidale – Solidarity Consumer Groups), buying from farmers or small local producers. There was much talk about how to change things in our own life, and the way in which we relate to one another, different from the idea that we take the government and from there we change the world.[217]

These groups played a crucial role in the 'genetic phase'[218] of the movement and were instrumental to the creation of local candidacies of Friends of Beppe Grillo, which predated the actual formation of the Five Star Movement. Yet, they lost much of their erstwhile power once the party entered parliament after the 2013 elections. In July 2015 their role was significantly redefined through a 'Letter to the Meetups' signed by the two figures in the party with most credibility with the grassroots base: Alessandro Di Battista and Roberto Fico.

This letter was fundamentally an internal organisational directive aimed at clarifying the remit of Meetup groups and setting some important limits to their scope of action.

> The Meetup Friends of Beppe Grillo are laboratories for sharing ideas and values consistent with the contents of the blog of Beppe Grillo. The purpose of the meetups is to create a culture of participation in public life. They are born spontaneously among people who want to take back an active role in their community and meet to imagine and realise together a better quality of individual and collective life. They organise according to the needs of the participants and take the most functional form to the habits of the territory and who participates in it.[219]

Despite a number of blandishing remarks about the importance of these local structures, the letter was adamant in the passage where it stated that 'the meetups alone are not the 5-Star MoVement'. Strict limits were set on the ability to use the logo of the Five Star Movement, whose ownership has often been used by Grillo to assert control over the party, and to sanction members accused of not following the party's guidelines. Thus, the letter made clear that 'meetups cannot use the Stars Movement logo, not even modifying it' and that 'elected spokespersons cannot be meetup organiser or assistant organiser'; 'organisers and assistants have an operative role and facilitators in relationships and internal organization, do not have the function of representation to the outside'. These instructions were accompanied by the assertion of the monopoly of communication by 'the staff specifically created to support the work of the representatives inside the institutions'. The letter was basically a complete slapdown on local groups, a redefinition of the party on the ground, motivated by the not too hidden intention of quashing grassroots' criticism.

No place for democracy?

This doing away with the party's local branch and the delegate system attached to it is seen by many, and in particular by older militants of left parties, as a net loss of democracy. They argue that the branch system is the only one that can guarantee that in-depth and qualified debate that leads to well-thought-out decisions in which all aspects of the questions can be carefully examined. But is this actually the case? To what extent can we consider the virtualisation of the party and the overcoming of the branch and delegation system as necessarily entailing an erosion of internal democracy?

To better ponder these issues, we can examine the motivations behind the organisational restructuring that took place in the Five Star Movement, by listening to the testimony of Matteo Canestrari, a long-time staffer at Casaleggio and an activist in Grillo's group. According to Canestrari, this move effectively 'disconnected the base from the vertices'. Thus, what this decision 'serves to is re-centralising the organisation both from the point of view of public appearance and from that of the effective power'. That includes the fact that 'the ability to speak on behalf of the movement is shifted from the base to the centre'. Canestrari proposes that this shift was a response to the brewing friction between the leadership of the party and local groups. 'Meetups were starting to ask questions and MPs were beginning to get annoyed'. In the period before the letter was issued, a M5S freshly minted MEP had coined the term *cattivisti* (bad activists) to talk about activists who 'break the balls', namely vocal participants in meetings accused of de-railing the movement and creating unnecessary polemics. Through the letter, the party and the new pillar of the party in office, with elected representatives of the Italian and European parliament, asserted itself as the only legitimate representative of the movement, inviting local groups to take a step back.

Although decisions, such as the one taken by the Five Star Movement, may appear as unmistakably anti-democratic and instrumental to the 'normalisation' of the party, its progressive embracing of a more managerial politics, and more moderate policy proposals, they also need to be understood in light of power struggles that have often arisen between the central leadership and rebellious local leaders as well as organised internal factions. Particularly instructive in this regard is the experience of Momentum and the internal fights around its deci-sion-making structure.

In December 2016, a controversy emerged within Momentum about whether to use a delegate system, with delegates coming from local groups, or whether to use an OMOV (one man, one vote) system. At a committee meeting, which turned into a heckling match, the vote went for the delegate system. However, this decision was opposed by

Momentum's founders, who feared this system would favour 'self-selecting "old hands"'. They denounced a hi-jacking attempt on Momentum by the Trotskyist fringe group Alliance for Workers Liberty. While opposed by delegates in the National Committee, the OMOV system seemed to be favoured by members, as 80 per cent expressed in a survey their preference for it. Eventually, only because Jon Lansman threatened to resign and a decision of the National Steering Committee opted for OMOV, what was perceived to be a takeover attempt was halted. Figures like Jill Mountford of the Alliance for Workers Liberty and Nick Wrack, a former member of the far-left faction Militant, called the move by Lansman a *coup*.

The conflicts that happened within Momentum and other formations are not merely internal power struggles sadly found in virtually any party. They also fundamentally have to do with different visions of internal democracy. The delegate system, favoured often by older and more politicised participants, lays emphasis on the primacy of the local group and representational democracy. The OMOV system, which has become extant in many organisations in recent years, with the diffusion of direct primaries and leadership elections, is based on the idea that all members should be allowed to vote directly, and more so given that now direct member participation has become more technologically feasible than in the past. Emma Rees, a Momentum staffer, argues that digital technology has substituted the functional role of 'regional centres of activity', decentralising things as much as possible down to the individual user. She highlights that 'the purposes of local groups often became quite sectarian, with different groups within Momentum try to outmanoeuvre each other' and argues that 'if we had continued down the road, of setting up a parallel party structures with local groups, with delegates from local groups going to national groups, we would have seen the level of activism diminishing'. Indeed, in present social conditions in which people are more reluctant or too busy to attend physical meetings than they were in the industrial era, local groups can become the Trojan Horse through which old sectarian groups infiltrate political organisations, by flooding meetings with their own dogged supporters, those whom Robert Michels sarcastically called the 'habituées of meetings'. It is also to avoid these despicable 'entryist' tactics that, across all these parties, the decision has thus been made to substitute the branch system with a 'superbase system', namely a digital assembly in which each individual member retains the right to vote on all important issues at a national level, rather than delegating it to a representative.

This said, there are well-motivated criticisms that can be made of the party's abandonment of the branch system, and in particular the risk of a virtualisation and individualisation of political participation. Taking away decision-making power from local groups, such a system runs the risk of making them feel superfluous, thus demoralising the most committed militants, with the ultimate result of depriving the party of those experienced activists that are fundamental to its success. Furthermore, there is a risk of individualising the experience of participation when the decision-making place becomes the screen of a computer or a smartphone, or any other 'personal device', rather than the collective space of a physical meeting. Thus, it is essential that online decision-making is accompanied by face-to-face activities at the local level, to facilitate a number of important tasks, such as debating political questions, and developing bonds of personal solidarity and collective identity that are fundamental to the life of political groups.

To be fair, many digital parties already have quite vibrant, though fickle, offline activities, as seen in the work of their local groups, and are trying to invest more in this aspect. For example, Podemos has started creating local party venues, called Casas Moradas, 'purple houses', which serve as a gathering point for local supporters, to debate on various political issues and organise events. These can be seen as initial attempts to fulfil the function of mass integration that, as described by authors such as Moisei Ostrogorski and Sigmund Neumann, was central to the mass party and which has been largely abandoned by the television party.[220] In the present society, with its unprecedented levels of atomisation, this would be a central task to ensure the social rootedness of the party in the long term. However, such a task requires a level of organisational solidity and a level of financial resources that digital parties in their present form are not able to afford.

6
Coding Democracy

The signature feature of digital parties is their development of participatory portals such as Liquid Feedback used by Pirate Parties, the Rousseau 'operating system' of the Five Star Movement and the Participa portal of Podemos. These online services allow party members to do a number of things including making decisions on leadership, candidates and policies; creating and joining local groups; donating to the movement; downloading campaign material and attending online training sessions for activists and prospective candidates. Often, they are also available on mobile apps, allowing easy access from any point and at any time.

These platforms can be viewed as the main plank of the *pars construens* of the digital party, which compensates for the *pars destruens* that was described in the previous chapter. The doing away of the old bureaucratic structure of the political party, of its branch and delegate system, of the central committee and of the cadres, is accompanied by a positive and creative process, establishing a new *architecture* of participation, or a new process (a term often used to distinguish it from the old *structure*) that serves to a large extent the functions that were previously fulfilled by the party's bureaucracy. Participatory platforms thereby become the party's digital heart, or to follow Gianroberto Casaleggio's description, the party's central nervous system of the collective intelligence of the movement. These online discussion and decision-making spaces are the gathering point for the digital assembly of party members, and thus by and large take on that intermediary role which Gramsci assigned to the intermediate level of the party.

To explore the meaning and consequences of digital platforms, it is necessary to begin from the actual architecture of these platforms, from the various functionalities that are embedded in their design. This is not merely to identify the features which they display, but also to understand the principles and overall 'philosophy' which underscores them. In fact, as developers and scholars in the emerging area of 'software studies' know very well, software is never a neutral machinery.[221] It always involves some considerations about the nature of the world, the subjects involved in it and a definition of aims and objectives that is by its nature profoundly political. Lines of code define the type of actions that can be performed, and the types of behaviour that are possible. They assign privileges and permissions to different categories of users, thus establishing hierarchies among participants. This has been widely demonstrated by analysing various algorithms, such as Google's PageRank, used to manage search queries, or Facebook's news feed algorithm, and the culturally laden assumptions that are hidden under the hood of software.[222]

This 'politics of software' can be most clearly seen in applications that are explicitly political, as is the case with decision-making platforms. It concerns the way in which these systems explicitly or implicitly define hierarchies, protocols and rules of behaviour. More generally, we know that all decision-making systems carry certain biases, as has been widely discussed in the comparative study of different electoral systems, where different arrangements (e.g. in methods that tend to emphasise majority options, or those that provide proportional representation over a large territory etc.) yield different logical and mathematical modelling of the people's will leading to different political consequences.[223] If we are to go beyond the illusion of the neutrality of the platform, which, as we have seen, is a key ideological component of the digital party, it is necessary to carefully scrutinise these biases.

The software of decision-making

The development of participatory platforms in digital parties is part of the long history of digital democracy as an array of practices aimed at improving, extending and deepening participation in the democratic process through the use of digital technology. Informed by a long-standing idealistic strain of democratic thinking, digital democracy offers the promise of addressing the growing disconnect between the citizenry and the political process, the so-called 'democratic deficit' which many hold as the main culprit for the situation of political apathy and dissatisfaction experienced by different polities.[224] While most of the early projects failed miserably, in recent years we have witnessed what may be termed a 'second wave of digital democracy'. This is having a far stronger impact than the first wave and bears a more credible promise of significantly reshaping the way in which decisions are made both at the institutional level and within specific organisations.

This field of experimentation includes a number of initiatives launched by local authorities, such as online participatory budgeting and crowdsourced city planning initiatives such as those waged by the city councils of Madrid, Barcelona, Paris and Reykjavik, as well as projects launched by national parliaments, for example the French parliament's *Parliament et Citoyens*, which enables citizens to express their views on legislation.[225] However, it is within new political parties emerging in response to the crisis of legitimacy of financial and political elites that these experimentations have delivered the most fruits, with the establishment of dedicated decision-making systems that are designed to substitute many of the intermediate layers of party bureaucracy that were previously central to their decision-making processes.

The pioneers in this wave of experimentation and organisational innovation have undoubtedly been the Pirate Parties. From the Pirate Party's early debates on electronic democracy, as part of their advocacy of digital rights, sprung the LiquidFeedback platform developed by the programmers of the Public Software group in Berlin that has strongly contributed to raising the question of digital democracy in the public imagination. While Pirate Parties, except for Sweden, Germany and few other countries, have remained a relatively fringe phenomenon, the spectacular growth of the Five Star Movement in Italy and Podemos in Spain has made their use of online decision-making platforms a topic of renewed interest. At its official launch in 2009, the Five Star Movement hosted a Skype discussion with Pirate Party activists to learn from their experience, and pledged to use digital democracy for its decisions. Other formations have soon followed the example. In Spain, Podemos recruited developers hailing from the 15-M protest movement to create its own participatory portal called Participa. More recently, similar trends have also been seen in France. Jean-Luc Mélenchon's left-wing party first used the political software NationBuilder and then went on to develop its own dedicated participatory platform so that supporters could be involved in various discussions and decisions. Similarly, Momentum has established its own digital democracy system, called My Momentum, to allow members to discuss and vote on various issues.

There are signs that digital democracy may soon transcend the space of digital parties and go mainstream. Besides anti-establishment formations, as Podemos, Five Star and France Insoumise, more mainstream parties have also demonstrated an interest in this area. Some social-democratic parties, such as the PSOE in Spain, the SPD in Germany and the Labour Party in the United Kingdom, have already begun internal discussions and limited experimentations with digital democracy tools, while neoliberal French president Emmanuel Macron, has been using online consultations on the website of his movement Republique en Marche. Finally, the Five Star Movement, now in government, intends to start introducing digital democracy mechanisms at the institutional level. Therefore, there could not be a more propitious time to assess the state of online democracy and examine the functioning of decision-making software.

The development of online democracy has grown on the back of a thriving scene of activists and developers, part of what is known in the United States as the 'civic tech' community. It is from this community that a great number of decision-making projects have emerged in recent years. These include Loomio,[226] DemocracyOS,[227] LiquidFeedback,[228] Your Priorities,[229] Nvotes,[230] Decidim[231] and Consul.[232] Although offering similar functions, each of these platforms has its own specificity, focusing on a certain type of interaction (deliberation, voting, referendum, ordering of priorities), and each of them betokens a different understanding of the motivations and objectives of online democracy.

As we know from political theory, in fact, there are different models of democracy, each of which comes with rather different assumptions about the nature of the democratic process and its aims and implications.[233] Simplifying a complex debate, for the purpose of our discussion, we can focus on three key democratic models that are particularly relevant for the understanding of platform parties: the deliberative or participatory one, which focuses on allowing for in-depth qualitative discussions; the representative model, which instead is concerned with allowing members a choice of the people and proposals that best represent them; and the plebiscitary one, which finally centers on measuring the opinion of citizens on key policy dilemmas, often through the use of plebiscites and Yes/No referenda.

For scholars such as Stephen Coleman, the real contribution of digital democracy lies not in the establishment of a direct democracy, opposed to existing representative democracy, but rather in the extension of representative democracy, with a better 'registration' of the opinion of citizens and a more responsive representation of their views.[234] Through the use of digital tools, it is believed, it may be possible to counteract some of the most problematic limits of representative democracy, enabling citizens to constantly monitor the actions of elected representatives. However, the bulk of the debate on online democracy adopts a more radical and 'participationist' approach, advocating the introduction of a direct democracy in which the very notion of a delegation, of a transfer of sovereignty and authority from the people to their elected representatives, may eventually be reversed. This promise of disintermediation and immediacy chimes well with the nature of digital culture, its anti-bureaucratic and anti-organisational spirit and its belief in individual autonomy and spontaneity. However, there is much controversy both within digital parties and among experts in the field as to what kind of directness digital democracy should actually aim for, and particularly whether this should be of the deliberative or the plebiscitary kind.

Deliberative democracy emphasises the importance of the process of in-depth discussion over the moment of 'preference expression' through voting.[235] According to John S. Dryzek, one of its main proponents, *deliberative democracy* is a participatory type of democracy which values deliberation over preference aggregation, and in which 'individuals participating in the democratic process are amenable to changing their minds and their preference as a result of the reflection induced by deliberation'.[236] Writing with David Schlosberg, Dryzek proposed that 'it would be possible to organize open electronic forums, where citizens could both offer their input and respond to that of others, having the chance to understand what others think and perhaps rethink and revise their own positions'.[237] What is proposed here is a digital re-enactment of Athenian democratic institutions or New England town hall meetings, with people participating in virtual assemblies rather than in real-world ones. This is the model of online democracy that dominated early debates and still enjoys much sympathy, especially among activists of more libertarian leanings.

A very different vision is inherent in the idea of 'plebiscitary' or 'plebiscitarian' democracy. This model of democracy focuses on the use of referendums and similar institutions such as plebiscites, through which the citizenry are asked to express their preference on specific policies or decisions, often in the form of a Yes/No vote. Referenda and plebiscites have been used in a number of countries, such as in Switzerland, California and Italy, where voters are asked to have a say on various questions, be they the abrogation of existing laws, the approval of new ones proposed by the citizenry or the recall of elected representatives.[238] In political science, it has long been debated whether referendums are democratic or authoritarian. Referendums have in fact been favoured by despots and dictators, starting with Napoleon I and III, continuing with Benito Mussolini and Adolf Hitler, and ending with authoritarian politicians in the present day, with the likes of Recep Tayyip Erdogan in Turkey and Viktor Orbán in Hungary recently resorting to this mechanism, to legitimise their governments.

Authors of the most different political persuasions have highlighted various risks inherent in the use of referendums. For some, the problem with the referendum lies in the excessive simplification of politics which it entails. British historian and Liberal politician James Bryce argued that the referendum 'gives no opportunity for amending a measure or arriving at a compromise upon it; it is the bill, the whole bill and nothing but the bill'.[239] Karl Kautsky, the Czech-Austrian Marxist philosopher who co-authored the Erfurt Program of the German Social Democratic Party of, criticised what he called 'direct legislation' for the way in which it militated against the development of a coherent and nuanced programme, which necessarily involved a compromise between different views.[240] Furthermore, he highlighted that if the resort to direct legislation were generalised, soon citizens would be so overwhelmed with questions appearing on their desk every week as to repent for their erstwhile enthusiasm. Other criticisms have instead focused on the authoritarian character of the referendum. Robert Michels said that though the referendum seems to submit the leader to the will of the mass, it in fact it leads to a strengthening of his leadership, allowing it to 'emancipate itself from the oversight of the masses'. By means of the referendum the leader secures indisputable legitimacy to pursue his strategy in any way he wishes. Referring to the case of Bonapartism, Michels denounced that 'the right of sovereignty born of the plebiscite soon becomes a permanent and inviolable dominion' and ends up favouring adventurist politicians. This is also because leaders can manipulate the will of the mass by 'clever phrasing of the questions and by reserving to themselves the right of interpretation in the case of replies which are ambiguous precisely because the questions have been ambiguously posed' and results can therefore be easily falsified.[241]

These pessimistic views on the referendum contrast with the opinion of many early idealistic socialists who saw it as a means to achieve something approximating the popular democracy proposed by Jean-Jacques Rousseau in *The Social Contract*.[242] Theorists such as Moritz Rittinghausen and Victor Considerant saw the referendum as an important means to avoid representatives becoming self-serving. Rittinghausen famously proposed a decision-making blueprint in which 'every law has one or more principles. The People vote on the principle of the laws. The votes are counted in each local section ... and the real and direct collective will of the People or of the majority is manifest. There is now a law. It only remains to draft it'.[243] Other authors, for example Thomas Paine, saw plebiscitary democracy as a useful complement to representative democracy, giving more grassroots legitimacy to important decisions. Besides being used at institutional level, referendums have come to be often used by trade unions, as in ballots regarding whether to strike or not, and in socialist parties regarding decisions about coalition making and the like.

Plebiscitary tendencies are not limited to the use of referendums, but can also be seen in the adoption of direct election mechanisms, for example for the purpose of leadership and candidate selection. This orientation is considered by political scientists as plebiscitarian because it involves a notion of directness of choice and is opposed to representational democracy, where these roles would be decided by a party committee supposed to represent members.[244] In recent years a number of parties, including the UK Labour Party, the Italian Partito Democratico and the Reform Party of Canada have become more plebiscitarian, because they have turned from a delegate democracy model to a one man, one vote democracy model, encompassing institutions as open primaries and direct leadership election. Thus, while plebiscitary democracy shares with deliberative democracy a suspicion towards political mediation, it tends to emphasise the process of preference aggregation and comes close to representative democracy in its acceptance and legitimation of hierarchies.

Although these different models of democracy may appear to be incompatible, in practice online decision-making platforms tend to integrate all of them and their most typical manifestations: deliberations on policies, elections of party officers or candidates and referenda on policy or strategy questions. Ultimately, as we know since the times of Aristotle, most political systems at both institutional and organisational levels tend to be mixed systems that need to attend to different tasks, each of which carries different requirements. When approaching the design of decision-making platforms, the question that begs asking is how these competing models of democracy are represented and associated with different tasks, and more generally what kind of narrative of democracy is mobilised, starting from such apparently trivial things as the language and the look and feel of user interfaces. In the following pages we analyse the platforms that have become the most prominent in recent years within digital parties. We begin with LiquidFeedback and Loomio, platforms that have developed in close contact with Occupy Wall Street and Pirate Parties, and contain a strong libertarian and deliberative twist. We then turn to the platforms utilised by the Five Star Movement and Podemos, which, while also hosting deliberative functions, tend to lean more on the moment of balloting, whether for the purpose of primaries and leadership election or for the purpose of policy development.

LiquidFeedback and Loomio

The platform that has to a great extent introduced the question of digital democracy to public debates beyond small circles of activists and developers is undoubtedly LiquidFeedback, a software produced by programmers connected to the Berlin-based Association for Interactive Democracy.

The software was first released in 2009 and is described by its creators as 'an open-source software, powering internet platforms for proposition development and decision making'.[245] It is written in Lua and uses PL/pgSQL for its database. The programme was brought to fame because of its use by the German Pirate Party between 2009 and 2011, but in the ensuing years it has been adopted by a variety of subjects, including co-ops, civic associations and companies, to gather ideas and register the sentiment of the base. It presents itself as a system of direct democracy that can supplement rather than completely substitute representative democracy.

The orientation of LiquidFeedback is strongly deliberative as it is chiefly concerned with 'proposition development', namely the development of policies to be adopted by parties or social organisations. To this end it adopts 'threaded conversations', meaning that discussions develop in multiple directions, which allows for more complexity in deliberation. Propositions proceed through three stages. First, 'initiators' can launch a proposal, providing a rationale and background for it, in order to gain support. If the proposal reaches a certain quorum, it passes to a revision stage in which other users can provide 'structured feedback' by making comments, proposing amendments as well as voting these. In the final stage the initiators revise the proposal, integrating some of the feedback, and the proposal goes to a vote. The discussion adopts a 'harmonic weighting' system aimed at the fair representation of minorities in order to avoid that minority ideas are too quickly brushed over.

One of the innovative features of LiquidFeedback is the mechanism of delegated, or proxy, voting, which it derives from the philosophy of 'liquid democracy', whose initial concept was proposed in 2000 by an anonymous internet user going under the name of Sayke. This means that users can delegate their votes on various issues to a person they trust on that area of expertise, as explained by Andreas Nitsche, one of the developers of the platform:

> The basic idea: voters can delegate their vote to a trustee (technically a transitive proxy). The vote can be further delegated to the proxy's proxy thus building a network of trust. All delegations can be done, altered and revoked by topic; e.g. I myself vote in environmental questions, Anne represents me in foreign affairs, Mike represents me in all other areas – but I can change my mind at any time. A dynamic scheme of representation takes place. Anyone can select their own way ranging from direct democracy to representative democracy. Basically, one participates in what one is interested (or expert) in but for all other areas gives their vote to somebody acting in their interest. One may make a bad choice once in a while but can change their mind at any time.

Proxy voting is thus presented as a pragmatic way to move beyond the delegate system of representative democracy, allowing for direct participation whenever users see fit, yet providing them the opportunity to delegate flexibly to people they trust where 'the decision for or against division of labour is left to the individual'.

The first large-scale application of Liquid Feedback was with the Berlin chapter of the German Pirate Party, at the time at which the German Pirates were touching their peak. As argued by Andreas Nitsche, this deployment of Liquid Feedback responded to the idea that 'empowering the ordinary members would make these parties more responsive to the demands of society'. However, in the case of the Berlin Pirate Party, a controversy soon emerged, as some party members wanted to have pseudonymous votes in order to protect the personal identity of participants.

> They demanded a pseudonymous use of LiquidFeedback which jeopardized the credible process based on recorded vote. They were unable to accept that political parties have a public mission but at the same time didn't want to abstain from using LiquidFeedback. Considering the temporary importance the Pirate Party had gained during the Berlin state election in 2011, we were uneasy with the pseudonymous use which we felt was irresponsible (as manipulations cannot be discovered in a pseudonymous system).

The validation of votes is indeed fundamental for the credibility of digital democracy and developers such as Nitsche feared that 'in digital participation without proper accreditation, a single resourceful person can create any number of sockpuppets and/or use bots to change the results to their liking which renders all results useless'. This controversy illustrates the tensions between different political values within digital democracy: the libertarian cypherpunk's desire to maintain anonymity for fear of state control and repression; and the requirements of a mass networked democracy, whose credibility rests on the possibility to verify participants' identity. Some pirates also complained about the fact that the introduction of LiquidFeedback in the movement had led to heated discussions, while some members of anarchist beliefs criticised the delegated voting process because of its creation of hierarchies, for how much they may be flexible and revocable.

Similar to LiquidFeedback in its privileging of deliberative processes is Loomio, a decision-making software written in Ruby and JavaScript, that was created by a group of developers based in New Zealand and inspired by the Occupy Wall Street movement's decision-making practices. This inspiration is seen in the emphasis laid on 'consensus-building' in the platform, with the aim of finding wide agreements through in-depth discussions, and in the use of Occupy Wall Street hand signals expressing dissent, consensus, abstention or blocking a proposal. From Occupy, Loomio derived the basic idea of 'leaderless deliberation in small groups where there's no leaders, there is nobody in charge telling people what to do' as explained by Richard Bartlett, one of its developers. However, it was also cognisant of some of the problems with the movement and the frustration experienced in Occupy Wall Street's popular assemblies, where often decision-making became 'super-frustrating', as Bartlett highlights. The idea was to transfer decision-making practices online, allowing people to participate more efficiently in the discussions.

Later, Occupy signals were abandoned, and the website came to encompass also more traditional voting functions. Loomio has since been adopted by a number of political groups, mostly for the purpose of small-group discussion, with groups mostly counting around 100 people. Pirate Parties such as the one of Greece have used it in local areas, and at one point, Podemos had 2,000 Loomio groups for its local circles. Loomio continue to thrive in such small-scale settings, for which it was initially designed. But at a larger scale, it has faced competition by other platforms designed from the start for the purpose of mass interaction.

Rousseau and Consul

The Five Star Movement and Podemos can be considered as the two formations in which the application of online mass decision-making has really come to maturation. They have established participatory processes that have seen the participation of tens if not hundreds of thousands of people, with e-ballots for referendums, primary elections or officers' elections held at the national level around ten times a year in the case of the Five Star Movement and three times a year in the case of Podemos. To understand how these decision-making systems operate, it is important to pay close attention to the software architecture of their platforms and the different functions they host.

The Five Star Movement utilises a platform called Rousseau after the Genevian political philosopher, which has been described as the 'Five Star Movement Operating System'.[246] While already existing de facto since 2012, in the form of separate decision-making applications for voting on primaries and referenda that were available on the movimento5stelle.it website, the platform was officially launched only in 2016, on the day of the death of its ideator, Gianroberto Casaleggio. Rousseau is based on Movable Type, a proprietary content management system written in Perl, first released by the company Six Apart in 2001. This use of proprietary software, which contradicts the Five Star Movement advocacy of Open Source software, has been criticised by many activists, including American free software activist Richard Stallman. It is impossible to know for sure what is the actual content of the software, given that it has been shrouded in some mystery. According to former employee at Casaleggio Marco Canestrari, who was involved in writing some of the initial lines of its code, Rousseau is fundamentally a 'fork' of the version 4.2 of Movable Type released in 2008, which now cannot be updated anymore, having been modified internally.[247] This 'deprecated' practice is one of the reasons for the serious security breaches that have plagued this platform, as seen in a streak of hacker attacks.

The current 2.0 version of Rousseau, released on 2 August 2017, enlists the following functions:

- Lex Nazionale: participation in the writing of national laws proposed by parliamentarians
- Lex Regionale: participation in the writing of regional laws proposed by regional councillors
- Lex Europa: participation in the writing of European laws proposed by MEPs
- Vote: vote in primary elections of candidates, or referenda on a variety of issues, held in an ad-hoc temporary area created for the time of consultations
- Fund raising: crowd-funding for election campaigns and events
- Lo scudo della Rete (Network Shield): fund raising for legal protection of the Five Star Movement or its members and elected representatives
- Lex Iscritti: law proposals by members who are then presented by the elected representatives at various levels
- E-learning: lessons on the functioning of institutions aimed at the elected representatives of the Five Star movement
- Sharing: an archive containing the different proposals (queries, resolutions, laws, etc.) put forward by party representatives at the municipal and regional levels
- Call to action: local groups (i.e. Meetup) and information on and from local groups on current initiatives
- Activism: propaganda materials to support Five Star Movement initiatives

Particularly interesting are the various law-making 'Lex' functions available on this platform. Digital democracy researcher, Marco Deseriis, has aptly described this function as a form to a 'direct parliamentarism', in which the focus rests on proposition development, allowing virtually all citizens to become lawmakers. Differently from Lex Iscritti, which was introduced in the 2.0 release and will be discussed later, in Lex Nazionale, Lex Europa and Lex Regionale only 'elected spokespersons', namely those by elected representatives of the parties, can put forward proposals. Proposals are introduced by a video, accompanied by an introductory text and the full draft of the proposal. Users can intervene by commenting on these proposals for 70 days after their posting in a number of ways: integration (adding new text); edit (amending the existing text); objection (raising questions about the validity of the proposal); suggestion (general comments about the proposal); formal vice (raising questions about the proposal's actual applicability).

Lex Iscritti builds on these functionalities by also allowing registered members to make law proposals. It has been presented as the most revolutionary function and an international first. Lex Iscritti 'allows anybody who has some experience and knowledge to make a proposal'[248] argues M5S MP and current transport minister Danilo Toninelli, and this point is emphasised by the slogan found on the feature's About page: 'You make the laws', and 'Citizens in parliament'. Thus, Di Maio, in presenting the new system, argued that it allows 'any citizen, from Lampedusa to Aosta, from the cities to a small town of 200 inhabitants on the top of the mountain, to become a lawmaker'.[249] Any proposal needs to be accompanied by a number of contextual data, on the state of the art of the legislation and on the financial implications of the proposal. Once it has undergone a technical assessment to establish its feasibility and alignment with party rules and pre-existing policy, the proposal is transferred to the relevant Lex sections (national, regional or Europe), according to the scale of competence.

As much as this may sound like an exciting feature, the various Lex functions have several shortcomings. The user interface, whose main menu is displayed in Figure 6.1, does not abide by basic criteria of usability. On the website, both proposals and comments on proposals are listed chronologically, with no popularity ranking, as happens, for example, with up-voted comments on Reddit. This type of paging makes it difficult for users to navigate the conversation, especially given that

Figure 6.1   The main menu of the Rousseau digital democracy platform.

in certain circumstances comments can come in the hundreds or even thousands. To this adds the fact that only few comments are pertinent and of sufficient quality to allow for serious consideration. Many of them are in the form of expressions of support, with phrases such as 'well done', 'great', 'continue this way'; more rarely, there are rejections: 'I don't like this', 'this is not good', and the like, rather than substantial interventions. To these limits of the process of deliberation, add the fact that the spokespersons ultimately have a lot of freedom for editing and selection. According to rules, they are only supposed to reject amendments that go against the principles of the Five Star Movement or the spirit of the proposal. But this power of selection leaves them quite some room for deciding which comments to integrate into the final proposal, a decision which is ultimately very political. On top of these more deliberative functions, Rousseau comprises a number of voting features that have been used in the occasion of online primaries and referenda.

Particularly concerning are the security issues of Rousseau, which derive from the amateurish decision of using the fork of a proprietary software, meaning that security updates can no longer be installed. These security weaknesses have made Rousseau vulnerable to hacker intrusions. In August 2017, a 'white hat' hacker, using the nickname Evariste Galois, alerted the public about the vulnerabilities of the system and the risk that people's personal data may be downloaded. A few days after, rogue_0, a 'black hat' using hacking for criminal purposes, revealed that he had already identified the vulnerabilities and had been on the system for a long time. He demonstrated that he had both reading and writing access to all the data and put on sale the entire database of Rousseau users for 0.3 Bitcoin, which at that point were convertible in around 1,000 euros. These events are testament to the rather amateurish character of Five Star Movement digital operations, themselves a consequence of the familial and opaque management of the movement.

Podemos's participatory platform is called Participa and is one of the sections of the main party website, Podemos.info. This platform integrates different software packages for the purpose of discussion and decision-making. It is divided into two parts: one for discussion and the other for actual decisions. Voting operations are supported by a software called Nvotes, previously known as Agora Voting, which self-describes as 'a project for open source, cryptographically secure voting', developed by the company Agora Voting, which offers a 'block-chain-based digital voting solution for governments and organizations'.[250] Significantly, some of the Agora Voting team, involving David Ruescas, Eduardo Robles and Lucas Cervera, hailed from hacker groups that were involved in the 15-M. The programme is written in Shell, with some components in Ruby on Rails, Python and Javascript. The main claim of this system is that it is tamper-proof, as it is based on mix-net and end-to-end encryption of voting operations, ensuring strong security. This system has been used several times for a number of purposes, including online primaries, election to party positions (e.g. secretary general) and internal referenda on policy and strategy. Agora voting services include the external verification of online votes, a function that has only been rarely used by the Five Star Movement.

The second component of Podemos participatory is Plaza Podemos, the area dedicated to internal party discussions, displayed in Figure 6.2. This forum initially hosted on Reddit which lent Podemos the moniker of 'Reddit party', as proposed by the *New Yorker*.[251] According to an article published in July 2014, soon after the European elections the forum had 'two thousand subscribers and significant traffic. About two hundred people were visiting the page at any given time, and there were a million page views in the month of July alone'.[252] More recently, the functionality moved to Plaza Podemos 2.0 supported by the Consul software written in Ruby on Rails and developed by the mayoralty of Madrid. Consul self-describes as 'the most complete citizen participation tool for an open, transparent and democratic government'.[253] It allows to open threads on various topics, thus permitting users to create separate 'rooms' in which people can discuss various issues of interest. Furthermore, it gives users the ability to create proposals which, when reaching

Figure 6.2   The early version of Plaza Podemos as it was still hosted on Reddit.

sufficient support by going beyond a certain 'threshold', can eventually be voted on. The software has been used for a number of consultations carried out by mayoralties the world over, including Paris, Madrid and Buenos Aires, while the city of Barcelona has developed a similar software called Decidim.[254]

The focus of Consul is proposition development through threaded discussions similar to the ones used by LiquidFeedback. In this context, as stated in the software's accompanying documentation, 'Once the proposal has been submitted and it has reached the number of necessary supporters, it goes to a vote. At this point it can be accepted or rejected by a majority vote from the citizens.'[255] In order to move to further consideration, proposals have to reach a certain threshold of support. In the case of the mayoralty of Madrid, for example, this support is set at 1 per cent of all participants on the platform. This process of filtering decisions attempts to strike a balance between the openness of the process of deliberation and the need to avoid the dispersion of attention and ensure that time is not wasted on proposals that will never achieve the necessary threshold. As we shall see, this system has been used by Podemos as part of its mechanism of Iniciativas Ciudadanas and Popular (ICP). However, its application has been quite disappointing given that no proposal eventually reached the necessary threshold of support that was required to go for a vote, as we will see more clearly in the next chapter.

France Insoumise provides another interesting case of online decision-making. A decision-making platform, displayed in Figure 6.3, was established on the official campaign website, jlm2017.fr, using the NationBuilder, a system developed in the United States to support political campaigns. The number of people registered to the platform grew rapidly during the campaign, moving from 30,000 people in February 2016 at the beginning of the campaign, to over 300,000 in March 2017, shortly before the presidential elections, and now it is above 500,000 members.[256] The system was used for a number of purposes, including the collaborative drafting of the Avenir en Commun, a programme that collected 3,000 contributions between February and August 2016.[257] Furthermore, it was used to consult the membership about a number of strategic choices, such as the stance to take in the second round, when Mélenchon was not anymore on the ballot. Since the presidential election, France Insoumise has gone on to develop its own dedicated

Figure 6.3 Screenshot of France Insoumise participatory process for the drafting of the programme.

software using Python and Django, which host a number of functions such as open text contributions to discussion, e-ballots and participation in local groups.

The challenges of decision-making platforms

Reviewing these different platforms, it can be seen that, although they are presented simply as neutral tools for decision-making, they inevitably carry some biases in their design. All digital parties have integrated in their participatory portals different features and functionalities that sit across different models of democracy, and in particular the representative, deliberative and plebiscitary ones. They include discussion mechanisms that are more deliberative in character, as they allow for different users to put forward arguments and engage with one another in their development; elections of candidates and internal officers that correspond to the classic representative democracy logic and finally, referendums on policy and strategy questions that correspond to the plebiscitary model of democracy.

None of the digital parties considered in this book concentrates exclusively either on deliberative, representative or deliberative functions, but all of them for different purposes. However, it is apparent that in their external presentation they tend to over-emphasise the importance of deliberative functions, through which the membership can qualitatively intervene on important choices, starting from policy development; at the same time, they underplay the role of balloting processes in the context of elections and referendums. This emphasis on deliberative elements is not surprising, given the way these mechanisms appear to better conform to the 'participationist' narrative, and are a more persuasive reason for the claim to be more innovative vis-à-vis traditional parties. Yet, as we shall appreciate more clearly in the ensuing chapter, balloting is very important, in fact strategically more important than the deliberative moment, as it is used to legitimise the leadership and its proposed course of action, including over dilemma choices, that have important political consequences.

The real challenge going forward, for activists and developers alike, is a more effective integration of deliberation and balloting, and of participation and representation, in a mixed model that may be described as a 'participatory representation'. As proposed by Yago Bermejo, one of the developers behind Podemos initial implementation of online decision-making, the key question is how to find a balance between participatory and representative processes, and also a means to balance the aristocratic tendencies of participationism.

> There are times when people are more motivated because there is a feeling that you can change things. Because suddenly the participation breaks and gets bigger. You will always have moments when you are going to inflate participation and times when you are going to deflate. And always when it is inflated the participation is more *representative* of the society that wants to represent that institution and that movement. It is the dilemma, when you have low participation you risk falling into the jar of activists who are not *representative* of society. There is a danger when participation means that the movement is controlled by a minority.

The ideal scenario is one in which an initial phase of open deliberation, involving active participation from the membership in qualitative debates about various subject matter, is ensued by a phase of aggregation of emerging proposals and their balloting, to verify their actual legiti-macy among members.

This is largely what has already been implemented in the develop-ment of threaded and ranked discussions, and the introduction of thresholds on such platforms as Consul and Decidim, which aim, on the one hand, to allow members to have a meaningful say, and on the other hand, to halt extreme manifestation of May's law of curvilinear disparity, according to which more active members tend to be unrepre-sentative of the party as a whole. We can envision that in the future further advances may be made at this level, integrating ever more so-phisticated forms of filtering and weighing in threaded discussions and proxy voting mechanisms as those utilised by LiquidFeedback. Thereby, discussions in deliberative and semantic polling may provide useful in-sights for a more syncretic approach, achieving a working compromise between participation and representation.[258]

A further challenge in the development of online decision-making platforms regards the security of voting operations. This risk has been most glaringly illustrated by the case of the Five Star Movement, where, because of poor encryption, hackers were able to break into the data-base. The fear is also that the party internal staff may analyse members' voting history and perhaps even 'profile' those voters that are not in line with the party leadership. More generally, some people, including the German Computer Chaos Club and free software activist Richard Stallman, question the very desirability of online democracy because it does not guarantee the same anonymity that is available with physical ballots. Although the more radical cypherpunk-oriented people will continue to distrust digital democracy, end-to-end encryption systems, such as the one used by Agora Voting, provide a reasonable degree of security against these risks. To ensure more security, some of these for-mations have also introduced two-step verification, whereby in order to vote, users have to enter a one-time password sent via a short message service (SMS), in the same way used for double-step verification on Gmail, Twitter or Telegram. Podemos used this system since the launch of its platform, whereas the more amateurish Five Star Movement has only introduced it with the 2.0 release of Rousseau.

A further question is external verification, namely the use of a third party validation of online consultations' results. This is necessary because of possible conflicts of interests, given that the staff responsible for managing participatory platforms is under direct control of the leadership. This risk is particularly evident in the case of the Five Star Movement, for example, the Rousseau association that manages the decision-making system is hosted at the office of Casaleggio Associati, the firm of late Gianroberto and of his son and successor Davide Casaleggio, who has been described by the *New York Times* as the 'mystery man who runs Italy's Five Star from the shadows'.[259] By relying on the services offered by Agora Voting, Podemos has had since the start external verification built into its voting operations. With the Five Star Movement, external verification has been adopted only in two circumstances, the Quirinarie primaries to select the M5S candidate for the president of the Republic in 2013 and the vote on amendments nonstatute in October 2016, for which it relied on the service of the Italian chapter of DNV GL, a Norway-based international accredited registrar and classification society. In other cases, including the nomination of the prime minister candidate in the 2018 elections, it has not used this system, without explaining the reasons for this choice. It can be envisaged that, in the future, pressure will grow in the M5S and beyond to ensure that external validation is consistently enacted, so as to confidently rule out the possibility of vote rigging.

7
Plebiscitarianism 2.0

In September 1905, hundreds of delegates of the SPD gathered for the annual party congress in Jena. The congress fell at a time of rapid growth for what was already the largest socialist party in Europe and a model for twin parties emerging in other countries. The debate centred on the relationship between trade unions and the political party. The event highlighted a division between a more moderate wing of the party, especially represented by trade unionists, who claimed autonomy and rejected the idea of a political mass strike, and a more radical wing, which acted also on the inspiration of the 1905 attempted revolution in Russia. Eventually, after a vociferous debate that involved a number of prominent party figures, including the party chairman, August Bebel, and the radical left-winger, Rosa Luxemburg, the party adopted a resolution which endorsed the use of the political mass strike as a political tactic in case of a coup d'etat. However, this decision was overturned at a secret meeting of the executive committee that took place in February 1906 and made some concessions to the cautiousness of union leaders.

The Jena congress of the SPD is one example of the democratic rituals that typify the history of mass parties. The annual congress, attended by the delegates, constitutes a key moment for developing the party strategy and electing key party officers. It operates according to the logic of representational democracy, with a number of delegates standing in for local constituencies, and is marked by a highly structured and bureaucratised system, and different specialised organs responsible for a variety of roles, in a system that resembles a state within the state in its complexity. The decision-making process of digital parties makes a stark contrast to the practice of traditional political parties. In some occasions, annual or bi-annual conferences are still celebrated. But the internal decision-making process is largely organised around the consultations that take place on online platforms, with daily discussions on a variety of policy and strategy questions, and important ballots convoking all members typically happening from 2 to 10 times every year.

Understanding how this digital process is managed and what are its results and consequences for party life constitutes a necessary complement of the analysis of decision-making software that has been completed in the previous chapter. The study of the design of software does not exhaust the analysis of online democracy. Online decision-making is not a static system, but a dynamic process, which, as with all processes, and in particular democratic processes such as elections and consultations, is never completely spontaneous and neutral. It involves a number of organisational acts of supervision, management, collection, verification and communication of results, which may appear as merely technical but are in fact highly political in their implications. At this level, a number of biases compounding those inherent in software design can be identified, which concern the supervision and management of consultations. These apparently 'technical' questions belie important power issues and often end up having a significant bearing on the quality and credibility of online decision-making.

As we see in the course of this chapter, the reality of online democracy to date paints a rather pessimistic picture. Despite the promise to allow for a more bottom-up involvement in the political process, with authentic engagement from the base of participants in important decisions, its implementation has been rather disappointing. It is true that digital parties have conducted interesting experimentations that may prefigure the shape of a future democracy to come. But for the most, online decision-making has ended up seriously under-delivering on its lofty promise. Although offering more responsiveness in certain respects and allowing members to contribute to party's internal discussions in novel ways, these parties have mostly delivered what may be described as 'plebiscitarianism 2.0', a top-down form of 'reactive democracy', styled after social media 'reactions' connected metrics, in which members' intervention often takes the form of ratification, reacting to proposals that are largely predefined by the leadership.

Deliberative discussions, those that have more qualitative depth, and allow for a more intense engagement from members, have been present as part of the participatory mix of these parties. Yet, it is more top-down forms of democracy of the representative and plebiscitary kinds that have ultimately prevailed in terms of the participation they have attracted and of the political impact they have produced. The most important occasions of online participation have been around online referendums, to decide over the expulsion of members or important strategic decisions, or yet to confirm the mandate of the leadership. As we shall see, these consultations have almost invariably ended with supermajority splits in favour of the line favoured by the leadership. The reasons for this pro-leadership bias can be largely detected in the strong control leaders exercise over the management of the decision-making process, and the way they are able to influence it in a number of ways.

To examine this issue, we begin by looking at discussions about the normative requirements of intra-party democracy identifying the elements present in two ideal types of party democracy: bottom-up, or membership-led, and top-down, or leadership-controlled. We then analyse bottom-up democracy as seen in deliberative and participatory practices, highlighting their serious limits in scope and ultimate effects. Finally, we discuss top-down practices, and in particular processes of representative and plebiscitary democracy, emphasising how these two, and in particular plebiscitary processes, take the lion's share in digital parties' decision-making, with serious consequences for the quality of the democracy that is practiced within these organisations and for their internal power balance.

The management of online democracy

Evaluating online democracy calls for an understanding of internal organisational mechanisms that are involved in managing the process of decision-making. American political scientist Susan Scarrow, a leading expert on this issue, lists three relevant dimensions – inclusiveness, centralisation and institutionalisation – that allow evaluation of democratic processes.[260] Inclusiveness 'tells us about how wide the circle of party decision makers is'. In certain parties, 'all are given the opportunity to decide on important issues'; in others, instead, decisions are very much centralised in the leadership. On this count digital parties may appear as highly inclusive, allowing party members to participate on decisions concerning candidates, leadership and policy. Yet, as Scarrow goes on to highlight 'more inclusive parties will [also] offer more opportunities for open deliberation prior to the decision stage' and this is a level where, as we shall see, platform parties may not appear as inclusive as they want to be seen.

Centralisation 'describes the extent to which decisions are made by a single group or decision body'.[261] At this level, it can be seen that decision-making in digital parties is highly centralised, as it is mostly assigned to the digital assembly of all members, instead of being sifted through local organisational subunits. Centralisation can also be seen to include the management of the decision-making process and whether control over this process is assigned to a procedures committee autonomous from the leadership, or to staff wholly subordinated to the party's leadership. As we shall see, in digital parties the second scenario is prevalent. Institutionalisation, finally, indicates the 'degree to which internal decision procedures are formalized'. In newer parties, as Scarrow notices, there often tends to be a low degree of formalisation of decision-making procedures. Although institutionalisation does not necessarily equate to democratisation, the lack of clear procedures can be used to control and distort the democratic process.[262]

These various dimensions need to be examined in connection with the analysis of the relationship between leadership and membership. At the end of chapter 1, we have highlighted the need to adopt a relational, rather than absolutistic, understanding of this process, which, as proposed by Angelo Panebianco, is best conceived as a relationship of conflict/negotiation or as a permanent tug-of-war between the two.[263] What matters ultimately is that the tension between the two can never be resolved, as the two poles are dependent on each other: the membership on the leadership for direction and the leadership on the membership for support. In different situations, and according to the prevalence of certain institutional mechanisms, the leadership, and (far less frequently) the membership, will be more or less well positioned to assert its will.

To examine these issues we need to take into account a number of factors which determine the respective sphere of influence of the leadership and the membership. These include: the role played by the party staff involved in managing the process of decision-making; the drawing up of initial decision-making procedures; the formulation of questions participants are called to express their opinion on, and of accompanying texts used in consultations; the launching and timing of discussions and e-ballots; the communications by party communication channels prior to consultations and the way they can set a certain agenda or mood which may end influencing the consultation; the collection and verification of online ballots and finally the publication of results. It is at this level that we can spot different forms of influence exercised by the leadership over the decision-making process, and conversely determine the room for intervention of the membership.

We can condense this host of questions in a simplified analytical framework organised around two ideal-type situations: top-down democracy (controlled by the leadership) and bottom-up democracy (controlled by the membership). *Bottom-up*, or *member-controlled*, democratic process practices will be more open and grassroots-oriented. They will emphasise the moment of participation over the moment of representation, and of deliberation over final decision, giving members the possibility to shape qualitatively the content of the issues they are called to decide upon, and providing them a say over the process as a whole. *Top-down*, or *leader-controlled*, practices will instead be strongly directed by the party staff assigned to the management of decision-making platforms, who will set the content, timing and framework of online consultations, leaving members just the option of expressing a preference over a limited and largely pre-defined set of choices.

Which of these two ideal scenarios do digital parties best approximate to? To what extent can the membership make a meaningful intervention on the process? Is digital democracy simply a confirmation by members of decisions already taken by the leadership, or is it a truly transparent and inclusive process?

A limited deliberation

Most of the parties and movements considered in this book display an important deliberative element that allows for a bottom-up intervention from members in internal discussions. This is the aspect of digital democracy that is often emphasised in their discourse, when celebrating the way common citizens can make proposals that may become policies pursued by the party and eventually even laws. And indeed, many of these formations have introduced mechanisms that allow the intervention of their members in policy deliberation in altogether novel ways. However, this intervention remains quite narrowly constrained by the wide room for manoeuvre retained by the leadership and the party staff and the comparatively low degree of participation of members in deliberative processes vis-à-vis e-ballots.

In the case of the Five Star Movement, as we previously discussed, deliberative elements are enshrined in a set of features available in the Rousseau platform: the various 'Lex' crowdsourced legislation functions. These, and in particular the Lex Iscritti function, are often mentioned as a demonstration of the authentic and open character of the Five Star

Movement's democracy. So far, over 30 proposals put forward through Lex Iscritti have gone on to become official party policy. However, there is no clear and transparent rationale for the way in which comments made by users are selected for integration. In the introduction page of Lex Parlamento, it is explained that the elected spokesperson does not have an obligation to use modification proposals, because 'the general system must remain faithful to the idea of the proponent', a formulation that leaves quite some room for top-down control. Furthermore, very few discussions actually attract a high volume of participation from the movement members. The proposal for a Citizen Income (basically a form of guaranteed minimum income) was the most commented, with a total of 4,328 interventions, a tiny fraction of the number of people intervening in e-ballots, and most of the other proposals had a far lower number of comments, with an average of few hundred comments, thus providing limited cues about the actual support and legitimacy of a proposal. Users have repeatedly complained on the movement's blog and on social media about the opaque procedure of selection and editing of proposals. This problem resurfaced few months after the elections, when it appeared that the party programme whose priorities had originally been voted online by members before the elections had been edited significantly, watering down some of the most radical positions.

In Podemos the participatory aspect has been manifested in the Plaza Podemos discussion area, where ongoing discussions about current events and internal party questions take place. One of the highlights of this effort has been the collaborative drafting of the party's policies in view of the national elections in 2015. The party's programme was organised around a number of axes, including economy, democracy, justice and social welfare, culture and international. Party members could make new policy proposals or integrate existing ones. All the proposals receiving 100 votes minimum had to be considered by the party leadership, and the Citizens' Council went on to select some of these measures for online voting. A total of 15,264 people actively participated in the participatory process, which may appear an impressive figure but still constitutes a mere 4 per cent of the 380,000 members at the time of the consultation.

The most ambitious deliberative mechanism in Podemos' decision-making structure is the instrument of *Iniciativas Ciudadanas Podemos* (Podemos Citizens' Initiatives) or ICPs. These are proposals which can be made by any member of the platform, both in terms of adoption of policy or modification of the statute. ICPs need to receive support from 0.2 per cent of the party members to move up to the homepage of the participation portal (participa.podemos.info). Once there, they are supposed to gain further visibility, and if they receive a 2 per cent support, an email is sent to all members announcing that the proposal is being discussed. After this stage, the proposal has 3 months to obtain the backing of 10 per cent of the members or 20 per cent of territorial circles. If this threshold is achieved, the proposal undergoes a phase of development, involving the proponent and a dedicated working group, lasting for a maximum of one month, after which the citizens' initiative is eventually put to the referendum vote of all the members. If the proposal wins in the referendum, it becomes binding on the party. However, to date, over four years since the introduction of the mechanism, no ICP has ever been approved. In fact, none has ever made it past stage two! According to Yago Bermejo, a developer who was involved in discussions for the introduction of the mechanism, the threshold of 10 per cent of supporters backing a proposal is too high, given the actual level of online participation. To amend the system this threshold should either be lowered or calculated over the census of active participants – namely those who have participated in the latest consultation – rather than over all nominal registered members, many of who are dormant.

In the case of France Insoumise, the participatory element has been more limited than in the previous two cases and concentrated on making contributions to the movement's programme called *Avenir en Commun* (Future in Common). The programme drew on Mélenchon's 2012 campaign programme, but it also encompassed a process of participatory programme drafting to ideally involve all the supporters in the writing of the programme. The idea was to adopt a procedure that was 'rich, collective, inclusive and unprecedented' in which 'the richness of shared experience would allow to make new proposals emerge'.[264] Around 3,000 contributions from supporters were collected on the website jlm2017.fr between February and August 2017. The content of these online proposals was gathered alongside other data (such as the input coming from a number of physical assemblies conducted by the party). Open text submissions were analysed and selectively adopted by the programme development team and then summarised in two documents which were published before the convention in Lille in October 2016. Their contributions were organised around seven thematic axes: the sixth republic, distribution of wealth, ecological planning, the exit from European treaties, an independent and alterglobalist France for peace, human progress and the new frontiers of humanity. Participants were then asked to vote which of the proposed measures they would prioritise, which led to the selection of 10 'emblematic measures'.[265] A total of 130,000 members on the platform participated in expressing their preference. Drawing from this process, a series of thematic books with wide circulation were published in December 2016. Thus, while integrating open-ended participatory elements, also in the case of France Insoumise, the extent of intervention of participants was quite limited and controlled by the programme facilitators, with most participants merely involved in voting the priorities among pre-established options.

What emerges from this analysis of management of deliberative mechanisms, is that they are quite tightly supervised by party staff, with little control for members over the process. All platform parties contain a deliberative element, giving the possibility to users for some *qualitative intervention* in the process of policy development, such as by drafting law proposals or providing comments and observations on existing proposals. However, ultimately the impact of this deliberative component is highly constrained. Although they provide the party with an effective means to crowdsource ideas for legislation, the leadership and the party staff remain in firm control, through their ability to initiate discussion on law proposals; to selectively choose among the proposals coming from members; and finally to filter user proposals that are deemed not to be in line with the party's principle and pre-established policy positions. This means that the membership has a limited degree of control even on those processes that are by definition more membership-led.

Digital acclamation

Despite the presence of deliberative, discussion-oriented and qualitative forms of online decision-making, the form of digital democracy that prevails in digital parties is clearly top-down: more concerned with balloting than discussing and favouring representative and plebiscitary democracy tendencies over deliberative democracy. This has been seen in the prominence which ballots on candidates, leadership and policies have acquired within a number of emerging formations, attracting far

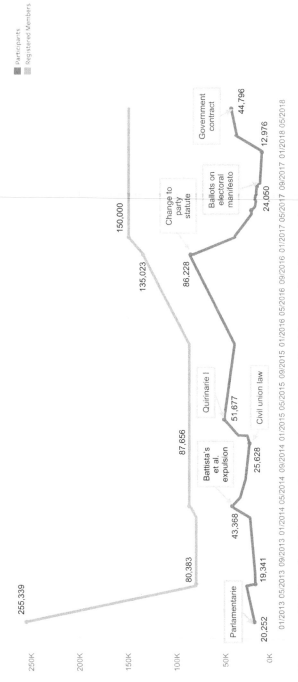

Figure 7.1 Number of participants and registered members in 5 Star Movement's online consultations.

higher levels of participation than deliberative discussions. As expressed by Guillaume Royer, the digital democracy coordinator of France Insoumise, although deliberative processes attract people in the 'thousands, balloting sees people participate in the tens or hundreds of thousands. Most people prefer to participate by voting than by sending a text'.[266]

In the Five Star Movement, since 2012 a total of 66 ballots have been carried out nationally, with many more conducted at the local level. These have included a number of issues, from primaries for candidates to stand in the national elections, to votes on the expulsion of elected representatives accused of misconduct. On 6 December 2012, the M5S held the Parlamentarie (parliamentary primaries), the first national online consultation organised by the movement. Registered members were invited to select from 1,400 candidates the ones to stand in the parliamentary elections, with 31,667 people participating in the consultation. Online primaries were also conducted on the occasion of ensuing rounds of local elections. In preparation of the local elections in Rome and other cities, online primaries were launched, where Virginia Raggi was nominated after receiving 45.5 per cent of the votes (1,764), ahead of Marcello De Vito at 35 per cent. Yet, Grillo retained ultimate say over this. On one occasion, the primaries for the mayoral elections in Genoa in April 2017, he arbitrarily disavowed Marika Cassimatis, the candidate selected by members. Having a limited central organisational structure, the Five Star Movement has used online elections on internal offices very sparingly. The only instance was the confirmative referendum on the creation of a Directorate (*Direttorio*) composed by Alessandro Di Battista, Luigi Di Maio, Roberto Fico, Carla Ruocco and Carlo Sibilia, which was approved by 91.7 per cent of members (34,050 votes).

Besides using the internet for online representative elections, the Five Star Movement has made heavy use of online referenda. One of the most famous or better infamous manifestations of this tendency have been the votes on expulsions of party representatives accused of having breached party rules of conduct. One of the first instances was the expulsion of the M5S MPs Lorenzo Battista, Fabrizio Bocchino, Francesco Campanella and Luis Alberto Orellana. Out of 43,368 registered users, 29,883 voted in favour and 13,485 against. It has been calculated that since 2012, 60 people have been expelled from the party, of which 18 are MPs and 19 are senators.

Online referenda have also been used for making political strategy choices. A referendum was called after the 2014 European elections to decide whether to join the Europe of Freedom and Direct Democracy (EFDD) group, with 78.1 per cent (23,121) of members voting in favour. In January 2017, Grillo called for a new consultation on this question, now proposing that the party move to the Alliance of Liberals and Democrats for Europe (ALDE) group; 78.5 per cent (31,914) voted in favour, but the move was never implemented because ALDE eventually refused the entry of Five Star MEPs in its ranks.

Since its inception Podemos has conducted around 20 digital ballots at the national level, with many more at the local level. The participatory platform has been used for a number of purposes, including the election party candidates at the national and local levels, the election of party officers, strategic choices and policy development. In November 2014, a few months after the first party conference in Vistalegre in Madrid, members were invited to choose a number of party officers, including the 62 members of the Citizens' Council, the equivalent of the party's central committee; the general secretary and the party's control committee (Comisión de Garantias), counting 10 members. Ninety thousand people, 80.71 per cent of 112,000 registered participants, voted for the organisational document proposed by Pablo Iglesias, and 88.6 per cent (95,311) for the latter as general secretary.

The members of the Citizens' Council and of the control committee were elected collectively as a closed list, according to a system described in Spanish as *lista plancha*, in which voters cannot express their preference for given individuals, but have to decide which team to vote collectively. In fact, it was possible for users to edit the composition of the team, but being more laborious it was only done by a minority of participants. The team 'Claro que Podemos', led by Pablo Iglesias, went on to fill the totality of the 62 members of the Citizens' Council and of the control committee. The participation portal was also used in the ensuing months in national, regional and local primaries. Also, in this context the closed list system was used and was abandoned only in April 2016, under the initiative of organisational secretary Pablo Echenique, who back in 2014 had withdrawn his list for the Citizens' Council in protest against the *lista plancha* system.

Podemos has resorted to online referendums to decide on important strategic questions, as illustrated in Figure 7.2. One example was the consultation held in April 2016 over a coalition government with the

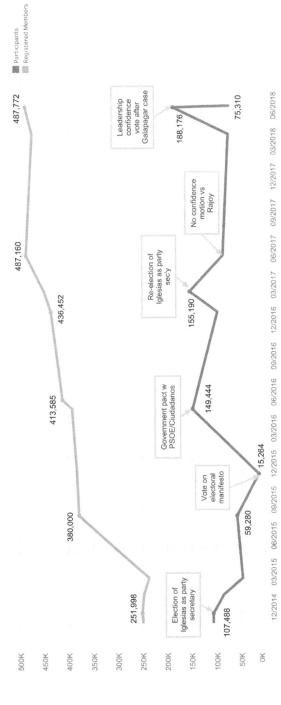

Figure 7.2 Number of participants and registered members in Podemos' online consultations.

Socialist Party and Ciudadanos. Out of 150,000 participants, 88.23 per cent voted against. In the following month, members were consulted on an alliance with Izquierda Unida in the ensuing elections, with 98 per cent of members voting in favour. The party also used the participatory platform to approve various political documents in view of the second congress held in February 2017. Of a total of 436,452 members, 99,162 party members (22.7%) participated in the vote, with 41.57 per cent of voters supporting the proposal of Pablo Iglesias, and 39.12 per cent for the one proposed by the party's second in-charge, Iñigo Errejón, in what amounted to one of the few cases of close referendum results in the history of the party.

An internal referendum was also called in May 2017 to decide on a no-confidence motion against Mariano Rajoy's government, in response to the prime minister's party involvement in a corruption probe. Although a high percentage, 97.4 per cent (85.310), voted in favour, only 87,674 out of 487,160 registered members participated (20%). In early 2018, a further consultation was held on a new no confidence motion proposed this time by the Socialist Party, returning an even higher percentage (98.94%) in favour of the proposition.

The most controversial case of use of online referendums has been the one held in May 2018 on the Galapagar controversy, whose voting interface is displayed in Figure 7.4. This recall referendum was launched after it was revealed that Podemos leaders Pablo Iglesias, the party secretary, and his partner, Irene Montero, the party's speaker in the Congress, had purchased a villa in Galapagar, in the outskirts of Madrid, worth 600,000 euros. In and of itself, there was nothing illegal about this action. But it was in contradiction, with the moralistic populist rhetoric adopted time and again by Iglesias and his party colleagues

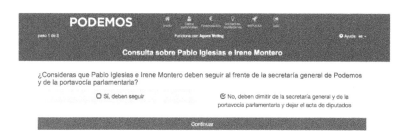

Figure 7.3   Screenshot of Podemos' consultation on Pablo Iglesias and Irene Montero.

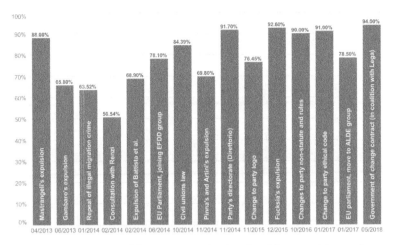

Figure 7.4 Percentage of the winning option in 5 Star Movement's internal referendums.

against their political opponents. In a speech before the 2015 general elections, Iglesias had famously criticised politicians who isolated themselves from the general populations, 'who live in Somosaguas [a luxury neighbourhood in Madrid], who live in chalets, who do not know what it is to take public transport'. The decision to purchase a chalet in the outskirts of Madrid seemed to contradict this stance and Iglesias and Montero were vehemently attacked in the media.

The consultation saw the participation of 188,176 people, the highest ever; 68 per cent of the members of Podemos voted for Iglesias and Montero to remain in their position. But the referendum was widely criticised as being preposterous and a manifestation of the worst plebiscitary and leaderistic tendencies of digital democracy. The question posed to party members, sent in an official email to all members, was the following anodyne one: 'Do you consider that Pablo Iglesias and Irene Montero should remain at the head of the General Secretariat and of the parliamentary spokesperson for Podemos?' But the accompanying text was rather tendentious in presenting Iglesias and Montero as the victims of a media persecution campaign. After the vote, the two continued in their positions despite the comparatively high number of members who had expressed dissatisfaction with the leadership and with the Anticapitalistas having called for an abstention.

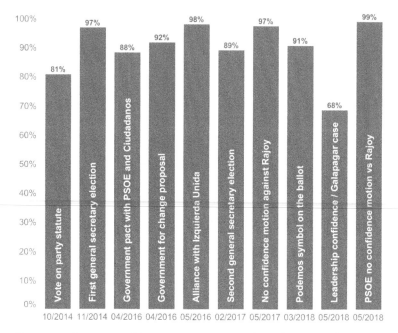

Figure 7.5   Percentage of the winning option in Podemos' internal referendums.

In the case of France Insoumise, the most important consultation was an internal and non-binding poll on the stance to take in the second round of the presidential elections, with three possibilities: abstention, voting for Macron and spoiling the ballot. Around 243,000 people, 55 per cent of the 440,000 'insoumis', participated in the consultation; 34.83 per cent voted for supporting Macron, 36.12 per cent for spoiling the ballot and 29.05 per cent for abstention.

These different referenda point to a strong control of the leadership over the process of consultation, making e-ballots resemble more of a rank-and-file stamp of approval for foregone decisions. Almost invariably they return supermajority results in favour of the leadership position, with most of them boasting 80 per cent or above majorities for the winning proposal, in a way that is reminiscent of sham elections in countries of the Soviet bloc. This situation seems to confirm Michels' assertion about the way the leadership uses referendums merely to impose its will on the membership. Different channels of influence are at the leadership' disposal to gear consultations towards the desired ends. This is seen in the biased formulation of some of the questions posed to the membership, and the way they are often designed to elicit a response favourable to the leadership. This state of affairs is further compounded by the way in which, on certain occasions, the leadership feels entitled to ignore the results of consultations, as with Grillo deciding to overturn the nomination of Marika Cassimatis as mayoral candidate in Genoa. More generally, the leadership can influence consultations indirectly by using their access to party communication to generate a mood favourable to their line. Davros David Puente, a former employee of Casaleggio, recounts how, in anticipation of important decisions, the staff and Grillo's blog would adopt a clear propaganda line with the aim of influencing the internal vote. 'It was enough for Grillo to say A and the members would vote A. It was enough for Grillo to say something and people wanted that.'

Online democracy betrayed?

What can be seen across this review is that online democracy in digital parties has had an unmistakable top-down bias, with the membership intervention being mostly reactive. Representation and plebiscitary consultations have had a far greater role than it has been the case with more participatory ones. Balloting, which by its nature involves choosing from a limited number of choices, has had a far greater weight than debating which allows participants to have a qualitative say on content.

It is fair to concede that deliberative processes such as crowdsourced policy development have shown promising elements. All these formations have established forms of grassroots intervention, such as through proposals which, after gaining a sufficient support, can go on becoming official party policy. But these measures appear ultimately incapable of rebalancing a process that is strongly skewed in favour of the leadership. These deliberative mechanisms have attracted rather small volumes of participation compared with online ballots. Furthermore, there are problems at the level of the leadership's responsiveness to deliberation, because of the wide room for selection and editing of proposals, and comments on existing proposals, that is retained by the central party staff. This has been seen in the case of the Five Star Movement, in which proposals can be filtered and edited if they are deemed not to be in line with the party's values or its strategy. In the case of Podemos, while there exist a binding mechanism (ICPs), which should allow for a reduction of such arbitrary intervention, a high threshold has resulted in the fact that no membership proposal was ultimately approved.

Online referendums, while attracting a high number of participants, are little more than the ratification of the decisions already taken by the leadership. Across Podemos and the Five Star Movement, there have been only two instances of successful rank and file rebellion: the first in the occasion of the consultation on the repeal of the crime of illegal migration; the second on a consultation with Matteo Renzi, when he was charged with the formation of a new government. In both circumstances the membership voted against the position explicitly favoured by Grillo and Casaleggio, with a 63% majority in the first case, and a narrow 50.5% one in the second. But these cases are more unique than rare. According to Davide Bono, a councillor for the Five Star Movement who has been collaborating with the team involved in managing the Rousseau's decision-making platform, the tendency of the membership to almost invariably agree with the leadership is due to the fact that 'the movement has a strong collective identity'. However, it is evident that this is also the result of the influence exerted by the leadership through a variety of means, including the timing of elections, sometimes announced by surprise, and with a short time span, as often happened in the Five Star Movement; the formulation of questions, which can be used to influence people's vote and the opinion campaigns waged by the party leadership in advance of the actual vote, suggesting a certain line to the base. Similar problems have been experienced in the context of online primaries and election of internal officers. The leadership has often displayed the intention to control such elections, by imposing a closed list system, as seen in the case of Podemos, or even disavowing the result of primary consultations as seen in the case of the 2017 M5S online primaries in Genoa.

These findings thus highlight that although these formations have waxed lyrical about the fact that they were introducing a direct democracy and making their organisations truly responsive to their members, the actual implementation is far less rosy. For the most, the digital democracy practiced by these parties has been strongly top-down, with balloting taking precedence over debating and the leadership maintaining a firm grip over the management of consultations, and very few instances of rank-and-file rebellion. This is a reflection of the fact that the leadership exercises direct control over the party staff responsible for managing participatory platforms. This situation leads people as former Casaleggio employee Davros David Puente to be very pessimistic about a form of democracy, where you 'express a vote but on something that has already been decided by others'.

In front of what by and large appears as a betrayal of the promise of democratisation put forward by these parties at their outset, it should not come as a surprise that there has been a significant drop in participation in online consultations. In the case of the Five Star Movement for example, although turnout in online polls averaged 60 per cent in 2012, it had gone down to 14 per cent in 2017.[267] Although Podemos did not experience such a significant drop, participation in online ballots has often appeared disappointing, not keeping up with the steady growth in membership experienced by the party. Party leaders should seriously take heed of this trend of low participation given that, as argued by Antonio Gramsci, one of the ways in which the base conveys its discontent is 'by dispersing or remaining passive before certain initiatives'.[268]

'Give people a vote and they will come' is a famous slogan used since time immemorial to advocate the introduction of democratic measures. But it is obvious that if members come to realise that their vote ultimately does not matter all that much, they will stop coming. We are thus already at the point where the initial enthusiasm associated with the salvific potential of digital democracy has started wearing off, and it is urgent to rethink more realistically what can actually be achieved through the use of these tools, as well as to devise clear and transparent mechanisms of members' control over online decision-making. If online democracy has to regain some credibility, it is imperative that its process is seriously reformed, introducing a number of guarantee rules, starting from assigning the management of all consultations to a party body independent from the leadership and trusted by the membership.

8

The Hyperleader

A round of applause reverberates through the halls of Clermont-Ferrand, Dijon, Grenoble, Montpellier, Nancy, Nantes and Le Port à La Réunion as France Insoumise leader, Jean-Luc Mélenchon, suddenly appears on the stage of all these cities' theatres simultaneously. Obviously, Mélenchon is not physically present in all of these places. He may well be a charismatic politician with a powerful rhetoric that make him resemble the tribunes of the people of ancient Rome or a Marat in the French revolution, but he is as of yet deprived of the gift of ubiquity. That night he happens to be physically present in Dijon. But his image is beamed as a hologram to other six locations, through a technique known as the Pepper's Ghost.[269] The audience in the halls that are packed to capacity follow the leader's speech, which covers some of the key proposals of France Insoumise and of the presidential campaign of 2017. As the speech ends with the words 'Allez les gens courage' (Come on people, take courage) the audience erupts into a roar, and then the meeting ends with a collective singing of the national anthem.

Enter the hyperleader: the new type of leader that stands at the forefront of digital parties. The tactic used by Mélenchon and other politicians, such as Indian right-wing leader and current prime minister, Narendra Modi, may just appear a matter of curiosity or a clever campaign stunt. But it is a powerful metaphor of leadership in the digital era. Far from having dissolved in the de-centralised networks of social media, platform parties' doings highlight that leadership is coming back with a vengeance acquiring new forms. This digitised leadership reflects the new possibilities for mass outreach and online crowding offered by social media, the rise of a digital celebrity culture that has emerged on platforms such as Facebook, Twitter, YouTube and Snapchat, and the continuing necessity of leadership in contemporary politics. This is clearly reflected in the plebiscitarian character of online consultations, as seen in the previous chapters, which often boil down to the leadership's need to stoke the support from members. The hyperleader and his magnetic influence over the organisation is the elephant in the room of online democracy. But what do we actually mean when talking about plebiscitarian and demagogic leadership in the digital age? What are the characteristics of the hyperleader? And what role does this figure play in the internal organisation and external projection of digital parties?

As we see in this chapter, like the hologram of Mélenchon beamed to different locations all over France, the hyperleader diffuses his image and words instantaneously through all sorts of communication networks and personal communication devices – computer, mobile phones, tablets – to an online crowd of internet supporters and sympathisers who, despite their physical dispersion, become united in following a single leader. The hyperleader becomes the symbolic centre of the movement, the pivot of the process of 'distributed centralisation' ushered in by digital parties; a figure which is the objective of a charismatic identification, charged with feelings of empathy and affection; his image being celebrated in thousands of memes, serious or joking; his face appearing in motion in hundreds of YouTube videos; his proposals being submitted to digital ballots open to all party members; his name being repeated incessantly in social media exchanges and turned into hashtags, all of which becomes a sort of symbolic rallying point for digital militancy.

Such development needs to be understood as a manifestation of a more systemic return of strong leadership in contemporary society, after a time at which prevalent processes of leadership took a technocratic and anti-charismatic form. Since the economic crisis, and amidst a condition of growing political and geo-political turmoil, we have instead been witnesses to the growth of strong leaders across the left/right divide. Think for example about politicians such as Donald Trump and Bernie Sanders, Marine Le Pen and Jean-Luc Mélenchon, Pablo Iglesias and Matteo Salvini, Xi Jinping and Vladimir Putin. Whatever you may think politically of these politicians, what is apparent is that they can hardly be considered as weak non-leaders, facilitators or distributed leaders. Hyperleaders are one specific manifestation of this return of strong charismatic leadership in our times, that also plays a crucial role in the functioning of platform parties.

No leader, no party

To understand the rise of the hyperleader, it is necessary first to do quite a bit of house cleaning, getting rid of some of the problematic assumptions that in recent years have been associated with the diffusion of digital technologies and their effect on politics. For a long time, it was widely assumed on both the left and the right that the diffusion of digital media would have militated against leadership and would have had strongly de-centralising effects. Techno-utopian pundits, neoliberal evangelists, neo-anarchist activists have all conspired in persuading the public that leadership and power were things of a technologically underdeveloped past, blemishes of a society not yet graced by the marvels of information technology. Manuel Castells, the theorist of the 'network society', whose work profoundly influenced the sociology of new media and the internet in the 1990s and 2000s, argued that the diffusion of new media meant that we were moving away from the pyramid to the network and that vertical power structures would give way to flat organisational structures.[270]

This idea was equally popular in many social movements that have developed in recent decades, and it continues to this day. Feminists, environmentalists, urban activists and the anti-globalisation movement all converged in suspecting leadership and in predicting its ultimate demise. At the height of the economic crisis, the idea was most famously expressed by Occupy Wall Street's claim to be a 'leaderless' movement. It was believed that the internet, empowering individuals and providing them with many-to-many channels of communication, would eliminate the presence of informational monopolies and therefore also the necessity for hierarchical and top-down command and coordination.

If we move beyond the delusion of the inevitability of 'leaderlessness', we are faced with a far more difficult task: ascertaining what leadership style has become prevalent in the present day and age. It is difficult to overstate how important leadership is within political parties. We know from long-standing scholarship how leaders accomplish a number of important roles for the party, including developing party policy, guiding internal organisation and presiding over key meetings, expressing publicly party views, liaising and negotiating with other parties, organisations and institutions, and in the case of electoral victories acquiring the role of government leaders. Within the representative system of modern democracy, the leader has thus embodied in his persona the role of the most important 'representative'; and in this capacity leaders have come to act as party symbols or short-hand references.

Although anarchists like to contend that leadership and any form of authority is in fact just an imposition that is irrational and can be eliminated, by glancing at the history of politics and political parties, it appears clear that it instead constitutes a fundamental necessity of political party, a necessary evil one may say, rooted in the impossibility of the masses to self-organise. For Weber an organisation can exist only if it *subordinates* itself to a leader and an organisational staff that represents it in the public arena. In other words, one cannot speak of organisation without some form of leadership, given that by its nature organisation involves a separation between the leaders and the led.

According to Robert Michels 'in the mass and even in the organized mass of the labour parties, there is an immense need for direction and guidance'.[271] This need stems from that passivity of the masses noticed by Gramsci, Michels and many elitist theorists. But there is also a fundamentally psychological reason for the necessity of leadership. According to Sigmund Freud, the leader acts as an 'external object' which produces a sense of community within the group and facilitates social solidarity. The leader thereby becomes a point of projection at which the desire for identification of the mass coalesces. Following this line of argument, talking of a 'leaderless organisation' is as meaningless as talking of a headless mammal or of a wingless bird.

Leadership, however, is not a monolithic entity. Throughout history, different typologies of leadership have emerged which differ on the basis of their legitimation and their consequences for organisational processes. According to Weber, in one of his typically schematic catalogues, three types of leadership and connected forms of 'legitimate domination' exist: traditional, charismatic and legal.

Traditional leadership rests on long-established customs and is legitimated by tradition and the past. It is the leadership of the king, the chieftain and the wizard. Legal-rational leadership constitutes instead the dominant form of leadership in modern and industrialised society, marked by complex bureaucracies and a legal system centring on the state, its parliaments and its courts. It rests on the legal-rationalistic process of election and office, whose legitimacy draws from a number of written rules and procedures established by political parties. Charismatic leadership is finally a type of leadership that is characteristic of many social and religious movements. It is fuelled by the charismatic or prophetic power of the leader, his possession of quasi-magical abilities and his capacity to harness an enthusiastic following.

Legal-rational leadership is the form that has been most closely associated with the mass parties of the industrial era. These large organisations were and still are characterised by the presence of large and impersonal bureaucratic apparatuses responsible for managing and processing vast amounts of information. They were often described as 'machines', precisely because of their mechanistic logic. As such, these organisations were not deprived of personal leaders assuming the role of guides for the party followers. Think, for example, about Russian Soviet leaders such as Leonid Breznev or Chinese Communist leaders such as Jang Zeming, or James Callaghan in the 1970s Labour, and there you will find a fitting example of the legal-rational leader, and its stereo-typical greyness. In recent decades, this legal-rational leadership has become widely suspected, as a function of the more general suspicion towards bureaucracy pervading the neoliberal era, but also of the actual quandaries of that arrangement.

Charismatic leadership is a type of leadership that has been widely associated with authoritarian leaders, with fascist dictators such as Benito Mussolini, Adolf Hitler or Francisco Franco. Franz Neumann famously asserted that within the National Socialist Party the 'leadership principle' dominated, namely the idea that in principle all decisions would be made by the Führer. However, charismatic leadership is not reducible to right-wing totalitarianism. Socialist and communist politics, despite their strong association with bureaucracy, also expressed charismatic leadership. Consider, for example, figures such as Stalin, Che Guevara and Mao Tse-tung, and it is evident how much their power was premised on personal charisma. These and other leaders in fact often legitimised themselves precisely in opposition to bureaucracy.

What kind of leader is the hyperleader? Is he a charismatic or a bureaucratic leader? Is he authoritarian or democratic? How does the hyperleader use digital communication to harness his leadership powers? What are the characteristics that are required to a politician to become a digital leader? What kind of interaction does the digital leader construct with the base?

Caesar 2.0

The hyperleader is an excessive leader, the purveyor of a spectacular, charismatic and highly personalised form of leadership that matches the changes in the public sphere as a consequence of the rise of digital hypermedia. Responding to the mercurial nature of social media communication, its obsession with personality and celebrity, and the widespread distrust towards organisations and bureaucracy that has become widespread in our society, the hyperleader presents himself as a departure from the technocratic and aloof politicians a disgruntled electorate is all too familiar with. The hyperleader floats above the party like a gas balloon and attempts to lift the party's militancy and its electorate all by himself – a balloon whose gas is the visibility of the leader, re-hashed almost every day through continuous participation in media representations, both on TV and on social media.

The term *hyperleader* emerged within debates taking place inside digital parties, and in particular within Podemos. Some of the intellectuals involved in the early conception of the movement, such as German Cano and Iñigo Errejón, discussed the idea of hyperleadership as a strategy to create a new political identity. Within this debate, the idea of a hyperleader stood to indicate the strongly 'mediatic' character of this leadership and 'the necessity at a time of profound social dispersion to have a person citizens of different walks of life could identify with', as argued by Cano. In the case of Podemos, conjecturing on the necessity of this form of leadership had to do with the circumstances of the initial founding group of Podemos. This was a group which counted few dozens of people and had very limited territorial penetration, to the point that it had to find an alliance with the Anticapitalistas Trotzkyist group which had a physical presence in different cities and regions around Spain. The idea was that to make up for such organisational weakness, it was necessary to resort to the seductive power of television and the media system more generally, its capacity to impress new faces and identities in the public sphere. Pablo Iglesias, who had by then acquired a media celebrity status as regular guest on a number of political talk shows, provided the concrete incarnation for this strategy.

The notion of hyperleadership is thus predicated upon a fundamental assumption: the centrality of the media system as the decisive battlefield in the struggle for power. According to this theory, hegemony is won not on the barricades of social movements, nor in the painstaking work of setting up a political movement, but rather through presence in TV studios and on social media platforms. This was openly theorised by Pablo Iglesias, who drew from his experience of Berlusconi's Italy during an Erasmus exchange in Bologna. Iglesias was struck by the way in which Berlusconi's ownership of the media and telegenic performances allowed him to win strong support despite his judicial problems and the failure of his stints in government. This led Iglesias to the persuasion that it was necessary to find space on national TV and gain visibility and consequently power; and this persuasion informed his participation in the alternative TV programme *La Tuerka*, which eventually acted as a springboard for his career as a talk-show guest. Yet, as many activists within Podemos themselves highlight, TV is by now certainly not the only stage where this struggle for media hegemony takes place. In recent years, TV has been increasingly challenged and complemented by social media, and this is having evident consequences for the nature of contemporary leadership. The hyperleader navigates the nooks and crannies of a hybrid media system in which TV videos are shared and wildly commented on in social media, and in turn social media posts often become the object of TV coverage.

From a political standpoint, the hyperleader may be described as a Caesarist figure, namely as a charismatic figure whose person is endowed with the power to represent an entire movement. Caesarism or Bonapartism hereby designates a type of leadership that befits situations of crisis, when the political structure of society is highly fragmented, and therefore the intervention of a charismatic leader is necessary to establish a new order. This is the point that is the most unpalatable in left circles as there is a justified worry that strong personalised leadership will lead to authoritarianism. The fear is that any form of strong leadership is a new instance of that 'leadership principle' which Franz Neumann saw as the dominant organisational logic in the Nazi party. However, this fear is ultimately exaggerated. In fact, as we have already seen, the charismatic leader type, and more specifically forms of Caesarist leadership, are not limited to authoritarian formations, but have also been seen in many democratic movements in times of profound crisis. Weber famously thought that all mass democracies were bound to go in a Ceasarist direction.

The Caesarist nature of the hyperleader needs to be understood in connection with the distrust towards bureaucratic organisation, which, as we have already highlighted at different points in the book, is one of the dogmas of neoliberalism and a prominent feature of digital cultures. Fear of collectivism and suspicion of totalitarian regimes has led to the perception that large-scale bureaucratic organisations are always bent on betraying the people they are supposed to serve, and are utterly inefficient and wasteful. In the case of political parties, this anti-bureaucratic sentiment stems from the crisis of traditional parties and the weakness of 20th-century ideological alignments organised around the opposition between labour and capital. Faced with this crisis of political collectivities, the hyperleader presents himself as an antidote to the party's weakness. It is indicative that in the European elections of May 2014, the symbol that the voters found on the card next to Podemos was not the overlapping circle logo of the party, but the photo of Pablo Iglesias with his determined, angry face. Furthermore, in many cases the leader's social media presence, as counted in number of likes and followers, is well above the popularity of the party he leads, signalling the fact that it is the leader propelling the party and not the reverse.

The leadership type that corresponds to the hyperleader is a clearly charismatic one. It corresponds, in Max Weber's terms, to the model of the charismatic-plebiscitary party, rather than the bureaucratic party. In the former the leader acquires the role of guide of the movement. It is charismatic because all questions of legal and rational legitimacy of the leader tend to come second vis-à-vis the emotional recognition and acclaim of the base. The leader's conflict with bureaucracy is easy to see when looking at a number of recent confrontations that have emerged within digital parties and beyond and have pitted the hyperleader against the party's oligarchy. Take the case of Jeremy Corbyn, who had to fight tooth and nail against the bureaucracy of the Labour Party, which has been trying in all possible ways to keep him out of power. Or consider the case of Bernie Sanders, who has had a similar confrontation vis-à-vis the Democratic National Committee, which did everything it could to prevent him from becoming presidential candidate.

Antonio Gramsci saw personal leadership, such as the one of the *condottiere* described by Niccolò Machiavelli, as something out of sync with the complexity of industrialised society, whose organisation necessarily required the presence of a structured apparatus capable of processing vast amounts of information, training political personnel and integrating a vast number of members. For him the bureaucratic mass party was the contemporary substitute to the demagogue. However, interestingly, Gramsci retained a space for leadership. For him 'in the modern world, only those historico-political actions which are immediate and imminent, characterised by the necessity for lightning speed, can be incarnated mythically by a concrete individual'.[272]

The moments when personal leadership is necessary are, as Gramsci goes on to explain, those periods of re-organisation of the political arena, such as after great crises that upset well-rehashed political balances of forces. But is not the moment we are currently traversing precisely a moment of profound transformation and therefore one in which personal leadership does have a place and a function? In this context, the Caesarism of the hyperleader may well appear as a necessary evil in order to pursue the task of organisational refoundation. The key strategic question is whether this organisational refoundation is actually carried out, whether the charisma of the leader is eventually 'routinised' in a more stable organisational structure that is not completely wed to the leader's ebbs and flows. The risk, evidently, is that if this does not take place, the party will end up perishing once the leader's charisma starts becoming opaque and when the love of the superbase for its spokesperson turns into suspicion and resentment.

The position of the hyperleader may be further understood by referring to Slavoj Zizek's famous idea of the 'vanishing mediator',[273] namely that in our society we are facing a crisis of mediations. To the contrary, the hyperleader is a mediator that does not want to vanish, but remains as resolute as ever in being the ultimate signifier of the political party and its collective intentionality. This activity of higher level mediation is what allows digital parties to get rid of other mediators who are felt to be superfluous and nefarious. In particular, here we refer to those intermediate ranks which as we have seen were reputed to constitute a key organisational structure for the political party, but also the source from which oligarchic tendencies emerged. The distrust towards the intermediate ranks translates into bestowing an unprecedented amount of power to the leader figure, and one might say that the party oligarchy, decried for its careerism and self-service, is substituted by a sort of plebiscitary dictatorship in which the leader acquires the role of sole depository of the membership trust.

The hyperleader's job description

Hyperleadership involves a redefinition of the skills and abilities that qualify a good leader, what we may describe as the 'identikit' of the political leader.[274] In a classic summary, Robert Michels included force of will, knowledge, strength of conviction and self-sufficiency as some of the key features of the effective leader. Many of these skills may be considered universal and applicable to all political leaders, and in fact most of the features listed by Michels are still relevant to the hyper-leader, provided we take into account the radically changed condition in which political leaders operate and the prominence of the media system, as the tribune's stage. Drawing on Michels' profile, we could describe the hyperleader's job description as follows: an ability to com-municate effectively on the media, especially on TV; an immaculate history of political engagement which gives the leader an impression of authenticity, ingenuity and honesty; a down-to-earth attitude, avoiding complex language, and presenting himself or herself as a common indi-vidual living like ordinary people do. The hyperleader does not simply need to be good at the media but also needs to be perceived as 'au-thentic', 'honest', and 'open' to the demands coming from ordinary citizens.

It is quite obvious that the hyperleader has to be 'media savvy', that he needs to be able to exercise a charismatic spell on media publics that come to identify themselves with his persona. Possibly the most in-structive cases are Beppe Grillo and Pablo Iglesias, and their leadership roles in the Five Star Movement and in Podemos, respectively. Beppe Grillo owed his celebrity prior to the creation of the movement to his work as a comedian involved in a number of memorable satirical one-man shows. The Five Star Movement would be unthinkable if it were not for the huge visibility that, prior to the appearance of the move-ment, was earned by Grillo both in the theatres and on the Web. Grillo has made use of his flamboyance and magnetic theatrical skills in po-litical rallies, which contain many of the typical elements one would find in one of his shows, such as ferocious gags or the mimicking of corrupt and unpopular politicians.

Grillo started as a rather typical 1980s variety show comedian who appeared on a number of famous prime-time programmes such as *Fantastico*. In one of the episodes of this show, Grillo made a joke about the corruption of the Italian Socialist Party, which was rumored to have taken bribes, as would be unveiled in the Tangentopoli scandal a few years later. After the show Grillo felt ostracised from national televi-sion. He stopped appearing on national TV channels, concentrating instead on his own theatre tours. He acquired the persona of a moral-ising Savonarola and presented himself as a martyr of a power system bent on silencing all forms of dissent. In the 1990s Grillo went on to wage campaigns against corrupt politicians such as Silvio Berlusconi, whom he called the 'psycho-dwarf', and against multinational corporations, and increasingly engaged with ecological issues, advocating the need to switch to electric cars, solar energy and recycling. He also delivered every year, starting in 2002, a series of *discorsi all'umanità* (speeches to humanity) that coincided with the annual speech of the Italian President of the Republic on New Year's Eve and that were televised on minor TV channels and broadcast on the internet.

Key in the political trajectory of Grillo was the leap from the theatre stage to the internet, with the creation of his personal blog – beppegrillo. it – which in a few years climbed the rankings of popular blogs to eventually enter the top 10 worldwide. The huge fame earned by Grillo as an actor went on to translate into Web celebrity. This turn was quite surprising given that at some points in his trajectory Grillo had appeared as an anti-technology Luddite, and during one of his shows he had famously hammered a computer to bits. Yet, his encounter with Web strategist Gianroberto Casaleggio after a theatre show changed this position. Casaleggio, who had previously worked at the Olivetti computer firm in Italy and was the owner of a small internet firm, Casaleggio Associati, persuaded Grillo to get on board with new technologies in order to give more outreach to his message. Once a customer of the Casaleggio and Associati digital consultancy firm, Grillo built a strong internet presence and intercepted a new public that was often younger and less politicised than the one going to his theatre shows. His posts growingly raged not just against Berlusconi but against the entire Italian political class accused of mismanagement and corruption, dubbed as the 'caste', a term taken from the title of a popular essay by Italian journalists Gian Antonio Stella e Sergio Rizzo.

Beppe Grillo's blog acquired great power in shaping the Five Star Movement, being between 2009 and 2018 the de facto house organ of the movement, to the point that critics derided it as the 'sacred blog', to describe the reverence displayed towards it by Five Star activists, and disparagingly assigned to the Five Star Movement the moniker 'blog party'. Although this fledgling organisation could initially rely on limited financial resources, made available by Grillo's commercial venture, advertising revenue from the blog and donors, the fame of Grillo provided a remedy for these weaknesses. Even the absence from TV of both Grillo and the candidates of the Five Star Movement – until

2013 M5S activists were severely discouraged to go on national TV – did not really matter. TV presenters and journalists were compelled to speak about Grillo and the movement anyway, given the public interest, sometimes broadcasting videos of large rallies such as those of the 'Tsunami Tour', which Grillo organised on the occasion of the 2013 national election campaign.

The rise to fame of Podemos's leader, Pablo Iglesias, though rather different, displays some clear similarities in the importance played by celebrity and the ability to use both old and new media to one's advantage. When Iglesias became known to the public, he was a young researcher in political science at the Complutense University in Madrid, a traditional hotbed of the radical left. But he was quite an unusual academic at that: not a person to content himself with the ivory tower, but rather first and foremost an activist interested in making an impact on the general public. Iglesias had a long standing in media and TV and possessed training as an actor. These abilities were put into service when he became the main host of the alternative TV show *La Tuerka*, a TV programme produced on a small budget, initially in a humble garage in the neighbourhood of Vallecas, where Iglesias himself lived. The show was launched in 2010, shortly before the beginning of the Indignados protest movement in May 2011, and was initially broadcasted on a small local cable network, TeleMadrid. It soon attracted a wide public by covering a number of critical political issues that were often ignored by mainstream parties, such as the abysmal economic situation experienced by Spain in the aftermath of the 2008 financial crisis, the difficult condition of youth facing unemployment and precarity, and widespread corruption of public officials.

This experience projected Iglesias into the role of a left-wing commentator, invited to appear on a number of mainstream shows. Keeping strictly to a recognisable dress code – with a ponytail, a white shirt and a red tie – Iglesias reached wide fame among the Spanish population, and rapidly gathered a public of fans following his media appearances. With his rebellious appearance, his searing attacks against opponents, his irony and his capacity to win rhetorically against older and often arrogant political commentators and leaders, Iglesias acquired a powerful aura that he has since been put at the service of Podemos. He is a leader in strong tune with popular culture and its ever-changing fashions, as seen in his references to television series such as *Game of Thrones*, whose DVD box set he even gifted to the king of Spain during a meeting. Furthemore, differently from left activists of previous generations he is capable of condensing complex political contents in simple slogans and soundbites.

For Pablo Iglesias, TV, rather than the internet, played a pivotal role in propelling him to celebrity. But the internet and social media were also instrumental to his rise. As recounted by Podemos activist German Cano, 'Social media were a key space where we could develop the conversation, including the discussion on topics that had been examined in TV appearances of Iglesias and other leaders.' La Tuerka itself ended up reaching most of its audience online, with its YouTube channel becoming one of the most followed in Spain. Furthermore, Iglesias and Podemos soon became the most popular of political social media accounts in Spain, with millions of followers on Facebook and Twitter. In other words, although the case of Iglesias points to the continuing centrality of TV in the system of political communications in the present era, it also highlights that TV is by now part of a hybrid media system[275] in which the internet is increasingly defining how TV is watched and the impact it has on political conversations and persuasions.

We can see how this identikit also applies to other typical leaders of digital parties, from Rick Falkvinge of the Pirate Party to Jean-Luc Mélenchon and Bernie Sanders. In fact, this media celebrity element is not limited to digital parties alone. Take, for example, the case of Donald Trump, who owes much of its ability to contest the U.S. presidential elections to the fact that he has been for 30 years a household name, a regular host in talk shows, and the presenter of the famous reality TV show *The Apprentice*. Furthermore, if we move to another example this time on the left, namely the case of Jeremy Corbyn, we may see how media charisma is not a given, but is more of a process that can evolve through time. Until the 2017 UK national elections, when Labour scored an impressive result, Corbyn was widely seen as an unattractive and grey figure, incapable of winning popular support. This was due, to a great extent, to the ferocious enmity of the news media against Corbyn, and a certain proneness to gaffes and lacklustre appearances. Since then, Corbyn seems to have learned a lot about how to use the media and social media to his own advantage, displaying more convincing performances in recent time. As suggested by UK activist Aaron Bastani, part of this ability may have to do with his own biography and the fact that he has three millennial children who have been advising their dad on how to become an attractive figure for the youth.

The typical misunderstanding that must be carefully avoided when affirming the centrality of media performance is thinking that here charisma is simply a matter of packaging, the like of which can be easily attained by hiring a good media consultant. However, this could not be farther from the truth. The charisma of the hyperleader is something that cannot be manufactured out of thin air. Rather, biography, reputation, a history of coherent conviction, and even the minutest details of his or her professional and political career are all-important to create the necessary trust from the base. It is sometimes sufficient for a minor revelation to emerge for the leader's charisma to obfuscate. Digital leaders put a lot of emphasis in demonstrating that they have nothing to hide, that they have an immaculate past and that all or most of their dealings happen in the open, and not in smoke-filled rooms, in which 'men in grey flannel' are known to meet. Thus, they respond to the sensibility of a public which has grown tired of the traditional political class and is eager to know all the details on politicians, searching the minutest information and rumours about politicians on the internet. At a time marked by high levels of public distrust towards existing institutions and traditional political parties, the hyperleader has good reasons to present himself as the total outsider, to highlight his lack of connections to the establishment, and exhibit his political virginity, even when it comes to career politicians such as Mélenchon, Corbyn and Sanders.

Possibly the Five Star Movement is the most radical in this direction in the way it has elevated the word *honesty* into a party slogan. Leaders of the party, such as Alessandro Di Battista and Luigi di Maio, have often paraded their unstained honesty and contrasted it with the widespread corruption of the Italian political class. Similar is the case of Podemos, and of various socialist candidates such as Corbyn, Mélenchon and Sanders, who owe much of their leadership aura to possessing an unblemished reputation as people who have never compromised their ideals to shrewd political convenience. As Bond and Exley have argued in reference to Sanders, 'Part of Bernie's effectiveness came from his matter-of-fact way of speaking and his old Brooklyn accent. But what allowed people to really trust him is that he has been saying the same thing for thirty years.'[276] This authenticity of Sanders was celebrated in a number of internet memes to show 'that Bernie Sanders is a representative of the 99% while Hillary Clinton is a representative of the 1%', as expressed by campaigner Winnie Wong. 'We did comparison video in which you could see how Hillary Clinton had changed her position on many issues while Bernie had been consistent on everything in his political career. It is important because it shows why Bernie was someone to trust. A key element here was trust, the credibility of the character, the fact that you thought he was someone in whom you could confide.'[277]

When this impression is disrupted, it has dire consequences for the leader's credibility. This was seen in the case of Podemos in the scandal embroiling Podemos's leaders and sentimental partners Pablo Iglesias and Irene Montero, when it was revealed that they had bought a 600,000-euros home in a rich town on the outskirts of Madrid, a behaviour that was in glaring contradiction with their moral fustigation of the political caste, which Iglesias had accused of 'hiding in villas'.

Finally, the hyperleader is a down-to-earth leader. He presents himself as a 'lad next door' or a 'geek next screen'. He abhors all the traditional pomp associated with party leadership, and presents himself as part of the people and as someone approachable. He tries to be seen as an ordinary person who has much in common with ordinary voters, yet also a person endowed with extraordinary conviction – the leader as a sort of everyday hero. In this light, leaders such as Grillo, Iglesias, Mélenchon and others have adopted a casual dress style that makes them look like ordinary people. Iglesias revealed that he bought his clothes at the cheap shop Alcampo. Similarly, Mélenchon has carefully avoided the bourgeoise suit and tie and made himself recognisable by wearing the 'Mao suit', similar to the one worn by Mao Tse-Tung. Curiously, this unassuming style of dress resembles the one of Silicon Valley executives such as Mark Zuckerberg, who famously often wears sneakers and a hoodie even in highly formal circumstances. Mélenchon has also used YouTube to convey a more personable and authentic image than the one sported on official occasions. As described by Antonie Leaument, coordinator of social media for France Insoumise, 'When I watch Mélenchon on YouTube, I see him the way he actually is. Elsewhere in the media, it is another Mélenchon, more concentrated, more controlled. On YouTube he allowed people to see the other Mélenchon.'

This effort of presenting oneself as common people chimes well with the dominant spirit of the digital society, suspicious of institutions, officiality and all sorts of mediation. And to this impression of approachability, the leader contributes through personal engagement on social media, sometimes also responding directly to user comments as if he were an internet user like all others. Similarly, selfies and the mediation of public appearances of the leader contributes in communicating the leader as 'one of us' rather than an aloof career politician, and this is why they have become such a recurrent feature of political campaigns across the entire political spectrum.

Founder, benevolent dictator, sockpuppet

This centrality of the leader is also due to the fact that the hyperleader is often the founder, the one without which the party would not exist. Grillo founded the Five Star Movement; Falkvinge, the Pirate Party; Iglesias, Podemos; Mélenchon, France Insoumise and Sanders, the Our Revolution campaign and many spin-offs from his presidential campaign. Hyperleaders are exceptional leaders also because they are almost invariably founding leaders.

This nature of the hyperleader qua founder is a type of authority that is not of the charismatic, but rather of the traditional type, as its legitimacy is based on the past and on the act of foundation. There are obvious similarities between the hyperleader and the figure of the 'benevolent dictator' seen in several digital personalities, such as Jimmy Wales, the founder of Wikipedia, or Linus Torvalds, the founder of Linux.[278] As is the case with these figures, the hyperleader presents himself as the ultimate guarantor of the party and its founding principles. This type of leadership is informed by a libertarian distrust for any form of authority and intermediation between the individuals and their collective action. In a way, in this context the leader denies his own existence, pretends not to be a leader. He acquires the form of a sort of caretaker and guarantor, a role that is very different from the imaginary of the leader qua conductor indicating the way to the movement as Caesar would command his legions.

The idea of a benevolent dictator is often premised on the promise to maintain the movement's initial spirit – a type of authority that has curious reminiscences of the traditional authority of the chieftain. Hereby, the leader bases his legitimacy on the past, on the history that has elapsed from the foundation of the movement, and one may say on its inherited tradition. The party staff thus comes to resemble a clergy which stands to defend the content of the Holy Scriptures against the risks of heresy that may arise at any point. The need for leadership seen in platform parties is similar to the needs of open source programmers

looking for a guarantor figure. As happens in open-source software communities, it is the very openness of the group, its attempt to draw people
from different sensibilities and ideological persuasions, that makes
the presence of the leader a necessary anchoring point, to focus the attention of all members and provide them with a reference point to
coordinate their collective action. Hereby, any serious controversy that
fundamentally affects the direction of the movement is directed to the
leader-founder and his judgement.

The almost paternalistic profile of the hyperleader, however, often
conceals a baffling reality, namely the fact that the hyperleader may not
necessarily be the strategist, the person who decides the path ahead
that the movement needs to take. In fact, one often finds concealed
behind the leader a hidden demiurge, who acts as a mastermind of the
party strategy, allowing the hyperleader instead to concentrate on the
physically and psychologically demanding task of throwing a permanent political show for the fruition of the media public. In this light the
hyperleader may sometimes appear as just a puppet manoeuvred by
someone acting behind the scenes.[279] Emblematic is the case of Gianroberto Casaleggio, the digital guru of Beppe Grillo. For a long time,
supporters and sympathisers of the Five Star Movement thought that
Grillo had complete control over the movement. Yet, rumours started to
develop around the role played by his media guru. As argued by Matteo
Canestrari, who worked at Casaleggio Associati, these rumours were
not mere conspiracy theory. In fact, Casaleggio was indeed the mastermind of the movement: 'He had developed all in his mind the vision of
the movement, and controlled his evolution and key dilemma moments',
argues Canestrari. 'Grillo would have never had the political intuition
and the understanding of digital media to do that.'[280] In the early phase
of Podemos, the situation was somehow similar. In fact, according to
various testimonies, Iñigo Errejón, who would act as campaign manager
in the 2014 European elections, was the real mastermind of the project
and was heavily responsible for setting up the party office in Madrid.
Iglesias was selected as leader only after the approach with Barcelona
activist and current mayor Ada Colau failed. Eventually Errejón
became tired of what he saw as Iglesias's diversion from the original
strategy and tried to mount a challenge to the leader, which, however,
was ultimately unsuccessful.

What this situation stands to show is that while the hyperleader acts
often more as a front of the movement, or even as a 'sockpuppet', a

digital culture term used to describe fake online identities, the most important decisions are often taken by 'nerds' such as Casaleggio and Errejón. The hyperleader performs the role of actor, and social media story-teller on the stage of the society of the hyper-spectacle, and must constantly feed the hunger for new appearances, for new tweets and social media posts, for new interventions, being prepared to constantly mix with voters, while always sporting a smile and a calm demeanour in the public eye. But it is often difficult for him to combine this demanding work of media actoriality with the more strategic organising that mostly happens in the party's shadowy backend. Thus, while it is true that the digital Caesarism of the leader may have partly side-stepped the oligarchy of the central committee and the cadre, it has not eliminated internal power struggles and conflicts happening behind the scenes. The leader's entourage often takes the form of a micro-oligarchy, a 'magic circle' that is not very different from the oligarchy of old. While promising total transparency and directness to voters, the hyperleader himself is thus caught in the opaqueness of power relations.

The risk more generally is that overdependence on the hyperleader may condemn the party to failure. It is thus crucial that digital parties establish measures to put some reins on hyperleadership, ensuring that it remains democratic and is influenced by internal discussion at all levels of the party. The ever-present danger is for the hyperleader to consume himself in a flame of boundless enthusiasm and hope that has, as their necessary counterparts moments of depression and despair; and that eventually supporters may get tired of the hyperleader as quickly as internet users do with a Netflix series after a bout of binge-watching. It will be seen in the near future which of the directions the hyperleader will take, whether his charisma will progressively be routinised in a more stable structure or whether it will continue in its actual form, and whether the dependency on the hyperleader will ultimately be to these parties' detriment.

9
The Superbase

Digital parties have been propelled to their impressive success by a swell of grassroots support, most clearly seen in the way in which they have been capable of recruiting hundreds of thousands of people as registered members. This return of mass participation in the internal life of political parties constitutes a surprising and largely unexpected event. We were used to a long trend towards the fall of party membership amidst the condition of political apathy that dominated the neoliberal era. What is the nature of the political participation that we see emerging here? And can we really say that these parties are more participatory, both quantitatively and qualitatively, than their predecessors?

As explained in this chapter, digital parties attract a vast and diverse group of supporters whom we can refer to as the *superbase*. The metaphor comes from chemistry, where the term *superbase* is utilised to describe a super-basic compound – such as lithium monoxide anion or methyl anion – that has high reactivity to protons. Superbases are very important in organic reactions, for example to facilitate catalysis, and are responsible for carbon dioxide fixation.

Deployed in the context of platform parties, the notion of *superbase* serves to express different characteristics of these formations' model of participation. First, most basically, these parties involve 'a return of the base'; they attempt to reconstruct a membership structure of support for political movements, in which members are once again considered as a necessary component of political organisation, a resource to be prized rather than merely a source of trouble and even embarrassment. This turn makes a stark contrast to the role of membership in the television party, which was viewed by political leaders as disposable at a time in which the party looked at its supporters, much in the same way TV producers look at spectators: as a tendentially passive mass from which the only thing one can exact are timid nods of approval.

Campaigns of digital parties owe much of their success to their ability to mobilise online large numbers of supporters. Counter to moralistic discussions on online participation as 'slacktivism', online campaigning has proven crucial to the success of these parties. New tactics have been created on top of predigital ones, such as door-to-door canvassing, posters, rallies, direct mail and phonebanking. Drawing inspiration from the organising practices developed in the protest movements of 2011, from the Indignados to Occupy Wall Street, and applying communication logics typical of social platforms, platform parties have managed to mount an impressive challenge against mainstream parties that are well staffed and well funded and often enjoy insider connections in mainstream news media.

The second meaning of *superbase* which is inspired by the use of the term in chemistry, lies in its being highly 'reactive' rather than 'active'. Although there is a marked increase in the quantity of participation, this does not directly correspond to an increase in the intensity of participation across the board. While hundreds of thousands have been involved, only a limited percentage of them, perhaps 1 per cent of the entire base, is really active. The superbase is far from being a homogeneous monolith. Where the militant of the mass party was subject to a strong discipline with compulsory attendance to meetings and similar activities, the digital militant finds in the Web, and the discussions that develop there the main space of political engagement. The digital participant, often conceived as a 'user', is far more unsteady and unpredictable than was the case with party militants of old.

The distinction between the militant, the normal member and the sympathiser becomes fuzzy, with highly porous lines dividing different categories of support. This is due to the greater ease of registration, where becoming a member is almost as simple as joining Facebook or other social networks. The digital party adopts the social media giants' free access model, leading to a wondrous increase in the number of nominal participants. But there exists a strong gradient of participation, ranging from people who participate a lot to people who participate very little. In truth, all political parties are confronted with a divide between active and passive membership. But here this tendency is pushed to an extreme. Only for a very few individuals does the digitisation of political activities unlock the possibility of a truly qualitative intervention in the life of the political party. Most of the base is instead simply *reactive*, namely it is mostly limited to a narrow and ad-hoc response to the stimuli coming from above, sometimes supportive, sometimes critical, and in other cases still apathetic, to the prompting messages launched by the party leadership, which, to keep with the metaphor, is the source of the protons that then go on producing a reaction in the superbase.

The changing communication structure in a digital era, with the diffusion of social media and their various interactive and *reactive* features (such as liking, sharing or commenting), provides new avenues of participation for people who would otherwise not be able to participate. However, as we shall see in the course of the chapter, this participation is highly uneven. The 'supervolunteer', the new digital hero of the party, a militant, who can avail ample amounts of his free time and labour and contribute at a distance in various tasks, is a powerful yet restricted and 'aristocratic' minority. Most participants stop at the level of 'lurking sympathisers', people who may agree with party contents and occasionally be 'engaged' by them, yet mostly abstain from making the leap to becoming active members.

The militant and the sympathiser

The presence of base, or of a *mass element*, to use the term of Antonio Gramsci, is a necessary feature of all political parties. Parties can hardly exist unless they are supported from below, and they have a social support base which guarantees their existence and legitimacy. Supporters provide political parties with a series of fundamental resources besides actual votes in the ballot box, including financial resources (through membership dues or donations), political labour (as seen in canvassing, leafleting or sharing of online propaganda) and, more broadly, social and reputational resources, lending their own credibility and access to personal networks of various kind in support of the party's cause.

This base of support involves different categories of people with varying degrees of involvement and loyalty, ranging typically from the party's electorate, whose participation is sometimes limited to casting the ballot for the party, to the party's militant, who is more highly involved, participating in meetings and dedicating time and labour on a regular basis to the political party, and in-between the two, to end with party sympathisers who express more occasionally their sympathy and support. There is constant flow in and out of the party, with some sympathisers becoming members, some members becoming activists, and in turn some activists and members falling in the external rungs because of dissatisfaction or for personal reasons. What has to be established thus is why people participate in different degrees and what the actual 'style of participation' at these different points of intensity consists in.

In the case of Duverger's analysis, discussed in Chapter 1, particularly important was the differentiation between sympathisers and militants. The French political sociologist proposed a picturesque analogy where militants and sympathisers stand to each other as marriage and concubinage respectively: the sympathiser engages in a more superficial relationship with the party, which can be ended with not much trauma; for the militant instead the relationship is deep and more stable. Typically, the concern of party organisers is how to turn electors or potential electors into sympathisers and sympathisers into members. However, this desire can run into serious difficulties. According to Duverger, the reason why many sympathisers do not become members is down to a repugnance towards the party discipline, with its quasi-militaristic connotations of hierarchy and conformity, obedience and discipline; a process towards which, as Duverger proposed, the petty-bourgeoisie harbours a strong suspicion because of 'the refusal to abandon [its] own individual independence'[281]

The resistance to *encadrement* Duverger diagnosed in the 1950s at the height of the industrial era, and at the time of a bureaucratic state and highly organised capitalism, when party obedience seemed only more natural, can only be considered stronger in the context of the present digital society, pervaded as it is by a deep-seated individualism. In a time in which suspicion towards organisations and collectivities has become widespread, are people really becoming once again more prone to being 'recruited' in a party?

To address this question, we need to start with the condition of widespread apathy and demobilisation that constitutes the terrain in which digital parties have emerged. As noticed by different political sociologists, in recent decades we have witnessed a decline of membership in political parties, and more generally a crisis of mass membership organisations. These have been challenged by advocacy organisations that instead of beseeching active participation of members content themselves with the financial contribution of dues-paying members. Many historical political parties that counted millions of members in their heydays have seen their membership rolls shrinking and shrinking.[282]

Paradigmatic is the case of the UK Labour Party before the revitalising arrival of Jeremy Corbyn as party leader in 2015. Labour had gone from over 1 million members in the 1950s to less than 200,000 at the end of Tony Blair's leadership. Many other political parties have experienced the same trajectory, with their membership base often more than halving. In Italy, the Partito Democratico saw a significant drop in members, from 539,354 in 2013 to 405,000 in 2016, and a further reduction in the last few years.

This reduction of membership is coherent with the transformation of the political party that took place at the same time. The turning of the party into an 'electoral/professional' organisation has led to a diminishing importance of membership. With campaigning by and large transitioning from rallies and door-to-door campaigning to the TV screen, and mainstream parties converging to the centre, there was not much space left for the militant in the party's strategy. Militants appeared as embarrassing vestiges of an hyperpoliticised past and were sometimes made to feel superfluous by the leadership. Digital parties seem to point towards an overcoming of this situation. But to what extent is this actually the case?

The return of mass political participation

Parties such as the Pirate Party, Podemos, the Five Star Movement and France Insoumise, and movements like Momentum, have managed to gather at their base in a few months or years a number of members that it had taken traditional parties several years, if not decades, to attract. Observers, analysts, journalists have often expressed their surprise at this trend, which seemed to contradict what many regarded as an unstoppable tendency towards the decline of party membership and growing political apathy. Many of them count several hundred thousand adherents, a level that locates them above many of their competitors who have been around for many more years.

In *Swarmwise*, Rick Falkvine relates that the Swedish Pirate Party managed to attract 13,000 members in its first three months of existence. Coinciding with the 2006 protests in support of Pirate Bay, the Pirate Party tripled its member count to 42,000 members, to become the third largest party in Sweden. As of 2018, just four years since its foundation, it counted over 500,000 members, more than double the number of members of PSOE, the second largest party in Spain (with below 200,000 members), and well above PP at less than 70,000.

France Insoumise managed in a very short span of time to recruit thousands of people and claimed 533,566 supporters as of May 2017, over ten times the membership of the Front National and the Parti Socialiste, both standing at around 40,000 members. The Five Star Movement also initially exhibited a spectacular growth, gaining 250,000 members in 2013, just a few years after its foundation in 2009. Since then membership has dropped to 80,000 members in 2013, and then picked up again to an estimate of 150,000, though no official figures have been released in recent years. The severe decline in membership between 2012 and 2013 is due to the fact that the Five Star Movement has by now adopted more restrictive rules on membership. Applicants need to meet a series of requirements, including not being members of any other parties or associations in opposition with the party's mission. However, as things stood in 2017, the Five Star Movement was the second largest party by membership in Italy, behind the Partito Democratico at 400,000 members in 2016. Furthermore, Davide Casaleggio has recently declared that the Five Star Movement will reach 1 million members, probably a bombastic promise, but still a demonstration of the ambition of mass growth characteristic of digital parties.

Considering the vote of these parties, the member/voter ratio is as follows: 20 per cent for the Swedish Pirate Party in 2009 (48,000 members and 225,000 votes in the 2009 European elections), 10 per cent for Podemos (500,000 members and 5 million votes in the 2016 elections), 7 per cent for France Insoumise (500,000 members and 7 million votes in 2017) and 1 per cent for the Five Star Movement (150,000 members and 11 million votes in the 2018 elections). On average, the ratio of members to voters for these parties is well above the one of mainstream parties, which often stands at just about 3 per cent. It can thus be said that indeed in most cases platform parties have managed to attain a quantitative increase in participation as measured by the number of party members, though this does not automatically equate to an improvement also at the level of the 'quality' of participation.

It is worth noting that the tendency of increase in members is not something limited to digital parties but is also experienced by more traditional parties that have undergone some form of renewal. Possibly the most spectacular case of the return of participation comes from the

Labour Party. With the rise to leadership of Jeremy Corbyn, the party has experienced a momentous growth. Since the low point of 2014, when it counted 180,000 members, it has now reached 550,000 registered fee-paying members, which puts it at the top of all parties in Western Europe by this measure. This phenomenon is interesting, bearing in mind the obvious differences between a traditional party such as Labour, and digital parties, because it suggests that the trend that we see in the most intense forms in digital parties is also influencing in the party system as a whole, and that we could be moving away from an era of political apathy to a new time of politicisation driven by growing preoccupation with the economy and social justice.

Why are digital parties attracting once again such a wide membership? Does it have to do simply with a return of interest for political affairs or also with the very redefinition of the notion of membership?

Both responses are true. It is evident that the surge in membership of digital parties, illustrated in Table 8.1, derives from the re-politicisation of society in the aftermath of the Great Recession. At times marked by growing economic trouble and connected social distress, produced by unemployment, falling wages, labour precarisation and cuts to public services, and growing political polarisation it is quite obvious that there will tend to be a return of interest and participation in political parties. In fact, similar trends of a return to political participation can be seen in the context of protest movements that have seen a significant growth in the last decade. One example is the case of the movements of the squares of 2011, the Arab Spring, Occupy Wall Street, the Indignados, widely considered as the largest wave of protest mobilisation for over 30 years.

The swell of support has, however, a second and possibly more important cause. It is a predictable result of the lower barrier to participation in these political parties, which constitutes a common feature of platform parties. These parties' redefinition of membership, where the

Table 8.1   Registered party members as of May 2017

Parties	Members
France Insoumise	533,566
Podemos	500,000
MoVimento 5 Stelle	150,000
Piratpartiet (Sweden)	3,500 (peak of 50,000 in 2009)

threshold for access is significantly lowered, and membership is de-linked from financial contribution, is a key factor in this growth in membership. In this, digital parties follow the model of social media giants such as Facebook and Twitter, but also innovations already at work in the field of online campaigning in digital advocacy organisa-tions such as MoveOn and Avaaz. MoveOn, for example, claims to have a whopping 5 million members, many of whom – as David Karpf high-lights – do not realise they are members at all, given that the definition of membership is so flexible as to include all mailing list recipients. It is significant that also the surge of Labour has been facilitated by a low-ering of entry fees to just three pounds to become party supporter (instead of full member), allowing subscribers to participate in leader-ship elections.

This connection between the rise in membership and easier registra-tion rules is corroborated by the negative case of the Five Star Movement and its low membership figures compared to other digital parties, which we may take as the proverbial exception that validates the rule. This is largely because party registration involves a laborious certifica-tion process, often taking several months. Some of the applications have been rejected simply because the scans of the ID document were not in the right format, which is required to be less than 100KB in size. This may seem like an apparently trivial requirement, but it can still prove quite a hurdle for people who are not digitally savvy and, in partic-ular, older people who have difficulties using a simple picture resize application online. This practice starkly contrasts with other parties such as France Insoumise and Podemos, in which the sign-up process is almost automatic, and just entails submitting one's name, email and identity card number. It has been reported that out of 500,000 people who made the request to become part of the Five Star Movement, only 130,000 have been certified and activated.[283]

The change towards a free membership model crucially involves lifting the customary connection between the member and the donor. Traditionally, political parties would make membership dependent on the payment of fees to the organisation, sometimes in the form of an annual membership fee, or even a monthly one, and this fee would be crucial to provide the party with the necessary resources for its func-tioning. However, this arrangement has been overcome in the context of digital party, which, in most cases, allows people to participate in the organisation without having to pay. Ultimately, as proposed by Miguel

Ardanuy, the participation organiser of Podemos, what characterises the digital party vis-à-vis older parties is a simple thing: you do not have to pay in order to participate. This logic, according to Ardanuy, would facilitate making 'your militants look more like the country', thus counteracting the tendency stated in the so-called 'May's law' about the disparity between the rank-and-file and the electorate.[284]

The significance and implications of this growth in membership can be better appreciated by considering the changing relationship between members and sympathisers. To this end, we can obtain an approximate measure of the sympathiser base from the number of 'likes' to their Facebook pages. This assumption is based on the understanding that by now Facebook has become extant among overwhelmingly young and internet-connected party supporters, and that liking a Facebook page is understood as expressing support, or at least interest, in a given formation. Obviously, this is not to say that all people liking a Facebook *are* sympathisers, nor that conversely all party sympathisers do like the party's Facebook page. However, the number of likes provides a tentative measure, perhaps a low estimate, of a party's sympathisers.

Looking at Table 8.2, which draws from data available as of 16 October 2017, it can be seen how these formations have a high number of Facebook likes, a figure positioning them among the top or top two political Facebook pages in their respective countries. The outlier here is France Insoumise, which has a very low level of likes, perhaps an indication of the comparatively younger age of the party and the fact that Facebook is less diffused in France among party activists than it is in other countries. If we are to take these figures as a rough estimate of the number of sympathisers to party members, it seems that there is quite a low sympathiser–member ratio here, which is 2 to 1, if we consider that Facebook likers feature full members too, who are assumed to like their party's Facebook page in very high numbers. This ratio suggests that,

Table 8.2 Facebook page likes

Organisation	Facebook Likes
Podemos	1,169,647
MoVimento 5 Stelle	1,089,622
France Insoumise	116,376
Piratpartiet (Sweden)	75,610

THE SUPERBASE · 171

within digital parties, sympathisers are more likely to become members than is the case in traditional parties, largely as a consequence of the adoption of a free membership model. Thus, it is indeed true that these parties are more open to society and set a lower barrier to participation. But, as is demonstrated in the continuation of the chapter, this quantitative change is accompanied by great disparity in the intensity of participation among members.

The supervolunteer

For all the suspicion one might have with the digital party, its virtualised politics and its shedding of previous sites and occasions of participation, it is undeniable that this organisational template leads to an opening to new members and allows people who were previously marginalised to take part in political campaigning. As recounted by Adam Klug, national co-ordinator of Momentum:

> People wanted something to do, and Momentum was giving them something accessible and proactive to do. What we had in mind right from the beginning was to transform this and engage people who were not involved before, particularly people from underrepresented backgrounds, to be active. For each of those people to have conversations in the communities and bring people into the movement.

Here participation online and participation offline in meetings, activities and canvassing operations becomes deeply interwoven, to the point of being indistinguishable. In this context, the flexibility afforded by digital media as a coordination tool allows 'people to do activities where they feel they are making an impact, that leads them to feel more energised and more enthused and to encourage other people they have relationship with to join and help shape it'. The militant becomes customised, able to more easily fit activism into his or her timeline and easily locate activities nearby, where people can participate.

This opening up of the party to new membership, however, does not translate into an even activation of all members. The greater flexibility of participation is accompanied by a highly uneven intensity of participation among nominal members, with a 'long tail' distribution in which a small number of members participates very actively, coming close to the contribution of full-time activists, while the great majority participates only occasionally, and often in limited ways, in the way of comments, online 'reactions' and involvement in the most popular consultations launched on the platforms. The divide between participants and non-participants is substituted by the divide between highly active participants and highly passive participants. The highly involved participants may be called 'supervolunteers', while the long end of the tail with low participation may be called the 'lurking supporters'.

Supervolunteer is a term that can be used to describe highly activated militants. The super volunteer may be seen as constituting the spear of the superbase, a hyperactive section of supporters which plays a central role within digital parties, allowing them to make up for their lack of a dependable organisational structure and a large and permanent salaried staff. The Five Star Movement, Pirate Parties and Momentum have heavily relied on the work conducted by unsalaried activists contributing to communication, event organisation, fund-raising and electoral campaigning.

The term *supervolunteer* was coined by Zack Exley and Bond, two staffers in the 2016 Bernie Sanders presidential primary campaign, to describe those highly involved volunteers that ended up playing a decisive role in the campaign.[285] They make a strong claim against thinking that one can substitute volunteers with paid staff, as seen in their expression 'The revolution will not be staffed'. They argue that volunteer leaders 'emerge ready to make change, and they bring their full selves, and life experience to task of building a movement that works'.[286] The supervolunteer is a volunteer who goes above and beyond the call of duty; a volunteer who does not stop at the simple and repetitive operations one would normally expect from an ordinary party militant, but sometimes also performs creative and supervisory roles generally attributed to party staffers. According to Bond and Exley three or four super-volunteers can substitute the work of a paid organiser. This reliance on supervolunteers is well represented across many of the movements discussed in this book.

In the case of Sanders' campaign, reliance on super volunteers was due to the extremely limited resources available to the campaign team. Sanders' campaign was forced to 'rely almost 100 per cent on the volunteer leadership that was already out there – among all the hundreds of local Bernie groups, many of whom were already months old and the tens of thousands of people who had already signed up to help'. The severe lack of paid staff, what from the perspective of a traditional campaign would had seemed a recipe for disaster, was taken as an inspiring challenge, forcing Sanders' team to develop a mass movement. 'Using conference calls, one-on-one calls, local Slack teams, and plain old email threads, we organized teams in several cities that were going to attempt to go beyond house parties to hold large public events.'

As Claire Sandberg, a digital campaigner who was party of Sanders' campaign team, relates, supervolunteers were doing virtually from remote locations 'a lot of the work a normal campaign would assume could only be managed by paid staff who were physically present'. This constituted a radical departure from the traditional forms of campaigning in which 'the only way that people can participate meaningfully is to relate directly to a staff person, and they are given a very low level of work, and the campaign volunteer tells them how to do it'. In this context, 'if there is not a field-staffer who is not in their physical community, there is not a way for them to get involved'. Contrary to community organising, where the idea is to slowly build people's leadership, in the Sanders' campaign the idea was 'Let's start from the people who want to do the most'. The highly active volunteers were called to organise 'barnstorms', events to discuss and share ideas for action, and to set up phonebanks to persuade voters. Falkvinge advocates a similar framework when discussing the role to be played by party leaders in local areas, and across other formations such as Podemos and the Five Star Movement we also see a heavy reliance on the work conducted by the most active militants, who are expected to heroically make up for the lack of a real territorial party infrastructure.

The choice to rely so much on supervolunteers is first and foremost a response to scanty economic resources. Deprived of steady funding, because of the absence of regular dues from members and the unpredictability of donation receipts, combined in certain cases with the refusal to access state funds (as is the case with the Five Star Movement), digital parties are severely constrained in terms of their staffing, both at the national and local levels. Hence, the necessity to rely on people who make their political labour available for free, despite all the problems that this choice involves, including the need to constantly train and retrain volunteers, and a certain 'aristocratic' tendency, favouring those with the privilege of time. In other words, these movements attempt to make up for the 'power of money', which they so sorely lack, with the 'power of people', to utilise the voluntary labour offered by the militancy as a means to compensate for their comparable lack of economic resources.

However, it is also more generally the conception of the role of the militant and of his position in the party organisational texture that is significantly different. Where the militant before constituted simply a soldier to be mobilised to achieve specific tasks commanded by the top of the party, and with limited room for autonomy in regard to whom to communicate the message and how, the digital militant is prized precisely for his ability to be personal, to bring his own life experience to the campaigning arena and, perhaps most importantly, for making available to the campaign his reputation and his network of contacts on social media. Militancy becomes personalised not only at the point of reception but also at the point of production and distribution, inviting the militant to repackage messages in ways that can better intercept his own personal network of sympathy and support.

It should, however, be noted that this 'creative militancy' goes with significant limitations. Although the supervolunteer is given freedom to adapt the message, he is not expected to have a decision-making position matching his level of commitment. This is because, as we have seen when discussing the virtualisation of the political party, local groups are supposed to be spaces of action, not spaces of decision, in line with the assertion that while work is distributed, planning strategy has to be strongly centralised. This disconnection is bound to create significant frictions given that often very active militants come to feel they should also have a greater say on decisions. This issue has been manifested in multiple incidents that have taken place within parties such as Podemos, the Five Star Movement and Pirate Parties, with ambitious local leaders often entering on a collision course with the national leadership.

The lurking supporter

At the opposite end of the super-volunteer one also finds an opposite ideal-type, what using a typical digital culture expression we name the *lurking supporter*. This term designates a person who is not very active, a mostly passive agent who is involved only occasionally in the life of the party, despite often being a fully registered member. It is a person who may occasionally participate in an online consultation or contribute to party communication by sharing a post or tweet, but only with great irregularity and often relapsing into latency. This is, to use the term of Chris Anderson, the 'long tail' of the party, which encompasses the great majority of supporters, and also of registered members.[287] To refer back to Jacob Nielsen's discussion of participation, this is the 90 per cent of party supporters, whose participation levels are mostly very low and mainly of a purely reactive type.

The presence of a vast passive membership within these parties has been seen when discussing online decision-making and noticing how levels of participation has been very low, often just 20 per cent of all registered participants taking part in consultations. There is an evident mismatch between the high number of nominal party members and the low number of those who actually participate assiduously in the movement.

Also, the participation that is actually performed is mostly of a reactive kind, in response to the stimuli coming from the leadership via the intermediate channelling provided by the super-volunteers. It takes the form of a reaction to a content that has already largely been 'pre-packaged', so to speak, something which the lurking supporter can like or not like, retweet or not retweet, or comment upon positively or negatively. Thus, the influence of lurking supporters is often rather limited in qualitative terms, and reducible to simple actions approximating a Yes/No vote, adding to the tallies. This situation highlights the serious pitfalls of participationism and suggests that counter to the idea that citizens want to participate rather than delegate, as argued by the likes of Casaleggio, the reality of the situation often seems to point to the contrary. Although many people want to be registered as members, and thus have the opportunity to intervene occasionally in decisions, only a small minority wants to participate actively, the majority contenting itself with delegating to others.

All political parties are faced with the obstinate presence of a passive membership, which despite all the best efforts seems impervious to activation, a state of affairs that seems to confirm Michels and other elitists scoffing about the passive mass. Yet, in the case of the digital party, these half-hearted participants are important for a number of reasons. First, they provide the party with a pool of potential active participants, from which new people may in time be recruited to higher levels of participation, thus making up for the inevitable sliding of some high-level participants into lower levels of participation. Second, platform parties need this pool of sympathisers because these formations need a diffuse 'cyber-army' of sharers and likers, allowing them to reach beyond the necessarily narrow rung of hardened militants.

This need is a consequence of the communicative architecture of social media and the fact that visibility is largely dependent on fans' contributions and the sharing of content on social media. Digital parties need to have recourse to the active cooperation of their base, as 'sharers', 'likers', and 'retweeters', lest their messages be widely circulated. From this viewpoint we can see how the superbase is in fact also a 'database', an array of users who are useful to the party as an accumulated repository even when they are not really active users in any significant way. The digital sympathiser comes to play a decisive role in what can be considered an all-important activity in digital campaigning, namely the 'transmission of trust' from the leader to the base. She puts her own reputation and online reputation, in particular, on the line by declaring her confidence in a given candidate and campaign. In so doing, she provides the campaign with access to people who, though not necessarily trusting a candidate or campaign that is far from them and about which they know very little, are far more likely to trust the 'Bob' or 'Lisa' whose messages they see appearing daily on their Facebook newsfeed, and whom they remember from their days in school or university.

In conclusion, the participationism of digital parties has yielded a quantitative increase in the number of participants, but with a great unevenness in levels of participation across different categories of participants. While some hyperactive participants, the aforementioned supervolunteers, have come to take a greater role than they would have had in previous party types, for the great majority of members participation is very low and infrequent and mostly of a purely reactive kind. It takes the form of involvement in digital ballots, or sharing and 'liking' social media material, but with little to no active or physical participation. Turning some lurking supporters into a more active militancy would definitely constitute an important headway for digital parties. However, this task is seriously obstructed by the fickleness of the experience of online participation and by the extremely agile structure of these formations, which constitute major obstacles to the process of mass integration and political education that would facilitate this conversion.

Conclusion

Digital parties promise a radical transformation of liberal democracy beyond the current dissatisfaction with this political form; a change that is expressed by a number of buzzwords found in participationist discourse: *openness, disintermediation, directness, transparency, responsiveness, choice, change, connection* and *community*. Political formations such as the Five Star Movement, Podemos and the Pirate Parties propose a solution to the systemic failings and imbalances of a society plagued by a crisis in political representation and legitimacy; they respond to a citizenry whose problems, interests, demands are not addressed by either old mass parties and trade unions or media-oriented centrist party organisations that have been the norm during the neoliberal era. To this end they project a new blueprint of political organisation and new democratic mechanisms embedded in their participatory platforms, which are presented as enablers of a more authentic political participation. But are digital parties delivering on their promise? Is online democracy better than the established representative democracy it aims to replace? And what are the key dilemmas that have emerged in the development of these parties?

At the outset of the book, we placed the digital party in the long history of theorising on the political party, which – despite the enmity that liberals and anarchists of all sorts have felt towards it – still constitutes the most important form of political organisation. The emergence of platform parties is a surprising development that defies the predictions of many analysts and commentators who thought the postmodern condition would lead to the ultimate death of the political party. Emerging formations stand to demonstrate that digital media do not result in the end of political hierarchies – inasmuch as the internet didn't bring the end of oligopolies, but is recasting in new guises all forms of organisation, including the political party. The party form is alive and well, and since the crisis of 2008 there has been an increasing demand for it among citizens who feel unheard and unrepresented.

The rise of new political parties reflects a new cleavage in society, stemming from technological and economic factors: a fracture between political and/or economic insiders and what I call *connected outsiders.*

This term refers to people who, though having levels of education and internet access above the average of the general population, often face serious economic hurdles, precarious working conditions, spells of unemployment, low wages and more generally a sense of alienation from the political system and its forms. Digital parties have championed a series of emerging wedge issues that are of interest to this constituency. These range from digital rights such as those championed by Pirate Parties, including privacy, freedom of communication and government transparency, to demands for new forms of political participation beyond the limits of representative democracy, which is perceived to be unresponsive and distant from the needs of ordinary citizens, and, finally and crucially, new mechanisms of welfare protection and economic regulation to weather the changing economic environment and the growing insecurity of the digital era.

To understand the specificity of the digital party, I have compared and contrasted it with the previous two party types in recent history: the mass party of the industrial era and the television party – or professional-electoral party – of the post-industrial era. We have seen that the digital party conjoins characteristics of both party types. On the one hand, it comes close to the mass party in its ambition of reconstructing a culture of mass political participation, by adapting it to the individualised experience of the digital society. On the other hand, it is reminiscent of the television party's anti-bureaucratic urge in its being media-focused and having a lean organisation and personalised leadership.

The similarity between the organisational logic of the digital party and the platform logic of digital oligopolies such as Facebook, Amazon and Google was then discussed. First, digital parties are data driven: they take the form of software operating on the back of an ever-expanding database and ever-more complex algorithms. Second, they adopt a free membership model, in which registration is delinked from financial contribution in a way that comes close to the sign-up process of social media. Third, they have, similarly to Silicon Valley firms, a limited central staff, which forces them to rely on the free labour provided by their members/users to communicate and interact with the electorate.

What is key politically in this context is the adoption of the platform as an organisational mechanism that allegedly allows the expression of the authentic will of the people. This goes hand in hand with a focus on process over content, best manifested in the changing meaning of the word *platform*, from the set of goals and policies included in a party's programme, to the set of procedures and mechanisms used to select political priorities and policy ideas. However, platforms are not neutral, and they imply new hierarchies and power relations. In fact, platformisation often appears as a sort of decoy used by party leaders to concoct the impression of a non-existing or weak and purely facilitatory leadership.

Participationist ideology provides an ethical and ideological justification for this turn towards the platform logic. Participationism is seen in the inordinate emphasis placed on the process of participation, which evolves from being merely a contribution of members to a collective task, to becoming the key attribute for the morally just politics these parties intend to pursue. This 'cult of participation', and the connected distrust towards representation, is accompanied by the adoption of the imaginary of the movement, and the aim of creating 'open spaces' for civic activation. Following the typical populist rhetoric of the people versus the elite, it is assumed that everybody can potentially intervene and that the direction of the movement is not carved in stone, but the performative product of the people's will at any point in time, without any firm ideological grid or unmovable political orientation restricting the field of possibilities.

Having fleshed out the technical and ideological orientation of the digital party, we have then explored the *pars destruens* of such organisational rearrangement, namely the demolition of the old party structure. The digital platform is the ram used to smash the gates of the traditional party bureaucracy, because of the way in which it seen as providing a substitute for the hierarchy of cadres and branches, taking on its work of registration of rank-and-file opinion and coordination of collective action. The rise of the digital party takes aim at all the manifestations of the party bureaucracy, that 'intermediate element' perceived as the redoubt of oligarchy, as famously denounced by Robert Michels in his theory of the party, distorting the free participation of members and the pursuit of an authentic democratic process.[288]

The major victim of this wrecking of party structures is the party cadre, the figure that played a fundamental role as intermediary between leadership and membership, as well as the complex system of party committees and local subcommittees which made traditional parties resemble governments in waiting, or a state within the state. The same destiny befalls the class of political professionals, freelance political consultants, spin doctors and pollsters that saw their influence grow in the epoch of the television party under high neoliberalism. But perhaps, most importantly, the wrecking ball of the digital party takes aim at the local party structures that still survive from the industrial era, especially for parties on the left: the panoply of local sections, branches, cells and sister organisations.

This enmity towards party bureaucracy does not merely proceed from the fact that it is perceived as being too costly financially, but also from the persuasion that it constitutes an unnecessary bottleneck between the party's periphery and its centre; it is a political architecture which is viewed as out of sync with present conditions of extreme temporal and spatial dispersion, and too often becomes monopolised by fanatic devotees who are not representative of the true will of the party base.

Upon the debris of old party structures, platform parties erect their own structures or, better, their own 'software' and 'process', one which is not translated into the hardware of buildings and offices, but rather informs the software of online decision-making platforms. Reviewing the participatory systems used by the Pirate Parties, the Five Star Movement and Podemos, we have come to appreciate the diversity that exists across different decision-making technologies and how different democratic visions and mechanisms are inscribed in software code. Furthermore, we have come to familiarise ourselves with the multiplicity of functions these different systems are aimed at fulfilling: from facilitating deliberative processes of open-ended discussions and supporting crowdsourced legislation, to conducting online primaries and elections of internal party officers, to finally voting on a number of referenda on strategic issues.

In their complex, these different functions are presented as a systemic way to allow the party to be directed by its members, approximating as much as possible to the ideal of direct democracy. However, as we saw in the ensuing chapter, looking at the management of the process and at its actual results, this edifying narrative does not correspond to reality. In fact, the more deliberative and open-ended mechanisms, in which members have a qualitative say on issues and actively participate in policy development have had far less importance than more top-down balloting mechanisms, such as elections and referenda. The most prominent form of consultation conducted within these movements has been what may be described as the 'dilemma referendum': Yes/No votes on highly divisive and symbolic issues, such as the expulsion of party representatives, the formation of alliances and coalition governments, or the recall of political leaders.

What is more concerning is the fact that almost invariably these consultations have resulted in highly expected results, with overwhelming majorities favouring the line proposed by the leadership. These findings stand to indicate that rather than the participatory and deliberative democracy that is promised on paper, digital parties correspond far more to the beleaguered model of 'plebiscitarian democracy', in which a demagogic leader periodically verifies his mandate by calling a referendum.

Such a plebiscitarian nature of digital democracy within emerging political parties can be better understood by looking at the changing nature of leadership and membership, discussed in the final two chapters. We have argued that the digital party is marked by an organisational polarisation that strengthens the party's centre and periphery at the expense of the intermediate bureaucratic element. Thereby, a charismatic hyperleader becomes allied with a digitally activated yet mostly reactive superbase, leading to a situation in which centralised and personalised leadership at the top exists in a state of tension with mass participation at the bottom.

The prominence of the hyperleader in the digital party is perhaps one of the most unexpected and counter-intuitive trends of these formations, given the way their adoption of a participationist ideology sometimes borders on proclaims of horizontality and leaderlessness. Yet, it is sufficient to look with unprejudiced eyes at the leadership role played in these movements by figures such as Falkvinge in the Pirate Party, Grillo and Di Maio in the Five Star Movement and Iglesias in Podemos, to appreciate that these are not merely spokespeople, facilitators or guarantors of grassroots democracy, and similar avatars of weak leadership. These figures more closely match the model of charismatic leadership, which constitutes an important role as a source of collective identity, and campaigning pivot. They can be seen as acting as anchoring points keeping together a dispersed and mercurial network whose presence makes up for the instability and hazy character of these movements' identity and policy objectives.

Discussing the party's superbase, we have come to see from close up the contradictory results of this organisational rearrangement on political participation. It is fair to say that these political parties have some reasons to claim that they have indeed expanded participation, starting from the vast base of registered members they have accumulated. This growth in party membership, resulting from the lifting of traditional barriers between the 'selectorate' and the electorate, constitutes a clear inversion from the falling membership trends experienced by most traditional political parties. Regarding instead the question of the 'deepening' of participation, which these parties have also promised to deliver, the situation is more complex. There exists a strong difference in the intensity of participation among registered members.

The openness of participation ushered in by participationism does not translate into more equality of participation, but in a steep distribution curve measuring the intensity of participation. In this context, the model of 'distributed organising' has allowed some supporters to become supervolunteers and make a huge contribution to these political parties in ways that are perhaps unprecedented. However, far more numerous are the 'lurking supporters', apathetic sympathisers who basically feature as party members only because of the ease of registration and who intervene only occasionally in internal decision-making. Although digital parties seem to deliver on the quantitative promise of affording more participation in internal party life, they only partly deliver on the promise of a deeper participation by party members.

These findings raise a number of important questions for activists on the Left, which has mostly reacted with suspicion to the rise of the digital party. Some claim that the abandonment of representative democracy in favour of more direct forms of democracy is in and of itself a democratic loss, one which can even pave the road towards authoritarianism. Furthermore, many have denounced that digital democracy has turned into a pure spectacle, with online ballots returning widely expected results, thus turning consultations into little more than grassroots acclamation for the leaders' decisions. A further controversy regards the risk inherent in the virtualisation and individualisation of participation produced by digital democracy. Some argue that platform parties do not propose a real solution to political disaffection because they are ultimately reproducing and exacerbating the individualising tendencies of contemporary society, in which people are connected at the same time as they are isolated from one another. This problem raises the question of 'social integration', a task which, as argued by Sigmund Neumann,[289] constituted one of the main strengths of mass parties, concerned as they were with the construction of community as much as with its mobilisation for electoral purposes. This question also carries implications for organisational sustainability, given that many critics argue that the virtualisation of participation means that these parties lack a strong organisational structure capable of weathering moments of crisis or low mobilisation. A final question proceeds from the process-oriented character of the platformisation of digital parties and the risk that it may lead to opportunism, or at least excessive eclecticism.

Disintermediation and distributed centralisation

The most fundamental problem of the digital party lies in the contradiction between the participationist narrative of radical disintermediation, sometimes bordering on proclamations of leaderlessness, and a reality in which leadership and hierarchy are very far from being dissolved into the ether or the cloud. In contesting representative democracy, digital parties raise questions not just about its legitimacy, but also of leadership and organisation, and promise a more direct, that is less mediated, kind of politics, where 'one is worth one', to refer to the Five Stars' famous slogan, striving for a collapse of all party hierarchies.

That the digital party is an agent of disintermediation is not altogether false. Similarly, to what happens with the digital economy and the way in which it claims to offer a 'leaner' and more customised service, doing away with pre-existing middlemen, the platformisation of the party does away with various 'political middlemen' and intermediate structures: the party bureaucracy, the party cadres and the local structure of organisation composed of cells, sections and other similar units. These structures of mediation are removed because of their prior role as 'gatekeepers' for access to party politics, seen as going against the imperatives of immediacy and directness of digital culture, that have been celebrated by Mark Zuckerberg's in his manifesto 'Building a Global Community'. The erection of the platform as the central organisational structure is presented instead as a neutral mechanism, a political 'operative system' allowing for the process of discussion and decision-making to proceed without restriction. Yet, there is much that remains concealed behind this edifying narrative.

The doing away with lower-level middlemen, that is party cadres, is accompanied by a centralisation of intermediation, or what I have termed a 'distributed centralisation' where supervisory power falls squarely in the hands of the party leadership and his or her personal staff. Mediation, far from disappearing, simply becomes more concealed, hidden as it is in the software of the platform or the process of management that takes place in its back end, managed by party staffers. This invisibility and impersonality of mediation make this process problematic, as unscrutinised power is notoriously even more pernicious and opaque than the power which everyone can see. Thus, much against the oft-heard claims about accountability and transparency the platformisation of the party can lead to the very opposite condition of opaqueness and irresponsibility.

Ultimately, this problem reflects more generally a conundrum of direct democracy which can never really be completely direct, as it depends on a set of rules, for instance to call a referendum or a popular initiative, and in the case of digital direct democracy, on the algorithms of participatory platforms. If Immanuel Kant famously rebuked Jean-Jacques Rousseau because the former thought the direct democracy of the latter did not have form, the criticism should be perhaps in the reverse.[290] Direct democracy may proclaim to be formless, but it always has a form, and this form carries questions of power; it always implies forms of mediation and hierarchy that continue to resurface in spite of digital parties' claims to the contrary.

Platforms allow members to participate directly in discussions and voting on policies, appointments and nominations. In this, digital parties seem to follow a tendency towards a more direct participation of their membership, and 'one man, one vote' procedures of internal democracy that have been introduced in many political parties in recent decades, as seen in the diffusion of primaries and the widening of the selectorate for leadership elections.[291] This constitutes arguably a positive innovation, especially when it is compared to the doings of more traditional parties, where, except for infrequent elections of delegates and poorly attended discussions at the branch level, members end up having little influence on the party centre. Furthermore, it also needs to be recognised that besides digital ballots, such as online primaries and online referenda, digital parties also usher in deliberative democratic processes that are altogether new – for example those connected with processes of 'open legislation', allowing theoretically any member to propose a law or comment on an existing proposal. These mechanisms harbour great potential to make politics more attuned with contemporary social experience, bringing crowdsourcing and its mass listening capabilities to the political arena. Especially, if they follow the more realistic model of a 'participatory representation', in which ideas proposed by the base are progressively refined and voted by members, to ensure a good balance of bottom-up input and collective representativeness.

However, the positives of digital parties stop here. First, the online democracy pursued on participatory platforms is far less participatory than the name would suggest. Although the official discourse of online democracy embraces deliberative democracy, its implementation comes closer to the model of plebiscitary democracy. Consultations often resemble electronic plebiscitarianism centering around referendums where members are asked to select a Yes/No binary *choice* and too often seems to a mere ratification of the will of the party leadership. Bottom-up initiatives, in which ordinary members have a qualitative say on policies and initiatives, have been either marginalised or altogether made impossible. Sometimes it feels as if these deliberative moments are merely cosmetic, scarcely hiding the overall plebiscitarian and top-down process of agenda setting and decision-making. Thus, though it may well be true that the digital party is the sworn enemy of party oligarchy, this comes at the cost of strengthening personalised leadership, the charismatic hyperleader and his immediate circle of the faithful. We seem to leave the iron law of oligarchy only to crash against the 'silicon law' of 'benevolent dictatorship'.

Hyperleadership and reactive democracy

Assessing digital parties thus require rethinking the role of leadership and hierarchy in a digital era. To do this it is necessary to clarify that demagogic leadership embodied in a charismatic leader is not necessarily anti-democratic. Demagoguery certainly has a very bad press, but as argued by Max Weber, it has been one of the most important democratic forms since the times of Alcibiades and Pericles;[292] because in order to be mobilised, people need to identify themselves collectively, and they often do so by identifying with a leading individual. This is seen in the function played by hyperleaders as social media storytellers constantly engaging and galvanising their base of support. At a time marked by profound suspicion towards collective organisations, the persona of the hyperleader provides at least with a temporary solution to the failure of collective identification. Furthermore, the importance of the hyperleader reflects the fact that the assertions of theorists of elites about the passivity of the mass continue to be relevant also in the digital age. The question is how the authoritarian risk involved in the nature of hyperleader as a 'benevolent dictator' can be restrained; and whether eventually the hyperleader will manage to find the new party and routinise his or her charisma, as Machiavelli's *condottiere* did by establishing a new state.[293]

The persistence of leadership and invisible mediations behind the façade of disintermediation leads to forms of bias or outright manipulation that raise serious questions about the democratic quality of consultations. This also stems from the fact that the platform is not a completely automated system. It is managed by a political staff, which reports to the party leadership, and retains different channels of influence in such apparently trivial operations as the calling and timing of consultations. The formulation of referendum's questions can have a strong manipulative effect on the electorate, given that it delimits the field of possibility and provides suggestions on preferred options. Coupled with the agenda-setting powers in the hands of the leadership, this power can have a strong influence on the outcome of digital ballots which, as seen in the case of online referendums, have almost invariably returned the desired answer sought by the leadership.

This does not mean, however, that the membership is completely powerless. The very fact that the leadership feels compelled to periodically seek the approval of the base demonstrates that some form of social contract exists between the hyperleader and the superbase, and in some circumstances the low support for proposals, or low levels of participation of the membership, with attendance figures being as important as the ultimate results, can act as rings of alarm for those at the top, forcing them to reconsider their position. However, within the digital party the initiative firmly rests in the hands of the leadership. We may thus picture participatory platforms as the site of a tug of war, or an uneven feedback circle, between membership and leadership, but one in which the latter almost invariably prevails over the former. Rather than a participatory democracy, the reality of platform parties is more of a 'reactive democracy', in which the power of the membership mainly consists of a veto power which is used very infrequently – the power to like or not to like.

It may thus be said that digital parties betray to a large extent their promise of radical democratisation. Their discourse of radical transformation of the way in which people take part in politics is seriously contradicted in practice. Where the discourse of online democracy proposes a vision in which digital technology is going to remediate the gaping hole between citizens and institutions, and allow the former a more direct participation in the latter, the reality points to a rather different situation. Top-down leadership continues to retain a primacy over the initiative of the base, whose *élan vital* is more of a fuel to sustain the goals of the organisation, rather than a steer. But here the problem lies as much with practical errors having to do with faulty implementation as it does with the unrealistic assumptions of the original conception. It would be wiser to take a more limited view of what can be achieved by digital democracy, and a more realistic acceptance of the persistence of leadership. By adopting the participationist utopia of leaderlessness and horizontalism, platform parties run the risk of following an all too well-known course from idealism to cynicism. What is required is thus more transparency about the power retained by the leadership, while clarifying the degree to which the membership can actually have a say.

The need for integration

The platformisation of the party means that decisions are taken collectively, but from the standpoint of physically isolated individuals, and this focus on online interactions runs the risks of exacerbating all those idiosyncrasies and psychopathologies that characterise online interactions, including trolling, flames and loneliness. This situation calls for a serious reflection about the sustainability of the organisational format at both the collective and individual levels.

It is evident that the digital form of participation that is favoured by the digital party combines great agility with great fragility. It may be, and it has demonstrated to be, highly effective for the purposes of short-term electoral struggle; the spectacular results registered by the movements discussed in this book are evident testament to this effectiveness. However, there is the risk that in the long term the lean organisational format used by the digital party may prove ineffective, as periods of latency follow in the trail of waves of enthusiasm. This is the risk that has been evidenced by Zeynep Tufekci when discussing the structural weakness of the internet-fuelled social movements of 2011, where their reliance on light and flexible organisational structures has ultimately made them vulnerable to state repression.[294] Faced with these hurdles, it is evident that digital parties also need to establish, alongside their digital platforms, new contexts of face-to-face discussion, physical environments and real-life events where members can rub shoulders, look one another in the eye and learn how to live together and feel integrated in a moral community whose purpose is not merely electoral performance, but the systemic transformation of society, within and without political institutions. The extreme degree of individualisation, social heterogeneity and sheer loneliness that we find in our societies call for a heavy investment in integrative processes, in moments of dialogue, in forms of popular education and in all sorts of activities allowing citizens to come together and form bonds of reciprocity and solidarity. However, attending to this task of social integration would require perforce significantly revising the organisational philosophy of these movements, and would entail access to economic resources which at the moment are well beyond their capacity.

The digital party may profit much from its being cloud-like, because this allows it to be capable of almost wondrous growth, similar to the fast expansion of successful start-up companies. However, by the same token it is also as inconsistent as the clouds. It can condense great popular anger and hope, and flash thunderbolts of rage, but just like a cloud it can also rapidly disperse into blue skies and thin air in response to the ever-changing winds of public opinion. Ultimately, unless the digital party manages to find a way to give solidity to its energy, by either routinising the charisma of the hyperleader or giving weight to its organisational structure, it risks experiencing the same mortality rate of start-ups or, worse, could end up becoming a party just like the others it so vehemently criticises.

Beyond the obsession with process

A final problem raised by the rise of digital parties concerns the relationship between political process and political content. In fact, as we have seen in the course of the book, the ideology of participation lays emphasis on the importance of a correct process. Participation is turned into a normative criteria because it is believed that unless a proper method of participation is established, politics will be biased and inauthentic. This is why the term *platform* comes to designate a process rather than a stable set of policies pursued by the party, as was its traditional meaning. This semantic shift summarises much of what is at stake in this organisational transformation.

The success of the digital party stems from the crisi of neoliberalism and the party form it fostered, the television party, which has alienated members and voters. Making once again the support and intervention of members a condition for the development of political strategy is therefore something that should be welcome by any true democrat. However, this obsession with process can easily turn into 'proceduralism', the excessive concern for process over content, which reflects the neoliberal enmity towards grand-narrative and systemic visions of the world, and a faith in the individual and his will as the ultimate normative criteria.[295] Furthermore, it belies a technocratic tendency to reduce politics to *techne*, thinking that as long as the mechanisms to make a decision are good, the decision will also be good, irrespective of their content.

Proceduralism leads these formations to problematic eclecticism, sometimes bordering on sheer opportunism. This has been most clearly seen in the context of the Five Star Movement and the way in which it has progressively transitioned from left-wing to right-wing policies, using the results of digital ballots to justify this change in political direction. This obsession with process, which is married with the suspicion of the very 'partisanship' of the party, can also be understood as premised on a moralistic illusion, which is also typical of neoliberalism, that politics can be changed through personal behaviour rather than through collective and systemic impact on the political system. Platform parties claim that they are going to solve the problem of democracy by changes to their own internal structure, much as the people who believe they are going to stop climate change by eating a more vegetarian diet. But this orientation comes worryingly close to a self-referential view of politics, in which it is overlooked that organisations are by their nature fraught with serious limits and that the real contribution of political parties to democracy is proposing alternative options to the electorate. This self-referentiality can also be seen as stemming from suspicion towards the party as representing a part of society and its implications for partisanship and conflict. The illusion which infects many activists is that digital parties can really represent anyone, irrespective of their class or political persuasion. But this persuasion in turn militates against the construction of a coherent strategy and a more stable and long-term project. Given their populist character, it is only natural that digital parties want to speak the people's voice. But as they grow and mature, they will need to guard themselves from following too closely the mutability of public opinion and of the political system: the *perpetuum mobile democraticum.*

A political to-do list

It may thus seem that the promise of digital parties of giving citizens a say in political affairs by overcoming the strictures and privileges of 'old politics' has turned sour. But the flaws and vulnerabilities of the digital party should not lead us to take an overly pessimistic view on its potential. The digital party has politicised and mobilised hundreds of thousands of people in ways that would have been unthinkable for outsider formations in previous eras. Coming from long years of apathy which had convinced many political scientists about the coming demise of the political party, one can only welcome this development and the way in which it has eventually attempted to address the failures of traditional organisational templates.

It is important to bear in mind that the root causes that led to the development of the digital party are all-too-real and that the proposed solutions have at the very least the merit of audacity, perhaps bordering on impudence, in trying to reinvent the political party. The digital party responds to a fundamental necessity: the need to radically update the organisational forms of politics and adapt them to the digital era. The question for progressives is how this historical necessity can be proficiently attended and how we can address the limits of the digital party and turn this party form into a means not just for digital democracy but for democracy broadly defined. This task is all the more urgent given that there are many signs that the digital party is far from being a flash in the pan, and this organisational blueprint will continue to spread in different political systems, also reshaping mainstream parties, which are likely to adopt some of its innovations in order not to slide into irrelevance.

This is seen in the initial experimentations with and overtures to electronic democracy made by social-democratic parties such as PSOE in Spain, SPD in Germany and Labour in the UK, as they try to integrate digital participation of members in their internal process. The emergence of the digital party reflects how more traditional and mainstream forces are also aware that traditional mechanisms of representation and organisation are failing. And it urges us to grapple with the serious difficulties that digital parties have encountered. There are four issues that constitute the most urgent for reflection and action in the coming years.

First, more weight needs to be given to bottom-up members' initiatives, with the possibility for more structured deliberative processes, with a binding mandate for proposals earning sufficient support. This would allow for a more active and meaningful participation of members in party life. Second, the management of decision-making platforms and processes should be assigned to a procedures or guarantee committee independent from the leadership. This would guard against the risk of the leadership manipulation of consultations and restore credibility in online decision-making. Third, it is necessary to establish new forms of social integration, to make the party evolve from being an electoral machine to a purveyor of political community and social solidarity. This process is decisive to give these parties more rootedness and turning some of their lurking supporters into active participants. But it would require a quite significant expenditure. Fourth, it is high time to shed the excessive prejudice against bureaucracy, as well as the obsession with participationism. We have to concede that if the digital party is to operate in an efficient and sustainable manner, it needs to create an apparatus, capable of analysing data and elaborating policies, managing members, and give itself a more solid and diffuse local structure, also to avoid relying too much on exploiting the free labour of party members.

Addressing these issues means going back to the promise of extended participation which platform parties put to the fore, while bearing in mind that participation happens in a mesh of power relations. These power relations may well be rearranged, but they can never be completely eliminated, regardless of the perfection and supposed neutrality of the tools that are utilised. Furthermore, personal leadership continues to be a central necessity of organisations, especially in present times of distrust towards collective organisations. The democrats and progressives who want to give a new lease of life to the party form, so that it can contribute to the urgent task of reorganising our society and a politics for the welfare of the greatest number, need to operate with this awareness in mind. They need to be conscious of the great potential that is inherent in the organisational template of the digital party, but also cognisant of the significant limits which it has displayed, avoiding the 'misoneism' or 'suspicion of the new' that too often has marked debates on this issue on the Left, but also the naïve techno-utopianism displayed by those libertarian activists who think that interaction and participation are an end onto itself. We can predict that this process of organisational reinvention will continue for the next years to come; and we should hope that it eventually culminates in an organisational template that is both democratic and strategically effective.

Appendix

This book is the product of research conducted along multiple years in different countries that have been host to the rise of digital parties, with a strong focus on European countries and, in particular, Italy, Spain, France and the United Kingdom. I have relied on three main primary sources. Archival material on the practices of digital parties, from newspapers, to various official party documents and the code of their digital platforms; interviewees with key informants, politicians, activists and developers involved in or collaborating with these formations; and observation of these parties' public events and offices. The method and approach are similar to the grounded theory which I have adopted in my previous work, such as *Tweets and the Streets* and *The Mask and the Flag*: the hypothesis emerged organically from the research rather than being a pre-constituted idea, as it happens with more rationalist and experimental social science research. In the next pages, the reader will find the list of key informants which were selected in order to cover the main case studies in the analysis, with particular reference to Five Star and Podemos, and with an eye at ensuring a good coverage of expertise and experience.

	Name	Responsibility	Organisation	Date of Interview
1	Julia Reda	Activist and MEP	Pirate Party	8 January 2018
2	Christian Engstrom	Activist and MEP	Pirate Party	3 June 2009
3	Birgitta Jónsdóttir	Activist and former MP	Pirate Party	13 May 2016
4	Davide Bono	Activist and local councillor	Five Star Movement	3 September 2018
5	Gioele Brandi	Social media manager	Five Star Movement	22 June 2017
6	Roberto Fico	Five Star Movement activist, current speaker of the Chamber of deputies	Activist, MP and president of the Italian Chamber of Deputies (since 24 March 2018)	22 June 2017
7	Roberta Lombardi	Activist and MP	Five Star Movement	22 June 2017
8	Marco Canestrari	Former employee	Casaleggio Associati	22 November 2017
9	David Davros Puente	Former employee	Casaleggio Associati	27 November 2017
10	Eric Labuske	Informatics coordinator	Podemos	26 June 2015
11	German Cano	Academic and activist	Podemos	23 June 2015
12	Sarah Bienzobas	Activist	Podemos	22 February 2016
13	Alejandro Cerezo	Activist and graphic designer	Podemos	20 February 2016
14	Jorge Moruno	Sociologist and activist	Podemos	21 February 2016
15	Segundo Gonzalez	Activist and MP	Podemos	18 February 2015

16	Miguel Ardanuy	Participation coordinator and Comunidad de Madrid councillor	Podemos	7 November 2017
17	Winnie Wong	Activist and communication strategist	People for Bernie Sanders	16 June 2017
18	Claire Sandberg	Digital organising director	Bernie Sanders presidential campaign	10 December 2017
19	Emma Rees	National organiser	Momentum	6 October 2017
20	Adam Klug	National organiser	Momentum	9 October 2017
21	Aaron Bastani	Media activist	Novara Media	6 March 2018
22	James Moulding	Activist	Digital Democracy – Labour	4 October 2017
23	Antoine Léaument	Social media coordinator	France Insoumise	15 January 2018
24	Guillaume Royer	Platform coordinator	France Insoumise	15 November 2017
25	Adria Rodriguez	Activist	Barcelona en Comú	22 February 2016
26	Alejandra Calvo Martínez	Activist	Ahora Madrid	20 March 2015
27	Eugenia Quilodran-Briones	Activist	Rede Sustenabilidade Brazil	21 October 2014
28	Richard Bartlett	Founder and developer	Loomio	25 October 2017
29	Andreas Nitsche	Developer and director	Association for interactive democracy	6 October 2017
30	Yago Bermejo Abati	Developer and activist	Medialab Prado	12 July 2017

Notes

1. 'M5S – Beppe Grillo incorona Luigi Di Maio, nuovo capo del Movimento 5 Stelle', YouTube, retrieved from https://www.youtube.com/watch?v=GUGtRjZ8750.
2. Beppe Grillo often described Five Star activists as *magnifici ragazzi* (wonderful boys), to emphasise both the youth and daring spirit of party activists.
3. 'M5S – Beppe Grillo incorona Luigi Di Maio'.
4. The *V for Vendetta* movie has famously become a symbol for protest movements and anti-establishment political groups in the aftermath of the 2008 financial crisis. This is discussed in my previous book on protest movements, *The mask and the flag: populism, citizenism, and global protest* (Oxford: Oxford University Press, 2017).
5. Jessica Aldred et al., 'The world's 50 most powerful blogs', *Observer*, 9 March 2008, retrieved from www.theguardian.com/technology/2008/mar/09/blogs.
6. Podemos was launched publicly on 16 January 2015. Its legal registration was on 11 March 2014 after collecting the necessary signatures for the official foundation as a political party.
7. 'Welcome to Momentum!', Momentum, retrieved 27 October 2016 from http://www.peoplesmomentum.com/.
8. David Karpf, *The MoveOn effect: the unexpected transformation of American political advocacy* (Oxford: Oxford University Press, 2012), pp. 6–9.
9. Mario Diani, 'Social movement networks virtual and real', *Information, Communication & Society* 3, no. 3 (2000): 386–401.
10. Becky Bond and Zack Exley, *Rules for revolutionaries: how big organizing can change everything* (Hartford, VT: Chelsea Green Publishing, 2016).
11. Jean-Jacques Rousseau, *Rousseau: 'the social contract' and other later political writings* (Cambridge: Cambridge University Press, 1997).
12. 'The Five Star Movement: an Italian Revolution – Davide Casaleggio presents the Rousseau application', YouTube, retrieved 5 May 2018 from https://www.youtube.com/watch?v=ZQe5j47GIsk.
13. David Karpf uses the term *passive democratic engagement* to indicate the type of participation seen in petition websites such as MoveOn, where user intervention is restricted to such limited acts as signing a petition or sharing a content. Karpf, *The MoveOn effect*, p. 50.
14. Russell J. Dalton and Martin P. Wattenberg, eds, *Parties without partisans: political change in advanced industrial democracies* (Oxford: Oxford University Press, 2002), p. 3.
15. Colin Crouch, *Post-democracy* (Cambridge, UK: Polity, 2004).
16. Peter Mair, *Ruling the void: the hollowing of Western democracy* (London: Verso books, 2013), p. 2.

17. Mair, *Ruling the void*, pp. 3–8.
18. Manuel Castells, *The rise of the network society*, Vol. 12 (New York: John Wiley & Sons, 2011).
19. Richard S. Katz and Peter Mair, 'Changing models of party organization and party democracy: the emergence of the cartel party', *Party Politics* 1, no. 1 (1995): 5–28, p. 23.
20. Michael Hardt and Antonio Negri, *Empire* (Cambridge, MA: Harvard University Press, 2001).
21. Thomas L. Friedman, *The world is flat: a brief history of the twenty-first century* (New York: Macmillan, 2005).
22. Richard S. Katz and Peter Mair, eds, *How parties organize: change and adaptation in party organizations in Western democracies* (London; Thousand Oaks, CA: Sage, 1994), p. 3.
23. P. C. Schmitter, 'Intermediaries in the consolidation of neo-democracies: the role of parties, associations and movements.' Working Paper No. 30. Barcelona: Institut de Ciencies Politiques i Socials, 1997.
24. Many of these critical interventions on the political party can be found in the collection *Perspectives on political parties: classic readings*, edited by S. Scarrow (New York: Springer, 2002). Also see Simone Weil, *On the abolition of all political parties* (New York: New York Review of Books, 2014).
25. Ralph Waldo Emerson, *Emerson in his journals* (Cambridge, MA: Harvard University Press, 1982), p. 78.
26. Simone Weil, *On the abolition of all political parties* (New York: New York Review of Books, 2014), p. 49.
27. A great deal has been written about totalitarian parties, a topic that is important for its general implications on the theory of the political party. Particularly important are the work of Hannah Arendt, Nicos Poulantzas, and Franz Neumann, *The origins of totalitarianism*, Vol. 244 (New York: Houghton Mifflin Harcourt, 1973); Franz Neumann, *Behemoth: the structure and practice of national socialism* (New York: Harper & Row, 1944) and Nicos Poulantzas, *The crisis of the dictatorships: Portugal, Greece, Spain* (London: NLB, 1976).
28. For the origins of this anti-bureaucratic and anti-authoritarian sentiment in the New Left, please see Wini Breines, *Community and organization in the New Left, 1962–1968: the great refusal* (Rutgers, NJ: Rutgers University Press, 1989).
29. Donatella Della Porta, Joseba Fernandez, Hara Kouki and Lorenzo Mosca, *Movement parties against austerity* (New York: John Wiley & Sons, 2017).
30. Friedrich August Hayek, *The constitution of liberty: the definitive edition*, Vol. 17 (Abingdon, UK: Routledge, 2013).
31. Clay Shirkey, *Here comes everybody: the power of organising without organisations* (London: Allen Lane, 2008).
32. W. Lance Bennett and Alexandra Segerberg, 'The logic of connective action: digital media and the personalization of contentious politics', *Information, communication & society* 15, no. 5 (2012): 739–768.

33. Jodi Dean, *Crowds and party* (London: Verso Books, 2016).

34. Seymour Martin Lipset and Stein Rokkan, eds, *Party systems and voter alignments: cross-national perspectives*, Vol. 7 (New York: Free Press, 1967).

35. On left-libertarian parties, see the most influential account by Herbert P. Kitschelt, 'Left-libertarian parties: explaining innovation in competitive party systems', *World Politics* 40, no. 2 (1988): 194–234.

36. Here I refer to the famous argument by Ronald Inglehart about the rise of post-materialist values paralleling the transformation from industrial to post-industrial society. See, in particular, Ronald Inglehart, *Culture shift in advanced industrial society* (Princeton, NJ: Princeton University Press, 1990).

37. Alexis De Tocqueville, *Democracy in America and two essays on America* (London: Penguin books, 2003); Moisei Ostrogorski, *Democracy and the organization of political parties*, Vol. 2 (New York: Macmillan, 1902); Maurice Duverger, *Political parties: their organization and activity in the modern state* (London: Methuen, 1959); Max Weber, *Economy and society: an outline of interpretive sociology* (Berkeley, CA: University of California Press, 1978); Sigmund Neumann and Frederick C. Barghoorn, *Modern political parties: approaches to comparative politics* (Chicago, IL: University of Chicago Press, 1956) and Vladimir Il'ich Lenin, *What is to be done? Burning questions of our movement* (Matawan, NJ: Panther Press, 1970).

38. This shift of focus in political science from the study of parties as organisations towards the study of party systems is seen most clearly in the work of Giovanni Sartori. See, for example, Giovanni Sartori, *Parties and party systems: a framework for analysis* (Colchester, UK: European Consortium for Political Research [ECPR], 2005).

39. Angelo Panebianco, *Political parties: organization and power* (Cambridge, UK: Cambridge University Press, 1988).

40. This argument about the trans-historical character of the party is particularly indebted to Max Weber's discussion of this issue in *Economy and society: an outline of interpretive sociology*. See, in particular, pp. 984–987 and 1343–1354.

41. Max Weber, 'The profession and vocation of politics', in *Weber: political writings* (Cambridge, UK: Cambridge University Press, 1994), pp. 309–369.

42. Elmer Eric Schattschneider, *Party government* (Piscataway, NJ: Transaction Publishers, 1942).

43. Susan E. Scarrow, 'The nineteenth-century origins of modern political parties: the unwanted emergence of party-based politics', in Richard S. Katz and William J. Crotty (eds), *Handbook of party politics* (Thousand Oaks, CA: Sage, 2006), pp. 16–24.

44. Edmund Burke, *Thoughts on the present discontents: the two speeches on America* (Oxford: Clarendon, 1878), p. 317.

45. Max Weber, *Economy and society: an outline of interpretive sociology*, Vol. 1 (Berkeley, CA: University of California Press, 1978), p. 284. 'The term "party" will be employed to designate associations, membership which

rests on formally free recruitment. The end to which its activity is devoted is to secure power within an organization for its leaders in order to attain ideal or material advantages for its active members. These advantages may consist in the realization of certain objective policies or the attainment of personal advantages or both.'

46. Joseph A. Schumpeter, *Capitalism, socialism and democracy* (Routledge, 2010), p. 283.

47. Giovanni Sartori, *Parties and party systems: a framework for analysis* (Colchester, UK: ECPR Press, 2005).

48. Robert Michels, *Political parties: a sociological study of the oligarchical tendencies of modern democracy* (New York: Hearst's International Library Company, 1915).

49. Richard S. Katz and Peter Mair, 'The evolution of party organizations in Europe: the three faces of party organization', *American Review of Politics* 14 (1994): 593–617.

50. For a summary of these functions, see Peter Mair, 'Party organizations: from civil society to the state'; and Katz and Mair, eds, *How parties organize*, pp. 1–22.

51. Russell J. Dalton and Martin P. Wattenberg, 'Unthinkable democracy' in R. J. Dalton and M. P. Wattenberg (eds), *Parties without partisans: political change in advanced industrial democracies* (Oxford: Oxford University Press, 2002), p. 6.

52. James Bryce, *Modern Democracies*, Vol. 1 (New York: Macmillan, 1921), p. 119.

53. This list of attributes is based on findings of the scholarship on the mass parties and in particular Duverger, *Political parties*; and Michels, *Political parties*.

54. Ostrogorski, *Democracy and the organization of political parties*; and Neumann and Barghoorn, *Modern political parties*.

55. Marco Revelli, *Finale di partito* (Turin, Italy: Giulio Einaudi Editore, 2013).

56. Otto Kirchheimer, 'The catch-all party', in Peter Mair (ed), *The West European party system* (Oxford: Oxford University Press, 1990), pp. 50–60.

57. Panebianco. *Political parties*.

58. Katz and Mair, 'Changing models of party organization', pp. 5–28.

59. Kirchheimer, 'The transformation of the Western European party systems'.

60. Panebianco, *Political parties*, p. 264.

61. Katz and Mair, 'Changing models of party organization'.

62. Katz and Mair, pp. 18–19.

63. The argument largely follows the analysis of Italian political scientist Marco Revelli in *Finale di Partito*.

64. Panebianco, *Political Parties*, p. 266.

65. Panebianco, *Political Parties*, p. 264.

66. Panebianco, *Political Parties*, p. 266.

67. Russell J. Dalton and Martin P. Wattenberg, eds, *Parties without partisans: political change in advanced industrial democracies* (Oxford: Oxford University Press, 2002).

68. Michels, *Political parties*, p. 342.
69. Michels, *Political parties*.
70. Michels, *Political parties*, p. 365.
71. Gaetano Mosca and Vilfredo Pareto were two social science academics, both active in Turin at the beginning of the 20th century, who emphasised the tendency of societies to be dominated by elite groups: Gaetano Mosca, *The ruling class (Elementi di scienza politica)* (New York; London: McGraw-Hill, 1939); and Vilfredo Pareto, *Manual of political economy* (Oxford: Oxford University Press, 2014).
72. Weber, *Economy and society*.
73. Michels, *Political parties*, p. 364.
74. Antonio Gramsci, *Selections from the prison notebooks*, Vol. 294, ed. and transl. by Quintin Hoare and Geoffrey Nowell Smith (London: Lawrence and Wishart, 1971).
75. Gramsci, *Selections from the prison notebooks*.
76. Max Weber, *Weber: political writings* (Cambridge, UK: Cambridge University Press, 1994), p. 164.
77. Joseph A. Schumpeter, *Capitalism, socialism and democracy* (London; New York: Routledge, 2010).
78. This point is well made by Panebianco, who suggested that we need to move from the view of the relationship between leader and led as one of domination, to a view of this relationship as based on a logic of 'unbalanced negotiation' between leadership and membership. Angelo Panebianco, *Political parties: organization and power* (Cambridge, UK: Cambridge University Press, 1988), pp. 21–24.
79. Michels, *Political parties*, pp. 87–88.
80. Maurice Duverger, *Political parties: their organization and activity in the modern state* (London: Methuen, 1959), pp. 134–135.
81. Duverger, *Political parties*, p. 136.
82. Weber, *Economy and society*, p. 1402.
83. Weber, *Economy and society*, p. 1417.
84. Michels, *Political parties*, p. 72.
85. Gramsci, *Selection from the prison notebooks*, p. 155.
86. Panebianco, *Political parties*, pp. 24–27.
87. Duverger, *Political parties*, p. 6.
88. Duverger, *Political parties*, p. 16.
89. Duverger, *Political parties*, p. 48.
90. Theda Skocpol, *Diminished democracy: from membership to management in American civic life*, Vol. 8 (Norman, OK: University of Oklahoma Press, 2013).
91. Gramsci, *Selections from the prison notebooks*, p. 151.
92. Guobin Yang. *The power of the internet in China: citizen activism online* (New York: Columbia University Press, 2009).
93. Stein Rokkan, *State formation, nation-building, and mass politics in Europe: the theory of Stein Rokkan: based on his collected works* (Gloucestershire, UK: Clarendon Press, 1999).

94. Talcott Parsons, *The social system* (Psychology Press, 1991).
95. W. Busch and J. P. Moreno, 'Banks' new competitors: Starbucks, Google, and Alibaba', *Harvard Business Review* 2 (2014): 1–3.
96. Swedish Pirate Party Declaration of Principles, 4.0 version, May 2012, retrieved from https://en.wikisource.org/wiki/Pirate_Party_Declaration_of_Principles/4.0.
97. Evgeny Morozov, *To save everything, click here: the folly of technological solutionism* (New York: PublicAffairs, 2013).
98. Richard Florida, *The great reset: how new ways of living and working drive post-crash prosperity* (Toronto: Random House Canada, 2010).
99. Schumpeter, *Capitalism, socialism and democracy*, pp. 81–83.
100. Clayton M. Christensen, 'The ongoing process of building a theory of disruption', *Journal of Product Innovation Management* 23, no. 1 (2006): 39–55.
101. The best starting point on the capitalist transformation of the internet is Robert W. McChesney, *Digital disconnect: how capitalism is turning the Internet against democracy* (New York: New Press, 2013).
102. James Titcombe, 'Apple's cash reserves swell to $250bn', *The Telegraph*, 1 May 2018, retrieved from www.telegraph.co.uk/technology/2017/05/01/apples-cash-reserves-swell-250bn/.
103. Nick Dyer-Witheford, *Cyber-proletariat: global labour in the digital vortex* (Toronto: Between the Lines, 2015).
104. A good account of this development is provided in Trebor Scholz, *Uberworked and underpaid: how workers are disrupting the digital economy* (New York: John Wiley & Sons, 2017).
105. Valerio De Stefano, 'The rise of the just-in-time workforce: on-demand work, crowdwork, and labor protection in the gig-economy', *Comparative Labor Law and Policy Journal* 37 (2015): 471.
106. Alex Foti, *General theory of the precariat: great recession, revolution, reaction* (Amsterdam: Institute of Network Cultures, 2017).
107. Nicholas Kulish, 'Direct Democracy, 2.0', *New York Times Sunday Review*, 5 May 2012, retrieved from www.nytimes.com/2012/05/06/sunday-review/direct-democracy-2-0.html.
108. Alessandro Gilioli, 'Chi sono gli elettori del Movimento 5 Stelle e di Beppe Grillo', *L'Espresso*, 30 January 2014, retrieved from espresso.repubblica.it/palazzo/2014/01/30/news/chi-sono-gli-elettori-del-movimento-5-stelle-1.150530#gallery-slider=undefined.
109. M. A. Elezioni, 'Genere, età, professione: identikit dei nuovi elettori a Cinque stelle', *Il Sole 24 Ore*, 6 March 2018, retrieved from www.ilsole24ore.com/art/notizie/2018-03-06/genere-eta-professione-identikit-nuovi-elettori-cinque-stelle-190100.shtml.
110. 'Perfil del votante de Podemos', *El País*, 31 May 2014, retrieved from elpais.com/elpais/2014/05/31/media/1401571468_769193.html.
111. Marcos Pinheiro, 'Podemos se apoya en los jóvenes de cara al 26J', *Eldiario.es*, 24 June 2016, retrieved from www.eldiario.es/politica/mitad-votantes-Podemos-anos_0_524948518.html.

112. Carlos Sánchez, 'La bomba demográfica estalla por primera vez en unas elecciones generales', El Confidencial, 2 December 2016, retrieved from www.elconfidencial.com/economia/2015-12-02/la-bomba-demografica-estalla-por-primera-vez-en-unas-elecciones-generales_1111267/.

113. Chris Curtis, 'How Britain voted at the 2017 general election', YouGov, 13 June 2017, retrieved from yougov.co.uk/news/2017/06/13/how-britain-voted-2017-general-election/.

114. O. Kirchheimer, 'The transformation of the Western European party systems', in J. LaPalombra and M. Weiner (eds), Political parties and political development (Princeton, NJ: Princeton University Press, 1966), pp. 177–200.

115. Nicola Maggini, 'Osservatorio Politico – Autunno 2014. Il bacino elettorale del M5s: caratteristiche socio-politiche e atteggiamenti tra continuità e mutamento', Centrol Italiano Studi Elettorali (CISE), 12 December 2014, cise.luiss.it/cise/2014/12/12/il-bacino-elettorale-del-m5s-caratteristiche-socio-politiche-e-atteggiamenti-tra-continuita-e-mutamento/.

116. José A. Carpio, 'El votante de Podemos, según el CIS: escorado a la izquierda, interclasista, urbano y formado', RTVE, 4 February 2015, retrieved from www.rtve.es/noticias/20150204/votante-podemos-segun-cis-escorado-izquierda-interclasista-urbano-formado/1093281.shtml.

117. Claire Gaveau, 'Présidentielle 2017: ouvriers, chômeurs, jeunes ... Qui a voté quoi?', RTL, 27 April 2017, retrieved from www.rtl.fr/actu/politique/presidentielle-2017-ouvriers-jeunes-ruraux-qui-a-vote-quoi-7788279034.

118. di Redazione TPI, 'Il M5S è il partito con più laureati, sia tra i candidati sia tra gli elettori', TPI news, 14 March 2018, retrieved from www.tpi.it/2018/03/14/m5s-partito-piu-laureati-candidati-elettori/.

119. Antonio Gurrado, 'Il M5s è il partito più votato dai laureati. Sorpresi?', Il Foglio, 7 March 2018, retrieved from www.ilfoglio.it/bandiera-bianca/2018/03/07/news/il-m5s-e-il-partito-piu-votato-dai-laureati-sorpresi-182776/.

120. Andrea Maccagno, 'Il voto nei capoluoghi e il cleavage centro-periferia', YouTrend, 15 March 2018, retrieved from www.youtrend.it/2018/03/15/il-voto-nei-capoluoghi-e-il-cleavage-centro-periferia/.

121. Álvaro Justo, '¿Quién vota a Unidos Podemos?', Politizen, 21 June 2016, retrieved from politizen.info/quien-vota-a-unidos-podemos/.

122. Luca Pinto and Rinaldo Vignati, 'Il successo e i dilemmi del Movimento 5 Stelle', Il Mulino 61, no. 4 (2012): 731–738.

123. Paola Alagia, 'Movimento 5 stelle, l'identikit degli eletti', Lettera 43, 6 March 2013, retrieved from www.lettera43.it/it/articoli/politica/2013/03/06/movimento-5-stelle-lidentikit-degli-eletti/77263/.

124. Xavier Coller, 'El nuevo congreso', El Pais, 12 December 2015, retrieved from politica.elpais.com/politica/2015/12/26/actualidad/1451146607_312379.html.

125. Luis Cano, '¿Qué han estudiado los diputados y de qué trabajaban antes de entrar en política?', ABC, 25 April 2017, retrieved from www.abc.es/espana

/abci-estudiado-diputados-y-trabajaban-antes-entrar-politica-2016011515
12_noticia.html.

126. Timothy Jordan, *Information politics: liberation and exploitation in the digital society* (London: Pluto, 2015).

127. Pirate Party's Declaration of Principles, retrieved 6 March 2018 from https://en.wikisource.org/wiki/Pirate_Party_Declaration_of_Principles/3.1.

128. Pirate Party's Declaration of Principles.

129. Ken Newton and Pippa Norris, 'Confidence in public institutions', in Susan J. Pharr and Robert D. Putnam (eds), *Disaffected democracies. What's troubling the trilateral countries* (Princeton, NJ: Princeton University Press, 2000).

130. Robert D. Putnam, 'Bowling alone: America's declining social capital', in *Culture and politics* (New York: Palgrave Macmillan, 2000), pp. 223–234.

131. Katz and Mair, eds, *How parties organize*, p. 9.

132. On this topic see Marina Sitrin and Dario Azzellini, *They can't represent us! Reinventing democracy from Greece to Occupy* (London: Verso Books, 2014); and my own book, Paolo Gerbaudo, *The mask and the flag: populism, citizenism, and global protest* (Oxford: Oxford University Press, 2017).

133. Beppe Grillo, Dario Fo and Gianroberto Casaleggio, *Il Grillo canta sempre al tramonto: Dialogo sull'italia e il moVimento 5 Stelle (Adagio)* (Milan: Casaleggio Associati, 2013).

134. Simon Tormey, *The end of representative politics* (New York: John Wiley & Sons, 2015).

135. Kenneth L. Hacker and Jan van Dijk, 'What is digital democracy', in K. L. Hacker and J. Van Dijk (eds), *Digital democracy: issues of theory and practice* (London; Thousand Oaks, CA: Sage, 2000), pp. 1–9.

136. Barry N. Hague and Brian Loader, eds, *Digital democracy: discourse and decision making in the information age* (London: Psychology Press, 1999).

137. Nathan Gardels, 'It's time to rethink democracy', *The Washington Post*, 23 March 2019, retrieved from www.washingtonpost.com/news/theworldpost/wp/2018/03/23/direct-democracy/?noredirect=on&utm_term=.a8360558f24f.

138. Podemos's electoral programme for the 2015 national elections, 'La sonrisa de un pais', retrieved from http://www.lasonrisadeunpais.es/programa/.

139. Podemos's electoral programme, 'La sonrisa de un pais', retrieved from lasonrisadeunpais.es/programa/.

140. Gareth Morgan, *Images of organization* (London; Thousand Oaks, CA: Sage Publications, 2014), p. 15.

141. James Jerome Gibson, 'Notes on affordances' in *Reasons for realism: selected essays of James J. Gibson* (Mahwah, NJ: Lawrence Erlbaum, 1982).

142. Karl Marx, *A contribution to the critique of political economy* (London: International Library, 1904).

143. Daniel J. Boorstin. *The image: a guide to pseudo-events in America* (New York: Vintage, 2012).

144. Joss Hands, 'Platform communism', *Culture Machine* 14 (2013).

145. Tarleton Gillespie, 'The politics of 'platforms', *New Media & Society* 12, no. 3 (2010): 347–364.

146. Network effect describes the way in which a product becomes more valuable as more people use it, hence the alternate definition as demand-side economy of scale. See Albert-László Barabási and Réka Albert, 'Emergence of scaling in random networks'. *Science* 286, no. 5439 (1999): 509–512.

147. Tiziana Terranova, 'Free labor: producing culture for the digital economy', *Social Text* 18, no. 2 (2000): 33–58.

148. Jaron Lanier, *Who owns the future?* (New York: Simon and Schuster, 2014).

149. Nick Srnicek, *Platform capitalism* (New York: John Wiley & Sons, 2017).

150. John Hagel and Marc Singer have coined the term *infomediaries* to point to the presence of new processes of intermediation or 're-intermediation'. John Hagel and Marc Singer, *Net worth: shaping markets when customers make the rules* (Cambridge, MA: Harvard Business School Press, 1999).

151. Benjamin H. Bratton, *The stack: on software and sovereignty* (Cambridge, MA: MIT Press, 2016).

152. Bratton, *The stack*, p. 44.

153. Bratton, *The stack*, p. 47.

154. Bratton, *The stack*, p. 374.

155. Bratton, *The stack*, p. 47.

156. Rick Falkvinge, *Swarmwise: the tactical manual to changing the world* (N. Charleston, SC: CreateSpace Publishing Platform, 2016), p. 23.

157. Falkvinge, *Swarmwise*, p. 19.

158. Becky Bond and Zack Exley, *Rules for revolutionaries: how big organizing can change everything* (Hartford, VT: Chelsea Green Publishing, 2016).

159. In this vein Florian Hartleb has spoken of Pirate Parties and the Five Star Movement as 'anti-elitist cyber-parties', Florian Hartleb, 'Anti-elitist cyber parties?', *Journal of Public Affairs* 13, no. 4 (2013): 355–369.

160. Bond and Exley, *Rules for revolutionaries*, p. 49.

161. Richard S. Katz, 'The problem of candidate selection and models of party democracy', *Party Politics* 7, no. 3 (2001): 277–296.

162. Falkvinge, *Swarmwise*, p. 19.

163. Andrew Chadwick, *The hybrid media system: politics and power* (Oxford University Press, 2017).

164. Davide Casaleggio, 'The 5 Star Movement – an Italian revolution', YouTube video, published 7 August 2017, retrieved from www.youtube.com/watch?v=ZQe5j47GIsk.

165. 'Releasing the code of Podemos's digital heart', Podemos, n.d., retrieved 2 February 2018 from podemos.info/releasing-the-code-of-podemos-digital-heart/.

166. 'Le Processus', L'Avenir en Commun, n.d., retrieved 15 April 2018 from avenirencommun.fr/le-processus/.

167. Swedish Pirate Party Declaration of Principles, 4.0 version, May 2012, retrieved from https://www.piratpartiet.se/principprogram/ (translated from Swedish).

168. MoVimento 5 Stelle, 'Libertà è partecipazione, intervista di Casaleggio a la Stampa', 20 November 2015, retrieved from http://www.ilblogdellestelle .it/2015/11/liberta_e_partecipazione_lintervista_di_casaleggio_a_la_ stampa.html.

169. Clarissa Gigante, 'L'iperdemocrazia a cinque stelle? È solo un sogno ad occhi aperti', *Il Giornale*, 19 September 2012, retrieved from http://www .ilgiornale.it/news/grillo-democrazia-partecipata-e-diffusa-838612.html.

170. Alessandro Di Battista, personal Facebook page post, 3 December 2013, retrieved from www.facebook.com/dibattista.alessandro/posts/45728 5577716845.

171. Podemos Statute.

172. France Insoumise Statute.

173. Momentum Statute.

174. Tim O'Reilly, 'What is Web 2.0? Design patterns and business models for the next generation of software', 30 September 2005, retrieved from www .oreillynet.com/pub/a/oreilly/tim/news/2005/09/30/what-is-web-20.html.

175. Henry Jenkins, *Convergence culture: where old and new media collide* (New York: New York University Press, 2006).

176. Mark Deuze, 'Participation, remediation, bricolage: considering principal components of a digital culture', *The Information Society* 22, no. 2 (2006): 63–75.

177. Bill Cooke and Uma Kothari, eds, *Participation: the new tyranny?* (London: Zed Books, 2001).

178. Nicolas Bourriaud, Simon Pleasance, Fronza Woods and Mathieu Cope- land, *Relational aesthetics* (Dijon: Les Presses du réel, 2002).

179. 'Non-statute of the 5 Star Movement', n.d., retrieved 5 March 2017 from https://s3-eu-west-1.amazonaws.com/materiali-bg/Regolamento-Movi mento-5-Stelle.pdf.

180. 'Non-statute of the 5 Star Movement', n.d.

181. 'Non-statute of the 5 Star Movement', n.d.

182. 'Non-statute of the 5 Star Movement', n.d.

183. Miguel Ardanuy, personal interview.

184. Jorge Lago, personal interview.

185. Falkvinge, *Swarmwise*, p. 19.

186. France Insoumise statute.

187. France Insoumise statute.

188. Emma Rees, personal interview.

189. Senator Vito Crimi, Ritorno alla base, 10 April 2015, Bicocca University, Milan.

190. Jean-Luc Mélenchon, 'L'insumission est un nouvel humanisme', *Le Un hebdomadaire*, 18 October 2017, retrieved from https://le1hebdo.fr/journal/ numero/174/l-insoumission-est-un-nouvel-humanisme-2481.html.

191. Birgitta Jonsdottir, personal interview.

192. Simone Weil, *On the abolition of all political parties* (New York: New York Review of Books, 2014).

193. Weil, *On the abolition of all political parties*, p. 14.

194. Adriano Olivetti, *Democrazia senza partiti*, Vol. 2. (Rome: Edizioni di Comunità, 2013).
195. Olivetti, *Democrazia senza partiti*, p. 23.
196. Olivetti, *Democrazia senza partiti*, p. 23.
197. Dario Fo, Beppe Grillo and Gianroberto Casaleggio, *Il Grillo canta sempre al tramonto* (Milano: Chiarelettere, 2013), p. 61.
198. Christopher Lasch, *The culture of narcissism: American life in an age of diminishing expectations* (New York: W.W. Norton, 1991).
199. Paolo Gerbaudo, *The mask and the flag: populism, citizenism, and global protest* (Oxford: Oxford University Press, 2017).
200. Guillaume Royer, personal interview.
201. Jakob Nielsen, 'The 90-9-1 rule for participation inequality in social media and online communities', Nielsen Norman Group, 2006, retrieved 16 September 2014 from www.nngroup.com/articles/participation-in equality/ .
202. Eszter Hargittai and Gina Walejko, 'The participation divide: content creation and sharing in the digital age', *Information, Community and Society* 11, no. 2 (2008): 239–256.
203. Manuel Vázquez Montalbán, *Murder in the central committee* (Brooklyn, NY: Melville House, 2012).
204. Falkvinge, *Swarmwise*, p. 278.
205. Roberto Fico, personal interview.
206. Falkvinge, *Swarmwise*, pp. 20–21.
207. Karpf, *The MoveOn effect*.
208. Falkvinge, *Swarmwise*.
209. Jorge Lago, personal interview.
210. L'Avenir en Commun, France Insoumise's electoral programme, retrieved 12 January 2018 from https://www.avenirencommun.fr/.
211. Charter of France Insoumise's action groups, France Insoumise official website, retrieved 2 January 2018 from https://lafranceinsoumise.fr/groupes -appui/charte-groupes-dappui-de-france-insoumise/.
212. Charter of France Insoumise' action groups.
213. Reda, personal interview.
214. Katz and Mair, 'Changing models of party organization', pp. 5–28.
215. Meetup, www.meetup.com/.
216. Fico, personal interview.
217. Fico, personal interview.
218. Panebianco, *Political parties*, p. 52.
219. Alessandro Di Battista and Roberto Fico, 'Lettera ai Meetup', blog delle Stelle, 19 July 2015, retrieved from http://www.ilblogdellestelle.it/2015 /07/lettera_ai_meet_up.html.
220. Ostrogorski, *Democracy and the organization of political parties*; and Sigmund Neumann and Frederick C. Barghoorn, *Modern political parties: approaches to comparative politics* (Chicago, IL: University of Chicago Press, 1956).

221. See, for example, Matthew Fuller, Roger F. Malina and Sean Cubitt, eds, *Software studies: a lexicon* (Cambridge, MA: MIT Press, 2008).

222. To delve into the vast scholarship on algorithms and politics, it is advisable to begin with Taina Bucher, 'Want to be on the top? Algorithmic power and the threat of invisibility on Facebook', *New Media & Society* 14, no. 7 (2012): 1164–1180; and Tarleton Gillespie, 'The relevance of algorithms', *Media technologies: essays on communication, materiality, and society* 167 (2014).

223. Arend Lijphart and Don Aitkin, *Electoral systems and party systems: a study of twenty-seven democracies, 1945–1990* (Oxford: Oxford University Press, 1994).

224. Pippa Norris, *Digital divide: civic engagement, information poverty, and the Internet worldwide* (Cambridge: Cambridge University Press, 2001).

225. Julie Simon, Theo Bass, Victoria Boelman and Geoff Mulgan, 'Digital democracy: the tools transforming political engagement' (London: NESTA, 2017), retrieved from www.nesta.org.uk/report/digital-democracy-the-tools-transforming-political-engagement/.

226. Loomio, www.loomio.org/.

227. DemocracyOS, democracyos.org/.

228. LiquidFeedback, https://liquidfeedback.org/.

229. Your Priorities, https://www.yrpri.org/.

230. nVotes, https://nvotes.com/.

231. Decidim, https://decidim.org/.

232. Consul, consulproject.org/en/.

233. David Held, *Models of democracy* (Cambridge, UK: Polity, 2006).

234. Stephen Coleman and Chris Rowe, *Remixing citizenship: democracy and young people's use of the internet* (Dunfermline, Scotland: Carnegie Young People Initiative, 2004).

235. John S. Dryzek, *Deliberative democracy and beyond: liberals, critics, contestations* (Oxford: Oxford University Press, 2000).

236. Dryzek, *Deliberative democracy*, p. 31.

237. David Schlosberg and John S. Dryzek, 'Digital democracy: authentic or virtual?', *Organization & Environment* 15, no. 3 (2002): 332–335.

238. See, among others, Karl Kautsky, *Der Parlamentarismus, die Volksgesetzgebung und die Sozialdemokratie* (Stuttgart, Germany: Dietz, 1893); Markku Suksi, *Bringing in the people: a comparison of constitutional forms and practices of the referendum* (Leiden: Martinus Nijhoff, 1993) and Mads Qvortrup and Matt Qvortrup, *A comparative study of referendums: government by the people* (Manchester, UK: Manchester University Press, 2005).

239. Bryce, *Modern Democracies*, p. 21.

240. Kautsky, *Parlamentarismus und Demokratie*.

241. Michels, *Political parties*, p. 310.

242. Jean-Jacques Rousseau and Gita May, *The social contract and the first and second discourses* (New Haven, CT: Yale University Press, 2002).

243. Moritz Rittinghausen, *Direct legislation by the people*, No. 87 (Berlin: Humboldt Library, 1897), p. 65.

244. Lisa Young and William Cross, 'The rise of plebiscitary democracy in Canadian political parties', *Party Politics* 8, no. 6 (2002): 673–699.

245. LiquidFeedback, https://liquidfeedback.org/.

246. Rosseau, Sistema Operativo 5 Stelle, https://rousseau.movimento5stelle.it/.

247. The Italian Data Protection Authority conducted an investigation after the 2017 data breach and established that the Rousseau system was using an obsolete version of Movable Type. 'Rousseau was made using a software product, the CMS Movable Type which, in the Enterprise version 4.31-en, [is] affected by indisputable technical obsolescence (the manufacturer identified on 31 December 2013 the 'end-of-life' date for versions 4.3x).' Garante della Privacy, 'Provvedimento su data breach', 21 December 2017, retrieved from https://www.garanteprivacy.it/web/guest/home/docweb/-/docweb-display/docweb/7400401.

248. Danilo Toninelli, 'Con Rousseau i cittadini diventano protagonisti', 2 April 2017, retrieved from http://www.ilblogdellestelle.it/2017/04/con_rousseau_i_cittadini_diventano_protagonisti_in_parlamento.html.

249. M5S, Di Maio presenta Lex: 'Si realizza il sogno di Casaleggio', La Repubblica, retrieved from https://video.repubblica.it/politica/m5s-di-maio-presenta-lex-si-realizza-il-sogno-di-casaleggio/240736/240682.

250. Agora Voting About page, retrieved 12 July 2018 from https://www.agora.vote/.

251. Jonathan Blitzer, 'In Spain, politics via Reddit', *The New Yorker*, 7 October 2014, retrieved from www.newyorker.com/tech/elements/spain-politics-via-reddit.

252. Blitzer, 'In Spain, politics via Reddit'.

253. Consul Project About page, retrieved 25 August 2018 from http://www.consulproject.org/.

254. Decidim, https://decidim.org/.

255. Decidim, https://decidim.org/.

256. La France insoumise, wikimonde.com/article/La_France_insoumise.

257. L'avenir en commun, https://avenirencommun.fr/le-processus/.

258. James S. Fishkin and Robert C. Luskin, 'Experimenting with a democratic ideal: deliberative polling and public opinion', *Acta Politica* 40, no. 3 (2005): 284–298.

259. Jason Horowitz, 'The mystery man who runs Italy's "Five Star" from the shadows', *New York Times*, 28 February 2018, retrieved from https://www.nytimes.com/2018/02/28/world/europe/italy-election-davide-casaleggio-five-star.html.

260. Susan E. Scarrow, *Political parties and democracy in theoretical and practical perspectives: implementing intra-party democracy* (Washington, DC: National Democratic Institute for International Affairs, 2005).

261. Susan E. Scarrow, *Implementing intra-party democracy* (Washington, DC: National Democratic Institute for International Affairs, 2005), p. 13.

262. Scarrow, *Political parties and democracy*, pp. 6–8.

263. Panebianco, *Political parties*, p. 22.
264. L'avenir en commun, https://avenirencommun.fr/le-processus/.
265. L'Avenir en commun About page, retrieved 6 March 2018, https://avenirencommun.fr/le-processus/.
266. Guillaume Royer, personal interview.
267. Lorenzo Mosca, 'Democratic vision and online participatory spaces in the Italian Movimento 5 Stelle', *Acta Politica* (2018): 1–18.
268. Gramsci, *Section from the prison notebooks*, p. 151.
269. Technically this was not exactly a hologram, but a 'pepper's ghost effect', an illusion used in museums, television and concerts.
270. Manuel Castells, *The rise of the network society. The information age: economy, society, and* culture, Vol. I (Information Age Series) (London: Blackwell, 1996).
271. Michels, *Political parties*, p. 88.
272. Antonio Gramsci and Quitin Hoare, *Selections from the prison notebooks*, Vol. 294 (London: Lawrence and Wishart, 1971), p. 145.
273. Slavoj Žižek, *For they know not what they do: enjoyment as a political factor* (London: Verso, 2002), p. 185.
274. Chadwick, *The hybrid media system*.
275. Becky Bond and Zack Exley, *Rules for revolutionaries*.
276. It is useful to go back to the criteria identified by Robert Michels that qualify a good leader: 'The chief is the force of will which reduces to obedience less powerful wills. Next in importance comes the following: a wider extent of knowledge which impresses the members of the leader's environment; a Catonian strength of conviction, a force of ideas often verging on fanaticism, and which arouses the respect of the masses by its very intensity; self-sufficiency, even if accompanied by arrogant pride, so long as the leader knows how to make the crowd share his own pride in himself; in exceptional cases, finally, goodness of heart and disinterestedness, qualities which recall in the mind of the crowd the figure of Christ, and reawaken religious sentiments which are decayed but not extinct. The quality, however, which most of all impresses the crowd is celebrity' (p. 100).
277. Winnie Wong, personal interview.
278. Jan Ljungberg, 'Open source movements as a model for organising', *European Journal of Information Systems* 9, no. 4 (2000): 208–216.
279. To understand the presence of an entourage not just supporting but sometimes also guiding the leader, it is useful to refer back to Max Weber's discussion of the 'charismatic staff' and the 'routinisation of charisma'. Weber, *Economy and society*, pp. 249–250.
280. Matteo Canestrari, personal interview.
281. Duverger, *Political parties*, p. 126.
282. Peter Mair, *Ruling the void: the hollowing of Western democracy* (London: Verso Books, 2013), pp. 4–5.
283. Nicola Biondo and Marco Canestrari, *Supernova: i segreti, le bugie e i tradimenti del Movimento 5 stelle: storia vera di una nuova casta che si pretendeva anticasta* (Milano: Ponte alle Grazie, 2018).

284. John D. May, 'Opinion structure of political parties: the special law of curvilinear disparity', *Political Studies* 21, no. 2 (1973): 135–151.

285. Bond and Exley, *Rules for revolutionaries*, p. 134.

286. Bond and Exley, *Rules for revolutionaries*, p. 2.

287. Chris Anderson, *The long tail: how endless choice is creating unlimited demand* (New York: Random House, 2007).

288. Michels, *Political parties*.

289. Sigmund Neumann and Frederick C. Barghoorn, *Modern political parties: approaches to comparative politics* (Chicago, IL: University of Chicago Press, 1956.).

290. Immanuel Kant, *Toward perpetual peace and other writings on politics, peace, and history* (New Haven: Yale University Press, 2006), pp. 74–75.

291. This turn towards plebiscitarian democracy has been documented across many parties in different geographic contexts. See, for example, Richard S. Katz, 'The problem of candidate selection and models of party democracy', *Party Politics* 7, no. 3 (2001): 277–296; Lisa Young and William Cross, 'The rise of plebiscitary democracy in Canadian political parties', *Party Politics* 8, no. 6 (2002): 673–699 and Susan E. Scarrow, 'Parties and the expansion of direct democracy: who benefits?', *Party Politics* 5, no. 3 (1999): 341–362.

292. Weber, *Economy and society*, p. 1130.

293. Nicoló Machiavelli, *The prince* (London: Penguin, 1961).

294. Zeynep Tufekci, *Twitter and tear gas: the power and fragility of networked protest* (New Haven, CT: Yale University Press, 2017).

295. This is a tendency I have already described in my previous work on social movements concerning their obsession with participation and spontaneity – Gerbaudo, *The mask and the flag*.

Bibliography

Alvarez, R. M., and T. E. Hall. *Electronic elections: the perils and promises of.* Princeton, NJ: Princeton University Press, 2010.

Arendt, Hannah. *The origins of totalitarianism*, Vol. 244. Boston, MA: Houghton Mifflin Harcourt, 1973.

Barbrook, Richard, and Andy Cameron. 'The Californian ideology.' *Science as Culture* 6, no. 1 (1996): 44–72.

Beck, Ulrich, and Elisabeth Beck-Gernsheim. *Individualization: institutionalized individualism and its social and political consequences.* London; Thousand Oaks, CA; New Delhi: Sage, 2002, pp. 291–318.

Bauman, Zygmunt. *The individualized society.* New York: John Wiley & Sons, 2013.

Bennett, W. Lance, and Alexandra Segerberg. *The logic of connective action: digital media and the personalization of contentious politics.* Cambridge, UK: Cambridge University Press, 2013.

Bogost, I., and N. Montfort. 'Platform studies: frequently questioned answers', paper presented at the *Digital Arts and Culture 2009* conference, Irvine, CA, 12–15 December 2009.

Bond, B., and Z. Exley. *Rules for revolutionaries: how big organizing can change everything.* Hartford, VT: Chelsea Green Publishing, 2016.

Bourriaud, Nicolas, Simon Pleasance, Fronza Woods and Mathieu Copeland. *Relational aesthetics.* Dijon: Les Presses du réel, 2002.

Breines, Wini. *Community and organization in the new left, 1962–1968: the great refusal.* Rutgers, NJ: Rutgers University Press, 1989.

Burke, Edmund. *Thoughts on the present discontents: the two speeches on America.* London: Clarendon, 1878.

Castells, Manuel. *The internet galaxy: reflections on the internet, business, and society.* Oxford: Oxford University Press, 2002.

Castells, Manuel. *Communication power.* Oxford: Oxford University Press, 2013.

Castells, Manuel. *Networks of outrage and hope: social movements in the internet age.* New York: John Wiley & Sons, 2015.

Tufekci, Zeynep. *Twitter and tear gas: the power and fragility of networked protest.* New Haven, CT: Yale University Press, 2017.

Chadwick, Andrew, and Philip N. Howard, eds. *Routledge handbook of internet politics.* London: Taylor & Francis, 2010.

Coleman, Stephen, and Chris Rowe. *Remixing citizenship: democracy and young people's use of the internet.* Dunfermline, Scotland: Carnegie Young People Initiative, 2004.

Cooke, Bill, and Uma Kothari, eds. *Participation: the new tyranny?* (London: Zed books, 2001).

Cross, William P., and Richard S. Katz, eds. *The challenges of intra-party democracy*. Oxford: Oxford University Press, 2013.

Crouch, C. *Post-democracy*. Cambridge, UK: Polity, 2004, pp. 70–76.

Dahlberg, L. 'Re-constructing digital democracy: an outline of four "positions".' *New Media & Society*, 13(6), 855–872. https://doi.org.10.1177/1461444810389569.

Dahlgren, P. *Media and political engagement*, Vol. 551. Cambridge, UK: Cambridge University Press, 2009.

Dal Lago, Alessandro. *Clic. Grillo, Casaleggio e la demagogia elettronica*. Naples: Cronopio, 2013.

Dalton, Russell J., and Martin P. Wattenberg, eds. *Parties without partisans: political change in advanced industrial democracies*. Oxford: Oxford University Press, 2002.

De Montesquieu, Charles. *Montesquieu: the spirit of the laws*. Cambridge, UK: Cambridge University Press, 1989.

De Stefano, Valerio. 'The rise of the just-in-time workforce: on-demand work, crowdwork, and labor protection in the gig-economy.' *Comparative Labor Law & Policy Journal* 37 (2015): 471.

De Tocqueville, Alexis. *Democracy in America*, Vol. 10. Washington, DC: Regnery Publishing, 2003.

Debray, Régis. *Media manifestos*. Trans. Eric Rauth. London and New York: Verso, 1996, p. 161.

Della Porta, Donatella, Joseba Fernandez, Hara Kouki and Lorenzo Mosca. *Movement parties against austerity*. New York: John Wiley & Sons, 2017.

Deuze, Mark. 'Participation, remediation, bricolage: considering principal components of a digital culture.' *The Information Society* 22, no. 2 (2006): 63–75.

Diani, Mario. 'Social movement networks virtual and real.' *Information, Communication & Society* 3, no. 3 (2000): 386–401.

Dryzek, John S. *Deliberative democracy and beyond: liberals, critics, contestations*. Oxford: Oxford University Press, 2000.

Duverger, Maurice. *Political parties: their organization and activity in the modern state*. London: Methuen, 1959.

Dyer-Witheford, Nick. *Cyber-proletariat: global labour in the digital vortex*. Toronto, Ontario: Between the Lines, 2015.

Epstein, Leon D. *Political parties in Western democracies*. Piscatawy, NJ: Transaction Publishers, 1980.

Fanon, Frantz. *Black skin, white masks*. New York: Grove Press, 2008.

Floridia, Antonio e Rinaldo Vignati, 'Deliberativa, diretta o partecipativa?', *Quaderni di Sociologia* 65 (2014): 51–74.

Foti, Alex. *General theory of the precariat: great recession, revolution, reaction*. Theory on Demand, 2017.

Friedman, Thomas L. *The world is flat: a brief history of the twenty-first century*. New York: Macmillan, 2005.

Fuchs, D. Participatory, liberal and electronic democracy. In T. Zittel and D. Fuchs, eds, *Participatory democracy and political participation: can participatory engineering bring citizens back in?* (pp. 29–54). London: Routledge, 2007.

Gareth, Morgan. *Images of organization*. Thousand Oaks, CA: Sage, 1997.

Gerbaudo, Paolo. 'From cyber-autonomism to cyber-populism: an ideological analysis of the evolution of digital activism.' *TripleC: Communication, Capitalism & Critique. Open Access Journal for a Global Sustainable Information Society* 15, no. 2 (2017): 477–489.

Gerbaudo, Paolo. *The mask and the flag: populism, citizenism, and global protest.* Oxford: Oxford University Press, 2017.

Gerbaudo, Paolo. *Tweets and the streets: social media and contemporary activism.* London: Pluto Press, 2012.

Gil de Zúñiga, H., A. Veenstra, E. Vraga and D. Shah. 'Digital democracy: reimagining pathways to political participation.' *Journal of Information Technology & Politics* 7, no. 1 (2010): 36–51.

Gillespie, Tarleton. 'The politics of "platforms".' *New Media & Society* 12, no. 3 (2010): 347–364.

Gladwell, Malcolm. 'Small change.' *New Yorker* (2010, 4 October) 42–49.

Golumbia, David. *The politics of Bitcoin: software as right-wing extremism.* Minneapolis: University of Minnesota Press, 2016.

Gramsci, Antonio. *Selections from the prison notebooks of Antonio Gramsci.* Ed. and transl. by Quintin Hoare and Geoffrey Nowell Smith. New York: International Publishers, 1971.

Gramsci, Antonio, Quintin Hoare and Geoffrey Nowell Smith. *Selections from the prison notebooks,* Vol. 12. London: Lawrence and Wishart, 1971.

Grillo, Beppe, Dario Fo and Gianroberto Casaleggio. 'Grillo canta sempre al tramonto.' *Dialogo sull'Italia e il MoVimento* 5 (2013).

Hacker, K. L., and J. van Dijk, eds. *Digital democracy: issues of theory and practice.* Thousand Oaks, CA: Sage, 2000.

Hacker, Kenneth L., and Jan van Dijk. 'What is digital democracy?' In Kenneth L. Hacker and Jan van Dijk, eds, *Digital democracy: issues of theory and practice* (pp. 1–9). London; Thousand Oaks, CA; New Delhi: Sage, 2000.

Hagen, M. (2000). 'Digital democracy and political systems.' In Kenneth L. Hacker and Jan van Dijk, eds, *Digital democracy: issues of theory and practice* (pp. 54–69). London; Thousand Oaks, CA; New Delhi: Sage, 2000.

Hague, Barry N., and Brian Loader, eds. *Digital democracy: discourse and decision making in the information age.* London: Psychology Press, 1999.

Hamilton, Alexander, James Madison, John Jay and Jack Richon Pole. *The federalist.* Cambridge, MA: Hackett Publishing, 2005.

Hands, Joss. 'Platform communism.' *Culture machine* 14 (2013): 1–24.

Hardt, Michael, and Antonio Negri. *Empire.* Cambridge, MA: Harvard University Press, 2001.

Hargittai, Eszter, and Gina Walejko. 'The participation divide: content creation and sharing in the digital age.' *Information, Community and Society* 11, no. 2 (2008): 239–256.

Hayek, Friedrich August. *The constitution of liberty: the definitive edition.* London: Routledge, 2013.

Held, D. *Models of democracy.* Cambridge, UK: Polity, 2006.

Hindman, M. *The myth of digital democracy.* Princeton, NJ: Princeton University Press, 2008.

Inglehart, Ronald. *Culture shift in advanced industrial society*. Princeton, NJ: Princeton University Press, 1990.

Jenkins, Henry. *Convergence culture: where old and new media collide*. New York: New York University Press, 2006.

Jordan, Timothy. *Information politics: liberation and exploitation in the digital society*. London: Pluto, 2015.

Karpf, David. *The MoveOn effect: the unexpected transformation of American political advocacy*. Oxford: Oxford University Press, 2012.

Katz, Richard S., and Peter Mair. 'The evolution of party organizations in Europe: the three faces of party organization.' *American Review of Politics* 14 (1994): 593–617.

Katz, Richard S., and Peter Mair. 'Changing models of party organization and party democracy: the emergence of the cartel party.' *Party Politics* 1, no. 1 (1995): 5–28.

Katz, Richard S., and Peter Mair, eds. *How parties organize: change and adaptation in party organizations in Western democracies*. Vol. 528. London; Thousand Oaks, CA; New Delhi: Sage, 1994.

Kirchheimer, Otto. 'The transformation of the Western European party systems.' In J. LaPalombra and M. Weiner, eds, *Political parties and political development* (pp. 177–200). Princeton, NJ: Princeton University Press, 1966.

Kitschelt, Herbert P. 'Left-libertarian parties: explaining innovation in competitive party systems.' *World Politics* 40, no. 2 (1988): 194–234.

Kojève, Alexandre. *Introduction to the reading of Hegel*. Ithaca, NY: Cornell University Press, 1980.

Kojève, Alexandre. *The notion of authority: a brief presentation*. London: Verso Books, 2014.

Lasch, Christopher. *The culture of narcissism: American life in an age of diminishing expectations*. New York: W.W. Norton & Company, 1991.

Lenin, Vladimir Ilich. *What is to be done?* London: Panther, 1970.

Levy, Steven. *Hackers: heroes of the computer revolution*, Vol. 14. Garden City, NY: Anchor Press/Doubleday, 1984.

Machiavelli, Niccolò, and Maurizio Viroli. *The prince*, Vol. 43. Oxford: Oxford University Press, 2008.

Macintosh, A., A. Malina and S. Farrell. (2002). 'Digital democracy through electronic petitioning.' In W. J. McIver Jr, William J. Elmagarmid and K. Ahmend, eds, *Advances in digital government* (pp. 137–148). New York: Springer, 2002.

Mair, Peter. *Ruling the void: the hollowing of Western democracy*. London: Verso Books, 2013.

Marx, Karl. 'A contribution to the critique of political economy'. In J. Sitton, ed, *Marx Today* (pp. 91–94). New York: Palgrave Macmillan, 2010.

McChesney, Robert W. *Digital disconnect: how capitalism is turning the internet against democracy*. New York: New Press, 2013.

Melucci, Alberto. *Challenging codes: collective action in the information age*. Cambridge, UK: Cambridge University Press, 1996.

Michels, Robert. *Political parties: a sociological study of the oligarchical tendencies of modern democracy*. New York: Hearst's International Library Company, 1915.

Moffitt, B., and S. Tormey. 'Rethinking populism: politics, mediatisation and political style'. *Political Studies* 62, no. 2 (2014): 381–397.

Morozov, E. *The net delusion: how not to liberate the world*. London: Penguin, 2011.

Morse, Anson D. 'What is a party?' *Political Science Quarterly* 11, no. 1 (1896): 68–81.

Mosca, Gaetano. *The ruling class (Elementi di scienza politica)*. New York; London: McGraw-Hill, 1939.

Mouffe, Chantal. 'Deliberative democracy or agonistic pluralism?' *Political Science Series 72* (Vienna: Institute for Advanced Studies, 2000).

Neumann, Franz Leopold. *Behemoth: the structure and practice of national socialism, 1933–1944*. Lanham, MD: Rowman & Littlefield, 2009.

Neumann, Sigmund, and Frederick C. Barghoorn. *Modern political parties: approaches to comparative politics*. 1956.

Newton, Ken, and Pippa Norris. 'Confidence in public institutions.' In Susan J. Pharr and Robert Putnam, eds, *Disaffected democracies: what's troubling the trilateral countries*. Princeton, NJ: Princeton University Press, 2000, 24–51.

Norris, P. (2011). *Democratic deficit: critical citizens revisited*. Cambridge: Cambridge University Press.

Norris, Pippa. (2001). *Digital divide: civic engagement, information poverty, and the internet worldwide*. Cambridge, UK: Cambridge University Press.

Nozick, Robert. (1974). *Anarchy, state, and utopia*, Vol. 5038. New York: Basic Books.

Olivetti, Adriano. *Democrazia senza partiti*, Vol. 2. Rome: Edizioni di Comunità, 2013.

Orwell, George. *George Orwell: a life in letters*. New York: W.W. Norton, 2013.

Ostrogorski, Moisei. (1902). *Democracy and the organization of political parties*, Vol. 2. New York: Macmillan.

Panebianco, Angelo. (1988). *Political parties: organization and power*. Cambridge, UK: Cambridge University Press.

Pareto, Vilfredo. *The mind and society*, Vol. 1. New York: Harcourt, Brace, 1935.

Pareto, Vilfredo. *Manual of political economy*. New York: Augustus M. Kelly, 1971.

Parry, G. *Political elites*. Colchester, UK: ECPR Press, 2005.

Poulantzas, Nicos. *Fascism and dictatorship: the third international and the problem of fascism*. New York: New Left Books, 1974.

Putnam, Robert D. 'Bowling alone: America's declining social capital.' In Lane Crothers and Charles Lockhart, eds, *Culture and politics: a reader* (pp. 223–234). New York: Palgrave Macmillan, 2000.

Qvortrup, Mads, and Matt Qvortrup. *A comparative study of referendums: government by the people*. Manchester, UK: Manchester University Press, 2005.

Revelli, Marco. *Finale di partito*. Turin, Italy: Giulio Einaudi Editore, 2013.

Rheingold, Howard. *The virtual community: finding connection in a computerized world*. Boston: Addison-Wesley Longman, 1993.

Sartori, Giovanni. *Parties and party systems: a framework for analysis*. Turin, Italy: ECPR press, 2005.

Scarrow, Susan E. 'Parties and the expansion of direct democracy: who benefits?' *Party Politics* 5, no. 3 (1999): 341–362.

Scarrow, Susan E. *Political parties and democracy in theoretical and practical perspectives: implementing intra-party democracy*. Washington, DC: National Democratic Institute for International Affairs, 2005.

Scarrow, Susan E., and Burcu Gezgor. 'Declining memberships, changing members? European political party members in a new era.' *Party Politics* 16, no. 6 (2010): 823–843.

Schattschneider, Elmer. *Party government: American government in action*. New York: Routledge, 2017.

Schlosberg, D., and J. S. Dryzek. 'Digital democracy: authentic or virtual?' *Organization & Environment* 15, no. 3 (2002): 332.

Schmitter, Philippe C. 'Intermediaries in the consolidation of neo-democracies: the role of parties, associations and movements.' Working Paper No. 30. Barcelona: Institut de Ciencies Politiques i Socials, 1997.

Scholz, Trebor. *Uberworked and underpaid: how workers are disrupting the digital economy*. New York: John Wiley & Sons, 2017.

Shirky, Clay. *Here comes everybody: the power of organizing without organizations*. New York: Penguin, 2008.

Simon, Julie, Theo Bass, Victoria Boelman and Geoff Mulgan. *Digital democracy: the tools transforming political engagement*. London: NESTA, 2017.

Sitrin, Marina, and Dario Azzellini. *They can't represent us! Reinventing democracy from Greece to Occupy*. London: Verso Books, 2014.

Solop, F. I. 'Digital democracy comes of age: internet voting and the 2000 Arizona Democratic primary election.' *Political Science & Politics* 34, no. 2 (2001): 289–293.

Srnicek, Nick. *Platform capitalism*. New York: John Wiley & Sons, 2017.

Suksi, Markku. *Bringing in the people: a comparison of constitutional forms and practices of the referendum*. Leiden: Martinus Nijhoff, 1993.

Teorell, Jan. 'A deliberative defence of intra-party democracy.' *Party politics* 5, no. 3 (1999): 363–382.

Tormey, Simon. *The end of representative politics*. New York: John Wiley & Sons, 2015.

Turkle, Sherry. *Alone together: why we expect more from technology and less from each other*. London: Hachette UK, 2017.

Turner, Fred. *From counterculture to cyberculture: Stewart Brand, the Whole Earth Network, and the rise of digital utopianism*. Chicago, IL: University of Chicago Press, 2010.

Van Biezen, Ingrid, Peter Mair and Thomas Poguntke. 'Going, going, ... gone? The decline of party membership in contemporary Europe.' *European Journal of Political Research* 51, no. 1 (2012): 24–56.

Van Selm, M., N. W. Jankowski and L. Tsaliki. 'Political parties online: digital democracy as reflected in three Dutch political party Web sites.' *Communications* 27, no. 2 (2002): 189–209.

Waldfogel, Joel, and Imke Reimers. 'Storming the gatekeepers: digital disintermediation in the market for books.' *Information Economics and Policy*, 31 (2015): 47–58.

Weber, Max. *Economy and society: an outline of interpretive sociology*, Vol. 1. Berkeley, CA: University of California Press, 1978.

Weber, Max. *Weber: political writings.* Cambridge, UK: Cambridge University Press, 1994.

Weil, Simone. *On the abolition of all political parties.* New York: New York Review of Books, 2014.

Wellman, Barry. 'Little boxes, glocalization, and networked individualism.' In M. Tanabe, P. van den Besselaar and T. Ishida, eds, *Digital cities II: computational and sociological approaches* (pp. 10–25). Berlin, Heidelberg: Springer, 2001.

Young, Lisa, and William Cross. 'The rise of plebiscitary democracy in Canadian political parties.' *Party Politics* 8, no. 6 (2002): 673–699.

Index

Printed and bound by CPI Group (UK) Ltd, Croydon, CR0 4YY

27/10/2024

14580223-0002